Migration, Human Rights, and Development

Migration, Human Rights, and Development:
A Global Anthology

Anne T. Gallagher, editor

International Debate Education Association

New York, London & Amsterdam

Published by
International Debate Education Association
105 East 22nd Street
New York, NY 10010

Copyright © 2013 by International Debate Education Association

Library of Congress Cataloging-in-Publication Data

Gallagher, Anne T.
  Migration, human rights, and development : a global anthology / Anne T. Gallagher.
     pages cm
  ISBN 978-1-61770-071-2
  1. Emigration and immigration--Government policy. 2. Human rights. 3. Emigration and immigration--Economic aspects. I. Title.
  JV6038.G35 2013
  325'.1--dc23
                          2012049043

 **IDEBATE Press**

Typeset by Richard Johnson
Printed in the USA

Contents

Introduction

Remember, remember always, that all of us, and you and I especially, are descended from immigrants and revolutionists.

Franklin D. Roosevelt

Homo sum: humani nihil a me alienum puto. (I am human, nothing human is alien to me.)

Publius Terentius Afer (Terence, 195/185–159 BCE)

Migration is the movement of people across a specified boundary for the purpose of establishing a new or semipermanent residence. Migration can of course occur within a country: in 2009 the total number of internal migrants was estimated at 740 million.[1] However, while acknowledging links and overlaps, this book is primarily concerned with the phenomenon of international migration: where people move from one country to another. In 2011 it was estimated that some 215 million people—close to 3 percent of the world population—live outside their countries of birth.[2] These figures are staggering but they are not unprecedented. The World Bank has noted that current migration flows, relative to population, are, in fact, weaker than those of the second half of the nineteenth century.[3]

The stories behind migration are as varied and numerous as the individuals themselves. Some people are forced to leave their countries because of war, conflict, or the threat of persecution; others migrate to escape poverty and support their families; some simply seek to take advantage of opportunities that are not available at home. Many migrants travel well and arrive safely. However, a significant proportion of the people who want to move do not have access to safe and legal migration channels. Human trafficking (moving a person into or holding them in a situation of exploitation from which they cannot escape) and migrant smuggling (the facilitated illegal movement of people across international borders for profit) can often be found where pressures to migrate are not matched by opportunities to do so safely and legally.

While migration is often caused by, and can cause, hardship and misery, that aspect is only part of the picture. Migration is a central plank of our new, globalized world. It supports national economies in countries of origin and destination. It has improved the lives of many millions of people immeasurably.

This anthology seeks to draw a broad but comprehensive picture of the phenomenon of international migration and the ways in which countries and institutions have responded to it. It does this by selecting relevant, interesting, and sometimes provocative writing on different aspects of migration and organizing these pieces in a way that helps the reader to understand the most important issues and controversies. The present introduction seeks to fill in some of the inevitable gaps: fleshing out a framework within which the articles can be considered and discussed.

What We Know About Migration Patterns and Trends

Reliable information on migration is not readily available. Some migration is hidden; some countries keep better statistics than others; definitions and data collection systems vary, making comparisons between countries difficult; and information quickly becomes outdated. However, our knowledge about migration is improving slowly. The following information on patterns and trends is drawn from several recent, authoritative, and publicly available reports from intergovernmental organizations working or researching in this area:[4]

- The top destination country for migrants in terms of absolute numbers is the United States, followed by the Russian Federation, Germany, Saudi Arabia, and Canada. The top destination countries, relative to population, are Qatar (87 percent of the population are migrants), Monaco (72 percent), the United Arab Emirates (70 percent), Kuwait (69 percent), and Andorra (64 percent).
- Mexico–United States is the world's largest migration corridor (11.6 million migrants in 2010). Migration corridors in the former Soviet Union—Russia–Ukraine and Ukraine–Russia—are the next largest, followed by Bangladesh–India.
- More people move between developing countries (known as South to South migration) than from developing countries to high-income countries. The highest rates of skilled emigration are from small countries. For example, almost all native-born doctors trained in Grenada and Dominica emigrate to work abroad very soon after finishing their studies.
- In 2010, refugees and asylum seekers (persons who are outside their country of origin and seeking asylum from persecution) made up 16.3 million, or 8 percent, of international migrants. This group makes up a higher percentage of the migrant population in low-income countries (average 14.6 percent) than high-income countries (average 2.1 per-

cent). Sixty-five percent of immigrants in the Middle East and Africa are refugees and asylum seekers.

• In 2010: (i) migrants sent home more than $440 billion, and (ii) most of this amount ($325 billion) was received by developing countries. A significant proportion of migrant remittances are not recorded, so the true figures are likely to be much higher. Recorded remittances in 2009 were nearly three times the amount of official aid delivered by all countries, and almost as much as foreign direct investment flows to developing countries.

• In 2010, the top recipient countries of recorded remittances were India, China, Mexico, the Philippines, and France. However, for some smaller countries, migrant remittances make up a much higher share of the gross domestic product. Measured in this way, countries such as Tajikistan (35 percent), Tonga (28 percent), Lesotho (25 percent), Moldova (31 percent), and Nepal (23 percent) were the largest recipients of migrant remittances (2009 figures).

• Remittances mainly come from high-income countries. The United States is by far the largest source of migrant remittances, with $48 billion in recorded outward flows in 2009. Saudi Arabia is next, followed by Switzerland and Russia. Remittance flows did not seem to be substantially affected by the global financial crisis of 2007–8—unlike other financial flows such as foreign direct investment, which fell sharply.

Understanding Why People Migrate

Data and statistics are important, but they don't tell us the full story of migration. The contributions in this book present a much more complex picture of human movement, including the many different incentives and pressures that cause migration as well as the factors that shape how migration happens and how it affects individuals, communities, and countries.

As noted above, people are sometimes forced to move because of threats to their security. Wars and conflicts will often result in mass migration and can turn whole populations into asylum seekers who are unable to return home because of fear of persecution. The political transitions in North Africa and the Middle East in 2011 provide a useful example of the complex movements that can result from instability. The civil conflict that accompanied these transitions led to mass movements of people within and from the affected countries. Many of these movements were temporary and residents were quick to go back home once the security situation improved. However, for others, returning home was not an option. It is estimated that during the upheavals of 2011, more than 1,500 migrants, including asylum seekers, died trying to cross the Mediterranean into Europe from North Africa.[5] Many migrants from Asia who had been working in the region for years found it impossible to return to their countries of employment because of ongoing instability and rising unemployment and instead were forced to go back to their country of origin, creating new pressures for already strained job markets.[6]

Dramatic political, economic, and social change, even without violence, is often a trigger for movement. A compelling example is provided by the mass migration that followed the fall of the Iron Curtain in central and eastern Europe in the early 1990s. Almost overnight, countries such as Italy, Greece, and Portugal, traditionally exporters of migration, became destination countries for migrants.

Much migration comes about through extreme economic and social pressures. When there are few or no opportunities to earn money at home, migration can represent an important—or even the only available—survival strategy. However, economic migrants remain vulnerable to external forces. For example, labor migration to industrialized countries fell sharply during the oil crisis of 1973–74. The impact of the 2007–8 global financial crisis had mixed impacts on migration.[7] Certainly, some opportunities have decreased. For example, more than half a million jobs, many of them filled by foreign workers, were lost in Spain.[8] However, research confirms that even when they lose their jobs, many migrants will remain in the host country, provided it is safe to do so, and will not return home where there are even fewer opportunities for employment.[9] This trend helped to shore up remittances which, as noted above, remained relatively steady during the worst of the financial crisis.

As early as 1990, the United Nations Intergovernmental Panel on Climate Change predicted that human migration could be the single greatest impact of climate change, with millions of people displaced by shoreline erosion, coastal flooding, and agricultural disruption.[10] While it is difficult to secure reliable estimates of current and future mobility triggered by environmental factors, there is widespread agreement that climate variability and change will likely increase internal displacement as well as cross-border migration.[11] Even when not directly linked to climate change, resource scarcity will often create similar migration pressures. For example, lack of water, along with deforestation and land degradation, have been identified as factors in pushing migration from Mexico to the United States and from Bangladesh to India.[12] Irrespective of the precise cause, mass movements of migrants can be a source of instability and conflict and thereby feed into further migration.

When considering who is migrating and why, it is important to acknowledge that not all migration is "survival migration." Many people migrate in search of personal autonomy; many are attracted to the adventure and possible prestige that may accompany a decision to leave their country of origin. Students are migrating in record numbers as tertiary education becomes increasingly internationalized. The new global economy depends heavily on a flexible and mobile workforce comprised of skilled workers and professionals drawn from a wide range of countries. Such workers may migrate to take advantage of better career opportunities as well as improved salaries, and countries will often compete to attract and retain the best and most productive workers. In some cases, however, this "brain drain" can cause burdens on countries of origin, where highly skilled and valuable workers are desperately needed but no longer available. This aspect of migration is discussed at several points in the anthology.

There can be little doubt that, whatever the initial trigger, migration causes migration. Individuals who have migrated, whether to escape persecution or to seek improved economic opportunities, will understandably wish their families to eventually join them. Ethnic migrant communities provide the contacts, structure, and familiarity that encourage and enable others to make a move. With the help of modern technology, these communities are often able to maintain strong contacts with their homes and families. In addition to facilitating further migration, migrant "diasporas" can exert substantial economic, social, and political power in their host country. Their influence may also be strongly felt in the country of origin through remittances and even through "circular migration," a term that seeks to capture the phenomenon of more fluid movements, including temporary and repeated migration.

SIGNIFICANT TRENDS IN MIGRATION

What are the most significant migration trends? In 2011 the International Organization for Migration (IOM) reported that while there have been surges of migration to some countries over the past decade, new migration flows in all regions weakened slightly because of the 2007–8 global financial crisis. The report noted, however, that the total "stock" of international migrants has remained stable and can be expected to grow in the coming years.[13]

Several macro trends deserve to be flagged in this introduction.
- **Shifting geography of migration.** As pressures to move increase, and as transport becomes easier, people are moving farther away from home. The Organisation for Economic Co-operation and Development (OECD), for example, has reported growing migration from physically

and culturally distant countries, especially in Asia.[14] The rapidly increasing number of migrant workers from Asia into the Gulf countries
provides further evidence of this trend. The changing geography of
migration is also a product of shifting demands. For example, aging populations in advanced industrialized countries require compensatory labor
immigration across all categories as well as in sectors such as nursing and
personal care. These demands often cannot be met without expanding
the migration pool well beyond the immediate region.

• **Continuing high levels of irregular migration and concern about
this phenomenon.** Not everyone who wishes or needs to migrate can
do so legally. Every country has the right to control its borders and most
countries have placed restrictions on who may enter and under what
conditions. These restrictions are enforced by a range of measures including visas, immigration checks, border controls, and sometimes even
patrols outside the territory of the destination country aimed at detecting
those seeking to enter without authorization. While such restrictions are
increasing, the levels of irregular migration are also continuing to rise.
Irregular migrants include refugees who are forced to flee conflict and
persecution. Under international human rights law, these persons have
a right to seek asylum and should not be returned home. Many other
irregular migrants are motivated by the simple desire for a better life
and the lack of any meaningful opportunities at home. Irregular migration can be risky for the individuals involved and is also argued to work
against the development goals of migration. However, as recognized by
several contributors to this anthology, the current mismatch between
migration pressures and opportunities means that it is difficult, perhaps
even impossible, to eradicate or substantially reduce such migration.

• **Gender in migration.** As our information position about who is
migrating and why has improved, so has our appreciation of the gendered aspects of migration. In short, it has become increasingly clear that
women and men migrate in different ways, often for different purposes,
and can face very different challenges. These differences are a reflection of how societies and labor markets are themselves highly gendered.
Traditionally, women migrated less than men and usually moved only as
part of a family group. Today, however, women are migrating more often,
on their own behalf, for both work and marriage. While gender divisions
in some aspects of the labor market are breaking down, women are still
heavily overrepresented in the informal economy and in occupations
such as domestic service that can present particular vulnerabilities. The

"feminization of migration" is an umbrella term often used to introduce discussion of women in migration. This issue is addressed at several points in this book.

• **National migration policies.** There is little doubt that policies of both sending and receiving countries profoundly affect how migration happens. Sending and receiving countries will, of course, have very different interests, concerns, and priorities. As a recent OECD report notes, for many industrialized countries, migration management has become "a difficult balancing act between attracting required skills without compromising domestic workers, firm border controls, effective integration of immigrants and satisfying public opinion."[15] Concern over irregular migration among this group of countries has become particularly acute in recent years, leading to a strengthening of migration controls and concerted attacks on migrant smuggling. Countries of origin must perform a similar balancing act, working to protect their migrating citizens from exploitation and abuse, maintain a steady flow of remittances, and ensure that sufficient skilled workers remain available at home to meet current and future needs.

• **Greater international and regional cooperation.** While the policy imperatives of countries of destination and origin are inevitably very different, there is a growing awareness of links and overlaps. This awareness is reflected in the various intergovernmental processes that bring different countries together with the goal of identifying common concerns and preserving common interests. The Global Forum on Migration and Development (GFMD), a voluntary and informal consultative process open to all United Nations member states, is an example of this type of process, although some critics charge that it is little more than a talk-shop that legitimizes continuing top-down strategies of migration control. Similar consultative processes on migration at the regional and subregional levels have been established in many parts of the world, providing a more tailored forum for groups of countries to come together on the basis of common (or at least complementary) interests in order to share information and develop agreed approaches. Civil society groups (comprised of migrants or their advocates, or involved in more general issues such as human rights protection) are also exercising a growing influence on policies and practices around migration.

• **Increased attention to aspects of human rights.** In recent years, the issue of migrants' rights, and how these rights can be protected and respected, has shifted up the international political agenda. This new level of attention reflects a growing realization of the extent to which certain categories of migrants are vulnerable to exploitation and abuse. For example, international and domestic laws now provide a range of protections to victims of trafficking[16] and countries of origin and destination are being pressured to ensure that migrants are protected from forced labor, sexual exploitation, and domestic servitude.[17] The obligation on countries not to return asylum seekers to persecution is increasingly being recognized, although still subject to frequent breach.

• **Ongoing human rights challenges, despite progress in some areas.** States generally continue to be reluctant advocates and inconsistent protectors of migrants and their rights. While recognizing the moral argument for justice and equality, many states also understand that the current system delivers them substantial economic benefits. It is relevant to note that the major United Nations treaty in this area, the International Convention on the Protection of the Rights of All Migrant Workers and Members of Their Families, took more than a decade to enter into force and has received almost no support from the wealthy countries of destination. Overall, the international system for protecting rights of migrants has been accurately described as "substance without architecture."[18] There is, in short, a substantial gap between the rhetoric of migrants' rights and the reality. Despite widespread agreement that migrants are entitled to basic rights and freedoms, many continue to suffer from an entrenched discrimination that undermines their rights and prevents them from accessing justice.

Different Perspectives on Migration

Migration is a complex area of study. It does not "belong" to—or allow itself to be easily captured by—one discipline. Rather, it cuts across many fields, from law to gender studies to anthropology, from geography to economics to international relations. The increasing diversity of migration and migration-related impacts creates additional barriers to neat classification. This reality is reflected in the breadth of articles selected for the present anthology, which are drawn from a wide range of disciplines and incorporate multiple perspectives, often on the very same issues.

As scholars and practitioners have come to appreciate the enormous complexities around migration and to understand underlying processes better, some of the more traditional and either/or modes of analysis and description (e.g., forced/voluntary, skilled/unskilled, regular (documented)/irregular (undocumented), origin/transit/destination, internal/cross-border, North/South) are being questioned. For example, it is now well understood that only in the most extreme cases of "forced" migration does the individual concerned lose all personal agency. Conversely, the apparently voluntary migrant may be subject to a range of pressures that operate to affect significantly the extent to which he or she is actually exercising control over whether and how migration takes place. The traditional division between internal and cross-border migration (followed in the present anthology) is coming up against a growing body of evidence that confirms significant and substantial links between internal and international migration.

The theoretical framework adopted by an institution working on migration—or indeed by an individual studying and writing about migration—will often reflect preexisting expertise, interests, and preferences. Some of these will be obvious. For example, migration research from the perspective of a country of destination may focus more heavily on issues of integration and labor market regulation and pay greater attention to the issue of irregular migration. Institutions in these countries and regions will often reflect such priorities in their research and other work. Countries of origin may prioritize consideration of how remittances can be facilitated as well as how their own human resources can be retained to meet national needs.

The two lenses through which this anthology considers migration, human rights, and development, are similarly weighted toward a particular theoretical framework. A focus on human rights in migration will likely place the individual at the center of any analysis: A human rights-based framework for examining migration will be *normatively based* on international human rights standards and *operationally directed* to promoting and protecting human rights. Such an approach will require an analysis of the ways in which human rights violations arise throughout the migration process, as well as of states' obligations under international human rights law. It will seek to identify and redress the discriminatory practices and unjust distributions of power that prompt migration in the first place and that deny justice for migration-related violations. While a development-focused consideration of migration may well touch on these issues, its primary framework is likely to be more centered on how migration affects the capacity of states to develop their societies and economies. It may pay more attention to the issue of remittances in increasing individual and community wealth; to the role of diasporas; and to the phenomenon of education-related migration.

A fundamental premise of this anthology is that the perspectives of human rights and development are—or should be—both complementary and interrelated. In other words, while their overarching theories may be different, they also share certain important ideas and values. It is hoped that in this way, the common themes that unite human rights and development, including justice, equality, improvement in the conditions and quality of life, and respect for the rule of law, can be recognized and promoted.

The following text box seeks to capture the rationale and guiding principles behind a unified vision of migration, development, and human rights.

Migration, development, and human rights: Some important links

- All persons, irrespective of their nationality and immigration status, are entitled to enjoy protection of their human and labor rights.
- A rights-based policy gives migrants an opportunity to be productive economically and to enrich their social lives.
- Equal protection of human rights for migrants and citizens enhances social cohesion and integration.
- Enjoyment of human rights enhances the capacity of migrants to contribute to their home and host society.
- Migrants' contributions to their country of origin can enhance the ability of people left behind to access their rights (for example, through remittances sent back that are used for education).
- Protection of human rights may reduce pressure to emigrate, as the violation of rights can create situations of poverty, poor governance, conflict, etc., all of which can provoke movement.
- Enforcement of labor standards in destination countries may curb the demand for irregular migrant workers who are at particular risk of human rights violations.

Adapted from Global Migration Group, *Mainstreaming Migration into Development Planning: A Handbook for Policy-Makers and Practitioners* (2010).

THE STRUCTURE OF THIS ANTHOLOGY

The anthology is divided into four parts: an initial part introducing key concepts and issues; two parts focusing on the development and human rights aspects of migration, respectively; and a final part that seeks to unite these two themes in looking to the future. Each part is prefaced by an introduction that provides a short overview of individual pieces as well as a set of questions for discussion.

Part 1: *An Introduction to the Issues* seeks to acquaint the reader with the most important concepts and themes of the anthology. The selected pieces are accordingly introductory and wide-ranging, addressing basic questions about what migration means, how it happens, and how it is linked to both human rights and development. The contributions to this part explain the political, social, and economic importance of contemporary migration. They also question the capacity of states to curb or even substantially affect migratory flows and trends. An underlying theme of this part is the recognition that properly managed migration, which seeks to promote development and respects basic human rights, can be, in the words of the United Nations Secretary-General Kofi Annan, a "triple win": for migrants themselves, for countries of origin, and for countries of destination.

Part 2: *Perspectives on Migration and Development* introduces the now widely recognized link between migration and development. It is important to note at this point that development means much more than increasing national wealth and economic security. The United Nations emphasizes "human development," which uses indicators such as life expectancy, access to education, and even political freedom to measure what it considers to be the real level of a country's development. The contributions to this part reflect on the migration–development nexus from both the country of origin and the country of destination. For countries of origin, priority issues include the causes of migration and its impacts, not just on the migrant but also on those who are left behind. Another central theme of this part is the role played by remittances, particularly in promoting development and reducing poverty. From the perspective of countries of origin, several contributions identify the many benefits of immigration, as well as the substantial costs that are associated with its control and management. The issue of irregular migration is, of course, a major concern for countries of destination and, as one contribution confirms, a source of growing public unease. The relationship between this form of migration and development is complex and contested, and the subject of a number of assumptions that need to be tested.

Part 3: *Human Rights in Migration* addresses the various ways in which issues of human rights intersect with migration and the extent to which international human rights law places constraints and limitations on many aspects of and responses to migration. For example, human rights law recognizes that all aliens, even those who are in another country without authorization, are entitled to have their basic human rights respected and protected, including the right to life, the prohibition on torture and inhuman or degrading treatment, and the prohibition on discrimination. International human rights law extends special and additional protections to certain categories of migrants, including unaccompanied children, migrant workers, and asylum seekers. The contributions to this part seek to identify the most pressing human rights issues for migrants and to flesh out the substantive content of the obligations owed to them by countries of destination and countries of origin. Importantly the articles in this section also confirm the many limitations on migrant rights and the significant obstacles to the effective implementation of those rights that are in fact recognized and accepted.

Part 4: *Toward the Future* seeks to encourage a broader and more thoughtful reflection on migration, human rights, and development with a selection of pieces that challenges traditional assumptions and present new ways of thinking about and dealing with migration. For example, is the long-held sovereign right of states to control their own borders actually justified in our newly globalized and interdependent world? Can we (and should we) find cheaper, more humane alternatives to current border control policies and practices? Is the view of irregular migration as a "problem" that can be "fixed" even a realistic one? How has the development–migration link evolved over the past decade and is it actually serving the interests of migrants and countries of origin? Finally, how can we promote a genuinely rights-based vision of migration, one that places the interests of individuals, families, and communities at the center of migration law, policy, and practice?

NOTES

1. United Nations Development Programme, *Human Development Report 2009—Overcoming Barriers: Human Mobility and Development* (New York: UNDP, 2009).

2. World Bank, *Migration and Remittances Fact Book 2011*, 2nd ed. (Washington, DC: World Bank, 2011).

3. World Bank.

4. World Bank; International Organization for Migration, *World Migration Report 2011: Communicating Effectively About Migration* (Geneva: IOM, 2011); Organisation for Economic Co-operation and Development (OECD), *International Migration Outlook: SOPEMI 2011* (Paris, OECD Publishing, 2011).

5. United Nations High Commissioner for Refugees (UNHCR), "Mediterranean Takes Record as Most Deadly Stretch of Water for Refugees and Migrants in 2011: Briefing Notes," http://www.unhcr.org/4f27e01f9.html (accessed November 20, 2011).

6. IOM 2011.

7. Bimal Ghosh, *The Global Economic Crisis and Migration: Where Do We Go from Here?* (Geneva: International Organization for Migration/The Hague Process, 2011).

8. IOM 2010.

9. IOM 2011.

10. IOM 2008.

11. United Nations, "17th Conference of the Parties to the United Nations Framework Convention on Climate Change, Implementing the Cancun Adaptation Framework: Vulnerability, Changing Populations and Human Mobility 2011" (COP17 2011), Interagency Concept Note, 6 December 2011, http://www.iom.int/jahia/webdav/shared/shared/mainsite/activities/env_degradation/cop17/Vulnerability-Population-Mobility-Concept-Note.pdf (accessed January 7, 2013).

12. Rafael Reuveny, "Climate Change-Induced Migration and Violent Conflict," *Political Geography* 26 (2007): 656–73.

13. IOM 2011.

14. OECD 2011.

15. Jean-Pierre Garson, and John Salt. "50th OECD Anniversary: International Migration and the SOPEMI," in *International Migration Outlook: SOPEMI 2011* (Paris, OECD Publishing, 2011), 14.

16. Anne T. Gallagher, *The International Law of Human Trafficking* (New York: Cambridge University Press, 2010).

17. U.S. State Department, *Trafficking in Persons Report: June 2012* (Washington, DC: Department of State, 2012).

18. T. Alexander Aleinikoff, "International Legal Norms on Migration: Substance without Architecture," in *International Migration Law: Developing Paradigms and Key Challenges*, ed. Ryszard Cholewinski, Richard Perruchoud and Euan MacDonald, 467–79 (The Hague: T.M.C. Asser Press, 2007).

REFERENCES

Aleinikoff, T. Alexander. "International Legal Norms on Migration: Substance without Architecture." In *International Migration Law: Developing Paradigms and Key Challenges*, edited by Ryszard Cholewinski, Richard Perruchoud, and Euan MacDonald, 467–79. The Hague: T.M.C. Asser Press, 2007.

Castles, Stephen. "Bringing Human Rights into the Migration and Development Debate." *Global Policy* 2, no. 3 (2011): 248–58.

———. "Understanding Global Migration: A Social Transformation Perspective." *Journal of Ethnic and Migration Studies* 36, no. 10 (2010): 1565–86.

Gallagher, Anne T. *The International Law of Human Trafficking*. New York: Cambridge University Press, 2010.

Garson, Jean-Pierre and John Salt. "50th OECD Anniversary: *International Migration and the SOPEMI*." In *International Migration Outlook: SOPEMI 2011*. Paris: OECD Publishing, 2011.

Ghosh, Bimal. *The Global Economic Crisis and Migration: Where Do We Go From Here?* Geneva: International Organization for Migration/The Hague Process, 2011.

Global Migration Group. *Mainstreaming Migration into Development Planning: A Handbook for Policy-Makers and Practitioners*. Geneva: International Organization for Migration, 2010.

Graham, Elspeth. "What Kind of Theory for What Kind of Population Geography?" *International Journal of Population Geography* 6 (2000): 257–72.

International Organization for Migration. *Migration and Climate Change*. Geneva: IOM, 2008.

———. *Migration and the Economic Crisis in the European Union: Implications for Policy*. Geneva: IOM, 2010.

———. *World Migration Report 2011: Communicating Effectively About Migration*. Geneva: IOM, 2011.

Legrain, Philippe. *Immigrants: Your Country Needs Them*. London: Little, Brown, 2007.

Organisation for Economic Co-operation and Development. *International Migration Outlook: SOPEMI 2011*. Paris: OECD Publishing, 2011.

Reuveny, Rafael. "Climate Change-Induced Migration and Violent Conflict." *Political Geography* 26 (2007): 656–73.

United Nations. "17th Conference of the Parties to the United Nations Framework Convention on Climate Change, Implementing the Cancun Adaptation Framework: Vulnerability, Changing Populations and Human Mobility 2011" (COP17 2011), Interagency Concept Note, 6 December 2011. http://www.iom.int/jahia/webdav/shared/shared/mainsite/activities/env_degradation/cop17/Vulnerability-Population-Mobility-Concept-Note.pdf (accessed January 7, 2013).

United Nations. "International Convention on the Protection of the Rights of All Migrant Workers and Members of their Families." United Nations Treaty Collection. http://treaties.un.org/Pages/ViewDetails.aspx?src=TREATY&mtdsg_no=IV-13&chapter=4&lang=en (accessed November 20, 2012).

United Nations Development Programme. *Human Development Report 2009—Overcoming Barriers: Human Mobility and Development*. New York: UNDP, 2009.

United Nations High Commissioner for Refugees. "Mediterranean Takes Record as Most Deadly Stretch of Water for Refugees and Migrants in 2011: Briefing Notes." UNHCR. http://www.unhcr.org/4f27e01f9.html (accessed November 20, 2011).

U.S. State Department. *Trafficking in Persons Report: June 2012*. Washington, DC: Department of State, 2012.

World Bank. *Migration and Remittances Fact Book 2011*. 2nd ed. Washington, DC: World Bank, 2011.

Part 1: An Introduction to the Issues

The purpose of Part 1 is to introduce the key issues and concepts to be explored further in the anthology, through a selection of introductory, wide-ranging pieces that address the most important questions: How does migration happen? What is the link between migration and development? Between migration and human rights? How do different countries experience migration? To what extent are the different interests around migration reflected in laws, policies, and institutions?

Part 1 begins with an address by the United Nations Secretary-General Kofi Annan to the High-Level Dialogue on International Migration and Development, which took place at the General Assembly in 2006. The Secretary-General highlights the growing awareness that properly managed migration brings "triple wins," for migrants, for the countries that receive them, and for their own countries of origin. He urges countries to view migration "through the prism of opportunity, rather than the prism of fear,"[1] recognizing common goals and working together to achieve them. While not dwelling on dangers and risks, the Secretary-General sounds some warnings: about migration-related practices, such as human trafficking and smuggling, that present grave risks to individual rights and freedoms; and about the costs to divided families and the problem of rising social tensions associated with migration.

In "Why Migration Matters," Khalid Koser places current discussions about migration in historical context before outlining the main reasons why migration is as important today as a political, social, and economic phenomenon. Koser discusses current migration dynamics, including the "feminization of migration"; the rapid increase in irregular migration; and the relationship between migration and globalization in terms of economic growth, development, and concerns about security. When looking to the future, Koser emphasizes the resilience of migrants and of migration: In his view, the 2007–8 global financial crisis is likely to have little lasting impact. However, the effect of climate change—and the way in which countries may respond to mass migration arising from climate change—is much less certain.

In his 2003 article, "Borders Beyond Control," Jagdish Bhagwati expresses the provocative view that the ability of countries to control borders has decreased dramatically, at the very time when their desire to do so has reached new heights. In his opinion, little can be done to effectively reduce or even significantly change migration, whether regular or irregular. He maintains that "governments must reorient their policies from attempting to curtail migration to coping and working with it to seek benefits for all."[2] A similar reorientation needs to take place in countries of origin; Bhagwati suggests that rather than trying to hold onto skilled labor, governments adopt a "diaspora model," which "integrates present and past citizens into a web of rights and obligations."[3]

The final article in Part 1 is a 2011 piece by Stephen Castles, "Bringing Human Rights into the Migration and Development Debate." Castles argues that migration management suffers from what he terms a "global governance deficit." Unlike other areas, such as trade and finance, of importance to all states, there is no international institution or arrangement to set and enforce internationally agreed standards. He charts recent developments, including the emergence of migration associations that are linking with established human rights organizations, and of intergovernmental processes that bring together countries of origin and destination. However, Castles questions whether these new developments will, in the end, bring significant benefits to migrant workers and their families. He identifies a risk that emerging global migration management strategies will be weighted toward the interests of states that may not prioritize protection of migrants from exploitation and other abuses of their rights. The central policy implication of Castles's analysis is that countries involved in importing labor "can no longer pursue migration policies that ignore the interests, needs and rights of migrants and their communities of origin."[4] Castles also maintains that states must take a broader view of migration and development: "Migration only benefits development if it is seen as part of a broader change process"[5] that includes strengthening institutions and improving rights and political participation. Like several other contributors to this anthology, Castles argues that the research agenda around migration has long been dominated by the interests of countries of destination and that real change will require a major reorientation of conceptual frameworks and data collection systems. This reorientation would affect how knowledge is produced and the way it is used for policy planning in the migration field.

As you read the articles in this part, consider the following questions:
• Why do people migrate? Think about economic and noneconomic factors in the origin and destination countries.
• Is gender only relevant for female migrants? For example, do male migrants face special issues or vulnerabilities that should be acknowledged and responded to?

- Several of the contributors to this section advocate a challenging of the assumptions that underlie much discussion around migration. Which assumptions do you think are the most important to challenge?
- What can countries do to discourage skilled professionals from going abroad? Or to encourage students who are studying abroad to return home after their studies? Think about the impact on the individual (shouldn't people be able to choose where they live and work?) and on the origin country (do citizens have obligations to their country of nationality or citizenship?).

NOTES

1. The United Nations Secretary-General, "The Secretary-General Address to the High-Level Dialogue of the General Assembly on International Migration and Development" (New York, September 14, 2006).

2. Jagdish Bhagwati, "Borders Beyond Control," *Foreign Affairs* 82, no. 1 (2003): 1.

3. Bhagwati, "Borders Beyond Control," 3.

4. Stephen Castles, "Bringing Human Rights into the Migration and Development Debate," *Global Policy* 2, no. 3 (2011): 248.

5. Castles, "Bringing Human Rights into the Migration and Development Debate," 248.

The Secretary-General Address to the High-Level Dialogue of the General Assembly on International Migration and Development

by the United Nations Secretary-General

Madam President, Excellencies, Ladies and Gentlemen:

Migration is a courageous expression of an individual's will to overcome adversity and live a better life. Over the past decade, globalization has increased the number of people with the desire and capacity to move to other places.

This new era of mobility has created opportunities for societies throughout the world, as well as new challenges. It has also underscored the strong linkages between international migration and development.

Just a few years ago, many people did not think it possible to discuss migration at the United Nations. Governments, they said, would not dare to bring into the international arena a topic on which their citizens are so sensitive.

Yet here you are, and I sense that the mood is changing.

More and more people are excited about the ways in which migrants can help transform their adopted and their native countries. More and more people understand that governments can cooperate to create triple wins—for migrants, for their countries of origin, and for the societies that receive them.

No one can deny that international migration has negative aspects— trafficking, smuggling, social discontent—or that it often arises from poverty or political strife. But by being here today you show yourselves willing to tackle migration's challenges through dialogue and cooperation, rather than antagonism and isolation.

Your presence is also a tribute to the infectious energy and visionary pragmatism of my Special Representative, Peter Sutherland. His efforts have reassured and inspired everyone. I am deeply grateful to him.

As you begin your Dialogue, let me suggest three reasons why this is the right moment for it.

First, to put it simply, we are all in this together. More countries are now significantly involved in, and affected by, international migration than at any time in history. And they are no longer so easily divided into "countries of origin" and "countries of destination". Many are now both. Countries that are very different in other respects face surprisingly similar migration challenges.

Second, the evidence on migration's potential benefits is mounting. With their remittances reaching an estimated 167 billion dollars last year, the amount of money migrants from the developing world send back to their families exceeds the total of all international aid combined. And money is far from being the whole story. Migrants also use their skills and know-how to transfer technology, capital, and institutional knowledge. They inspire new ways of thinking about social and political issues. They form a dynamic human link between cultures, economies, and societies. As a result, we are better positioned than ever to confront the challenges of migration, and seize its opportunities.

Third, Governments are now beginning to see international migration through the prism of opportunity, rather than of fear. You are focused on magnifying the positive, mutually beneficial aspects of migration: on sharing your experiences, developing practical ideas, building partnerships.

For all these reasons—and also because people migrate not only between neighbouring countries or within regions, but from almost every corner of the world to every other—international migration today cries out for a global discussion.

Of course, it also stirs passionate debate. It can deprive countries of their best and brightest. It can divide families. It can generate social tensions. Sometimes criminals and terrorists exploit it. But the answers to many of these problems can be found through constructive engagement and debate.

That's why I think the dialogue you are starting today should not end tomorrow. I am especially delighted that so many of you have embraced my proposal for a Global Forum on Migration and Development, and asked me to help set it up. And I am particularly grateful to the Government of Belgium for offering to host the first meeting next year.

I believe such a Forum can foster practical, evidence-based cooperation among governments. It can give you a chance to frame the issues in a way that allows you to move forward together, to discover areas where you agree, and to find ways of improving cooperation.

Clearly, there is no consensus on making international migration the subject of formal, norm-setting negotiations. There is little appetite for any norm-setting intergovernmental commission on migration. But, as I understand the thinking of the countries that back it, the Forum would be the opposite of that. It would be informal, voluntary, consultative. Above all, it would not make binding decisions.

The Forum would allow us to build relationships of trust, and to bring together the best ideas that different countries have developed: facilitating remittances; engaging diasporas; exploring new ways to reduce poverty; building educational partnerships; and so on.

Finally, it would show that Governments are now willing to address this complicated, volatile issue in a thoughtful, constructive fashion.

The Forum must be led and overseen by States. But the United Nations System, and I personally, stand ready to support it. I have decided to extend the mandate of my Special Representative on Migration beyond this Dialogue. I trust that the Special Representative will form an essential link between the proposed Forum and the entire United Nations system. Also, I stand ready to create a voluntary Trust Fund to help support the Forum's work, should you find this useful.

The United Nations is rising to the challenges of international migration in other ways as well. Last spring, I established the Global Migration Group, which brings together UN offices, Funds, Programmes, and Agencies engaged in various aspects of international migration and development, as well as the International Organization for Migration. You are no doubt familiar with the important work done by the constituent members of the Group—from supporting labour migration to helping developing countries connect better with migrant communities abroad, from outstanding demographic analysis to research on remittances, from efforts to secure the rights of migrants to combatting trafficking in human beings. The Global Migration Group is working to ensure stronger coordination and greater coherence among its members.

Ladies and gentlemen,

This High-level Dialogue will succeed to the extent that it ushers in an era of sustained, thoughtful consideration of international migration and development issues. For far too long, migration policy has been based on hunches, anecdotes, and political expediency. It is now time to turn to the evidence, and use it to build a common understanding of how international migration can bring benefits to all.

Thank you very much.

The United Nations Secretary-General. "The Secretary-General Address to the High-Level Dialogue of the General Assembly on International Migration and Development." New York, September 14, 2006. Available at www.un.org/migration/sg-speech.html. © United Nations 2006.

Reprinted by permission.

Why Migration Matters

by Khalid Koser*

"The world total of international migrants has more than doubled in just 25 years; about 25 million were added in just the first 5 years of the twenty-first century."

Migration has always mattered—but today it matters more than ever before. The increasing importance of migration derives from its growing scale and its widening global reach, but also from a number of new dynamics. These include the feminization of migration, the growth of so-called irregular migration, and migration's inextricable linkages with globalization in terms of economic growth, development, and security. Climate change, moreover, is certain to raise migration still higher on nations' and international institutions' policy agendas.

The history of migration begins with humanity's very origins in the Rift Valley of Africa. It was from there that Homo sapiens emerged about 120,000 years ago, subsequently migrating across Africa, through the Middle East to Europe and Central and South Asia, and finally to the New World, reaching the Bering Straits about 20,000 years ago. Then, in the ancient world, Greek colonization and Roman expansion depended on migration; significant movements of people were also associated with the Mesopotamian, Incan, Indus, and Zhou empires. Later we see major migrations such as those involving the Vikings along the shorelines of the Atlantic and North Sea, and the Crusaders to the Holy Land.

In more recent history—in other words, in the past two or three centuries—it is possible to discern, according to migration historian Robin Cohen, a series of major migration periods or events. In the eighteenth and nineteenth centuries, one of the most prominent migration events was the forced transportation of slaves. About 12 million people were taken, mainly from West Africa, to the New World (and also, in lesser numbers, across the Indian Ocean and the Mediterranean Sea). One of the reasons this migration is considered so important, other than its scale, is that it still resonates for descendants of slaves and for African Americans in particular. After slavery's collapse, indentured laborers from China, India, and Japan moved overseas in significant numbers—1.5 million from India alone—to work the plantations of the European powers.

European expansion, especially during the nineteenth century, brought about large-scale voluntary migration away from Europe, particularly to the colonies of settlement, dominions, and the Americas. The great mercantile powers—Britain, the Netherlands, Spain, and France—all promoted settlement of their nationals abroad, not just workers but also peasants, dissident soldiers, convicts, and orphans. Migration associated with expansion largely came to an end with the rise of anticolonial movements toward the end of the nineteenth century, and indeed over the next decades some significant reverse flows back to Europe occurred, for example of the so-called *pieds noirs* to France.

The next period of migration was marked by the rise of the United States as an industrial power. Between the 1850s and the Great Depression of the 1930s, millions of workers fled the stagnant economies and repressive political regimes of northern, southern, and eastern Europe and moved to the United States. (Many fled the Irish famine as well.) Some 12 million of these migrants landed at Ellis Island in New York Harbor. Opportunities for work in the United States also attracted large numbers of Chinese migrants in the first wave of the so-called Chinese diaspora, during the last 50 years of the nineteenth century.

The next major period of migration came after World War II, when the booming postwar economies in Europe, North America, and Australia needed labor. This was the era when, for example, many Turkish migrants arrived to work in Germany and many North Africans went to France and Belgium. It was also the period when, between 1945 and 1972, about 1 million Britons migrated to Australia as so-called "Ten Pound Poms" under an assisted passage scheme. During the same era but in other parts of the world, decolonization continued to have an impact on migration, most significantly in the movement of millions of Hindus and Muslims after the partition of India in 1947 and of Jews and Palestinians after the creation of Israel.

By the late 1970s, and in part as a consequence of the 1973 oil crisis, the international migrant labor boom had ended in Europe, though in the United States it continued into the 1990s. Now, with the global economy's momentum shifting decisively to Asia, labor migration on that continent has grown heavily, and it is still growing. How much longer this will be true, given the current global financial crisis, is a matter open to debate.

MORE AND MORE

As even this (inevitably selective) overview of international migration's history should make clear, large movements of people have always been associated with significant global events like revolutions, wars, and the rise and fall of empires; with epochal changes like economic expansion, nation building, and political transformations; and with enduring challenges like conflict, persecution, and dispossession.

Nevertheless, one reason to argue that migration matters more today than ever before is sheer numbers. If we define an international migrant as a person who stays outside his usual country of residence for at least one year, there are about 200 million such migrants worldwide. This is roughly equivalent to the population of the fifth-most populous country on earth, Brazil. In fact, 1 in every 35 people in the world today is an international migrant.

Of course, a less dramatic way to express this statistic is to say that only 3 percent of the world's population is composed of international migrants. (In migration, statistics are often used to alarm rather than to inform.) And it is also worth noting that internal migration is a far more significant phenomenon than is international migration (China alone has at least 130 million internal migrants). Still, the world total of international migrants has more than doubled in just 25 years; about 25 million were added in just the first 5 years of the twenty-first century.

And international migration affects many more people than just those who migrate. According to Stephen Castles and Mark Miller, authors of the influential volume *The Age of Migration*, "There can be few people in either industrialized or less developed countries today who do not have personal experience of migration and its effects; this universal experience has become the hallmark of the age of migration." In host countries, migrants' contributions are felt keenly in social, cultural, and economic spheres. Throughout the world, people of different national origins, who speak different languages and practice different customs and religions, are coming into unprecedented contact with each other. For some this is a threat, for others an opportunity.

Migration is also a far more global process than ever before, as migrants today travel both from and to all of the world's regions. In 2005 (the most recent year for which global data are available) there were about 60 million international migrants in Europe, 44 million in Asia, 41 million in North America, 16 million in Africa, and 6 million each in Latin America and Australia. A significant portion of the world's migrants—about 35 million—lived in the United States. The Russian Federation was the second-largest host country for migrants, with about 13 million living there. Following in the rankings were Germany, Ukraine, and India, each with between 6 million and 7 million migrants.

It is much harder to say which countries migrants come from, largely because origin countries tend not to keep count of how many of their nationals are living abroad. It has been estimated that at least 35 million Chinese currently live outside their country, along with 20 million Indians and 8 million Filipinos. But in fact the traditional distinctions among migrants' countries of origin, transit, and destination have become increasingly blurred. Today almost every country in the world fulfills all three roles—migrants leave them, pass through them, and head for them.

A WORLD OF REASONS

The reasons for the recent rise in international migration and its widening global reach are complex. The factors include growing global disparities in development, democracy, and demography; in some parts of the world, job shortages that will be exacerbated by the current economic downturn; the segmentation of labor markets in high-income economies, a situation that attracts migrant workers to so-called "3D" jobs (dirty, difficult, or dangerous); revolutions in communications and transportation, which result in more people than ever before knowing about life elsewhere and having the ability to travel there; migration networks that allow existing migrant and ethnic communities to act as magnets for further migration; and a robust migration industry, including migrant smugglers and human traffickers, that profits from international migration.

In addition to being bigger, international migration today is also a more complex phenomenon than it has been in the past, as people of all ages and types move for a wide variety of reasons. For example, child migration appears to be on the increase around the world. Migrants with few skills working "3D" jobs make important contributions to the global economy, but so do highly skilled migrants and students. Some people move away from their home countries permanently, but an increasing proportion moves only temporarily, or circulates between countries. And though an important legal distinction can be made between people who move for work purposes and those who flee conflict and persecution, in reality the two can be difficult to distinguish, as members of the two groups sometimes move together in so-called "mixed flows."

One trend of particular note is that women's representation among migrants has increased rapidly, starting in the 1960s and accelerating in the 1990s. Very nearly half the world's authorized migrants in 2005 were women, and more female than male authorized migrants resided in Europe, North America, Latin America and the Caribbean, the states of the former Soviet Union, and Oceania. What is more, whereas women have traditionally migrated to join their partners, an increasing proportion who migrate today do so independently. Indeed, they are often primary breadwinners for families that they leave behind.

A number of reasons help explain why women comprise an increasing proportion of the world's migrants. One is that global demand for foreign labor, especially in more developed countries, is becoming increasingly gender-selective. That is, more jobs are available in the fields typically staffed by women—services, health care, and entertainment. Second, an increasing number of countries have extended the right of family reunion to migrants, allowing them to be joined by their spouses and children. Third, in some countries of origin, changes in gender relations mean that women enjoy more freedom than previously to migrate independently. Finally, in trends especially evident in Asia, there has been growth in migration of women for domestic work (this is sometimes called the "maid trade"); in organized migration for marriage (with the women sometimes referred to as "mail-order brides"); and in the trafficking of women, above all into the sex industry.

MOST IRREGULAR

Another defining characteristic of the new global migration is the growth of irregular migration and the rapid rise of this phenomenon in policy agendas. Indeed, of all the categories of international migrants, none attracts as much attention or divides opinion as consistently as irregular migrants—people often described as "illegal," "undocumented," or "unauthorized."

Almost by definition, irregular migration defies enumeration (although most commentators believe that its scale is increasing). A commonly cited estimate holds that there are around 40 million irregular migrants worldwide, of whom perhaps one-third are in the United States. There are between 3.5 million and 5 million irregular migrants in the Russian Federation, and perhaps 5 million in Europe. Each year, an estimated 2.5 million to 4 million migrants are thought to cross international borders without authorization.

One reason that it is difficult to count irregular migrants is that even this single category covers people in a range of different situations. It includes migrants who enter or remain in a country without authorization; those who are smuggled or trafficked across an international border; those who seek asylum, are not granted it, and then fail to observe a deportation order; and people who circumvent immigration controls, for example by arranging bogus marriages or fake adoptions.

What is more, an individual migrant's status can change—often rapidly. A migrant can enter a country in an irregular fashion but then regularize her status, for example by applying for asylum or entering a regularization program. Conversely, a migrant can enter regularly then become irregular by working without a permit or overstaying a visa. In Australia, for example, British citizens who have stayed beyond the expiration of their visas account for by far the largest number of irregular migrants.

THE RICH GET RICHER

International migration matters more today than ever because of its new dimensions and dynamics, but even more because of its increased impact—on the global economy, on international politics, and on society. Three impacts are particularly worth noting: international migration's contribution to the global economy; the significance of migration for development; and the linkages between migration and security.

Kodak, Atlantic Records, RCA, NBC, Google, Intel, Hotmail, Sun, Microsoft, Yahoo, eBay—all these US firms were founded or cofounded by migrants. It has been estimated that international migrants make a net contribution to the US economy of $60 billion, and that half of the scientists, engineers, and holders of Ph.D. degrees in the United States were born overseas. It is often suggested (though this is hard to substantiate) that migrants are worth more to the British economy than is North Sea oil. Worldwide migrant labor is thought to earn at least $20 trillion. In some of the Gulf states, migrants comprise 90 percent of the labor force.

Such a selection of facts and figures can suggest a number of conclusions about international migration's significance for the global economy. First, migrants are often among the most dynamic and entrepreneurial members of society. This has always been the case. In many ways the history of US economic growth is the history of migrants: Andrew Carnegie (steel), Adolphus Busch (beer), Samuel Goldwyn (movies), and Helena Rubenstein (cosmetics) were all migrants. Second, migrants fill labor market gaps both at the top end and the bottom end—a notion commonly captured in the phrase "Migrants do the work that natives are either unable or unwilling to do." Third, the significance of migrant labor varies across countries but more importantly across economic sectors. In the majority of advanced economies, migrant workers are overrepresented in agriculture, construction, heavy industry, manufacturing, and services—especially food, hospitality, and domestic services. (It is precisely these sectors that the global financial crisis is currently hitting hardest.) Finally, migrant workers contribute significantly more to national economies than they take away (through, for example, pensions and welfare benefits). That is, migrants tend to be young and they tend to work.

This last conclusion explains why migration is increasingly considered one possible response to the demographic crisis that affects increasing numbers of advanced economies (though it does not affect the United States yet). In a number of wealthy countries, a diminishing workforce supports an expanding retired population, and a mismatch results between taxes that are paid into pension and related programs and the payments that those programs must make. Importing youthful workers in the form of migrants appears at first to be a solution—but for two reasons, it turns out to be only a short-term response. First, migrants themselves age and eventually retire. Second, recent research indicates that, within a generation, migrants adapt their fertility rates to those that prevail in the countries where they settle. In other words, it would not take long for migrants to exacerbate rather than relieve a demographic crisis.

THE POOR GET RICHER

International migration does not affect only the economies of countries to which migrants travel—it also strongly affects the economies of countries from which migrants depart, especially in the realm of development in poorer countries. The World Bank estimates that each year migrants worldwide send home about $300 billion. This amounts to triple the value of official development assistance, and is the second-largest source of external funding for developing countries after foreign direct investment. The most important recipient countries for remittances are India ($27 billion), China ($26 billion), Mexico ($25 billion), and the Philippines ($17 billion). The top countries from which remittances are dispatched are the United States ($42 billion), Saudi Arabia ($16 billion), Switzerland ($14 billion), and Germany ($12 billion).

The impact of remittances on development is hotly debated, and to an extent the impact depends on who receives the money and how it is spent. It is indisputable that remittances can lift individuals and families out of poverty: Annual household incomes in Somaliland are doubled by remittances. Where remittances are spent on community projects such as wells and schools, as is often the case in Mexico, they also have a wider benefit. And remittances make a significant contribution to gross domestic product (GDP) at the national level, comprising for example 37 percent of GDP in Tonga and 27 percent in both Jordan and Lesotho.

Most experts emphasize that remittances should not be viewed as a substitute for official development assistance. One reason is that remittances are private monies, and thus it is difficult to influence how they are spent or invested. Also, remittances fluctuate over time, as is now becoming apparent in the context of the global economic crisis. Finally, it has been suggested that remittances can generate a "culture of migration," encouraging further migration, and even provide a disincentive to work where families come to expect money from abroad. It has to be said, even so, that the net impact of remittances in developing countries is positive.

International migration, moreover, can contribute to development through other means than remittances. For example, it can relieve pressure on the labor markets in countries from which migrants originate, reducing competition and unemployment. Indonesia and the Philippines are examples of countries that deliberately export labor for this reason (as well as to obtain remittance income). In addition, migrants can contribute to their home countries when they return by using their savings and the new skills they have acquired—although the impact they can have really depends on the extent to which necessary infrastructure is in place for them to realize their potential.

At the same time, however, international migration can undermine development through so-called "brain drain." This term describes a situation in which skills that are already in short supply in a country depart that country through migration. Brain drain is a particular problem in sub-Saharan Africa's health sector, as significant numbers of African doctors and nurses work in the United Kingdom and elsewhere in Europe. Not only does brain drain deprive a country of skills that are in high demand—it undermines that country's investment in the education and training of its own nationals.

SAFETY FIRST

A third impact of international migration—one that perhaps more than any other explains why it has risen toward the top of policy agendas—is the perception that migration constitutes a heightened security issue in the era after 9/11. Discussions of this issue often revolve around irregular migration—which, in public and policy discourses, is frequently associated with the risk of terrorism, the spread of infectious diseases, and criminality.

Such associations are certainly fair in some cases. A strong link, for example, has been established between irregular migrants from Morocco, Algeria, and Syria and the Madrid bombings of March 2004. For the vast majority of irregular migrants, however, the associations are not fair. Irregular migrants are often assigned bad intentions without any substantiation. Misrepresenting evidence can criminalize and demonize all irregular migrants, encourage them to remain underground—and divert attention from those irregular migrants who actually are criminals and should be prosecuted, as well as those who are suffering from disease and should receive treatment.

Irregular migration is indeed associated with risks, but not with the risks most commonly identified. One legitimate risk is irregular migration's threat to the exercise of sovereignty. States have a sovereign right to control who crosses their borders and remains on their territory, and irregular migration challenges this right. Where irregular migration involves corruption and organized crime, it can also become a threat to public security. This is particularly the case when illegal entry is facilitated by migrant smugglers and human traffickers, or when criminal gangs compete for control of migrants' labor after they have arrived.

When irregular migration results in competition for scarce jobs, this can generate xenophobic sentiments within host populations. Importantly, these sentiments are often directed not only at migrants with irregular status but also at established migrants, refugees, and ethnic minorities. When irregular migration receives a great deal of media attention, it can also undermine public confidence in the integrity and effectiveness of a state's migration and asylum policies.

In addition, irregular migration can undermine the "human security" of migrants themselves. The harm done to migrants by irregular migration is often underestimated—in fact, irregular migration can be very dangerous. A large number of people die each year trying to cross land and sea borders while avoiding detection by the authorities. It has been estimated, for example, that as many as 2,000 migrants die each year trying to cross the Mediterranean from Africa to Europe, and that about 400 Mexicans die annually trying to cross the border into the United States.

People who enter a country or remain in it without authorization are often at risk of exploitation by employers and landlords. Female migrants with irregular status, because they are confronted with gender-based discrimination, are often obliged to accept the most menial jobs in the informal sector, and they may face specific health-related risks, including exposure to HIV/AIDS. Such can be the level of human rights abuses involved in contemporary human trafficking that some commentators have compared it to the slave trade.

Migrants with irregular status are often unwilling to seek redress from authorities because they fear arrest and deportation. For the same reason, they do not always make use of public services to which they are entitled, such as emergency health care. In most countries, they are also barred from using the full range of services available both to citizens and to migrants with regular status. In such situations, already hard-pressed nongovernmental organizations, religious bodies, and other civil society institutions are obliged to provide assistance, at times compromising their own legality.

IN HARD TIMES

What might the future of international migration look like? Tentatively at least, the implications of the current global economic crisis for migration are beginning to emerge. Already a slowdown in the movement of people at a worldwide level has been reported, albeit with significant regional and national variations, and this appears to be largely a result of declining job opportunities in destination countries. The economic sectors in which migrants tend to be over-represented have been hit first; as a consequence migrant workers around the world are being laid off in substantial numbers.

Interestingly, it appears that most workers are nevertheless not returning home, choosing instead to stay and look for new jobs. Those entitled to draw on social welfare systems can be expected to do so, thus reducing their net positive impact on national economies. (It remains to be seen whether national economic stimulus packages, such as the one recently enacted in the United States, will help migrant workers get back to work.) Scattered cases of xenophobia have been reported around the world, as anxious natives increasingly fear labor competition from migrant workers.

In the last quarter of 2008 remittances slowed down. Some project that in 2009 remittances, for the first time in decades, may shrink. Moreover, changes in exchange rates mean that even if the volume of remittances remains stable, their net value to recipients may decrease. These looming trends hold worrying implications for households, communities, and even national economies in poor countries.

Our experience of previous economic downturns and financial crises—including the Great Depression, the oil crisis of the early 1970s, and the Asian, Russian, and Latin American financial crises between 1997 and 2000—tells us that such crises' impact on international migration is relatively short-lived and that migration trends soon rebound. Few experts are predicting that the current economic crisis will fundamentally alter overall trends toward increased international migration and its growing global reach.

HOT IN HERE

In the longer term, what will affect migration patterns and processes far more than any financial crisis is climate change. One commonly cited prediction holds that 200 million people will be forced to move as a result of climate change by 2050, although other projections range from 50 million to a startling 1 billion people moving during this century.

The relationship that will develop between climate change and migration appears complex and unpredictable. One type of variable is in climate change events themselves—a distinction is usually made between slow-onset events like rising sea levels and rapid-onset events like hurricanes and tsunamis. In addition, migration is only one of a number of possible responses to most climate change events. Protective measures such as erecting sea walls may reduce the impact. Societies throughout history have adapted to climate change by altering their agricultural and settlement practices.

Global warming, moreover, will make some places better able to support larger populations, as growing seasons are extended, frost risks reduced, and new crops sustained. Where migration does take place, it is difficult to predict whether the movement will mainly be internal or cross-border, or temporary or permanent. And finally, the relationship between climate change and migration may turn out to be indirect. For example, people may flee conflicts that arise over scarce resources in arid areas, rather than flee desertification itself.

Notwithstanding the considerable uncertainty, a consensus has emerged that, within the next 10 years, climate-related international migration will become observably more frequent, and the scale of overall international migration will increase significantly. Such migration will add still further complexity to the migration situation, as the new migrants will largely defy current classifications.

One immediately contentious issue is whether people who cross borders as a result of the effects of climate change should be defined as "climate refugees" or "climate migrants." The former conveys the fact that at least some people will literally need to seek refuge from the impacts of climate change, will find themselves in situations as desperate as those of other refugees, and will deserve international assistance and protection. But the current definition of a refugee in international law does not extend to people fleeing environmental pressures, and few states are willing to amend the law. Equally, the description "climate migrant" underestimates the involuntariness of the movement, and opens up the possibility for such people to be labeled and dealt with as irregular migrants.

Another legal challenge arises with the prospect of the total submergence by rising sea levels of low-lying island states such as the Maldives—namely, how to categorize people who no longer have a state. Will their national flags be lowered outside UN headquarters in New York, and will they be granted citizenship in another country?

The complexities of responding to climate-related movements of people illustrate a more general point, that new responses are required to international migration as it grows in scale and complexity. Most of the legal frameworks and international institutions established to govern migration were established at the end of World War II, in response to a migration reality very different from that existing today, and as a result new categories of migrants are falling into gaps in protection. New actors have also emerged in international migration, including most importantly the corporate sector, and they have very little representation in migration policy decisions at the moment.

Perhaps most fundamentally, a shift in attitude is required, away from the notion that migration can be controlled, focusing instead on trying to manage migration and maximize its benefits.

*Khalid Koser is deputy director and academic dean at the Geneva Centre for Security Policy. He is an expert in international migration, refugees, asylum, and internal displacement.

Koser, Khalid. "Why Migration Matters." Current History 108, no. 717 (April 2009): 147–153.

Borders Beyond Control

*by Jagdish Bhagwati**

A Door That Will Not Close

International migration lies close to the center of global problems that now seize the attention of politicians and intellectuals across the world. Take just a few recent examples.—Prime Ministers Tony Blair of the United Kingdom and Jose Mar'a Aznar of Spain proposed at last year's European Council meeting in Seville that the European Union withdraw aid from countries that did not take effective steps to stem the flow of illegal emigrants to the EU. Blair's outspoken minister for development, Clare Short, described the proposal as "morally repugnant" and it died amid a storm of other protests.—Australia received severe condemnation worldwide last summer when a special envoy of the UN high commissioner for human rights exposed the deplorable conditions in detention camps that held Afghan, Iranian, Iraqi, and Palestinian asylum seekers who had landed in Australia.

Following the September 11 attacks in New York City and Washington, D.C., U.S. Attorney General John Ashcroft announced several new policies that rolled back protections enjoyed by immigrants. The American Civil Liberties Union (ACLU) and Human Rights Watch fought back. So did Islamic and Arab ethnic organizations. These groups employed lawsuits, public dissent, and congressional lobbying to secure a reversal of the worst excesses.

The Economist ran in just six weeks two major stories describing the growing outflow of skilled citizens from less developed countries to developed countries seeking to attract such immigrants. The "brain drain" of the 1960s is striking again with enhanced vigor.

These examples and numerous others do not just underline the importance of migration issues today. More important, they show governments attempting to stem migration only to be forced into retreat and accommodation by factors such as civil-society activism and the politics of ethnicity. Paradoxically, the ability to control migration has shrunk as the desire to do so has increased. The reality is that borders are beyond control and little can be done to really cut down on immigration. The societies of developed countries will simply not allow it. The less developed countries also seem overwhelmed by forces propelling emigration. Thus, there must be a seismic shift in the way migration is addressed: governments must reorient their policies from attempting to curtail migration to coping and working with it to seek benefits for all.

To demonstrate effectively why and how this must be done, however, requires isolating key migration questions from the many other issues that attend the flows of humanity across national borders. Although some migrants move strictly between rich countries or between poor ones, the most compelling problems result from emigration from less developed to more developed countries. They arise in three areas. First, skilled workers are legally [immigrating], temporarily or permanently, to rich countries. This phenomenon pre-dominantly concerns the less developed countries that are losing skilled labor. Second, largely unskilled migrants are entering developed countries illegally and looking for work. Finally, there is the "involuntary" movement of people, whether skilled or unskilled, across borders to seek asylum. These latter two trends mostly concern the developed countries that want to bar illegal entry by the unskilled. All three problems raise issues that derive from the fact that the flows cannot be effectively constrained and must instead be creatively accommodated. In designing such accommodation, it must be kept in mind that the illegal entry of asylum seekers and economic migrants often cannot be entirely separated. Frustrated economic migrants are known to turn occasionally to asylum as a way of getting in. The effective tightening of one form of immigrant entry will put pressure on another.

SOFTWARE ENGINEERS, NOT HUDDLED MASSES

Looking at the first problem, it appears that "developed countries" appetite for skilled migrants has grown—just look at Silicon Valley's large supply of successful Indian and Taiwanese computer scientists and venture capitalists. The enhanced appetite for such professionals reflects the shift to a globalized economy in which countries compete for markets by creating and attracting technically skilled talent. Governments also perceive these workers to be more likely to assimilate quickly into their new societies. This heightened demand is matched by a supply that is augmented for old reasons that have intensified over time. Less developed countries cannot offer modern professionals the economic rewards or the social conditions that they seek. Europe and the United States also offer opportunities for immigrant children's education and career prospects that are nonexistent at home. These asymmetries of opportunity reveal themselves not just through cinema and television, but through the immediacy of experience. Increasingly, emigration occurs after study abroad. The number of foreign students at U.S. universities, for example, has grown dramatically; so has the number who stay on. In 1990, 62 percent of engineering doctorates in the

United States were given to foreign-born students, mainly Asians. The figures are almost as high in mathematics, computer science, and the physical sciences. In economics, which at the graduate level is a fairly math-intensive subject, 54 percent of the Ph.D.'s awarded went to foreign students, according to a 1990 report of the American Economic Association.

Many of these students come from India, China, and South Korea. For example, India produces about 25,000 engineers annually. Of these, about 2,000 come from the Indian Institutes of Technology (IITS), which are modeled on MIT and the California Institute of Technology. Graduates of IITS accounted for 78 percent of U.S. engineering Ph.D.'s granted to Indians in 1990. And almost half of all Taiwanese awarded similar Ph.D.'s had previously attended two prestigious institutions: the National Taiwan University and the National Cheng Kung University. Even more telling, 65 percent of the Korean students who received science and engineering Ph.D.'s in the United States were graduates of Seoul National University. The numbers were almost as high for Beijing University and Tsinghua University, elite schools of the People's Republic of China.

These students, once graduated from American universities, often stay on in the United States. Not only is U.S. graduate education ranked highest in the world, but it also offers an easy way of immigrating. In fact, it has been estimated that more than 70 percent of newly minted, foreign-born Ph.D.'s remain in the United States, many becoming citizens eventually. Less developed countries can do little to restrict the numbers of those who stay on as immigrants. They will, particularly in a situation of high demand for their skills, find ways to escape any dragnet that their home country may devise. And the same difficulty applies, only a little less starkly, to countries trying to hold on to those citizens who have only domestic training but are offered better jobs abroad.

A realistic response requires abandoning the "brain drain" approach of trying to keep the highly skilled at home. More likely to succeed is a "diaspora" model, which integrates present and past citizens into a web of rights and obligations in the extended community defined with the home country as the center. The diaspora approach is superior from a human rights viewpoint because it builds on the right to emigrate, rather than trying to restrict it. And dual loyalty is increasingly judged to be acceptable rather than reprehensible. This option is also increasingly feasible. Nearly 30 countries now offer dual citizenship. Others are inching their way to similar options. Many less developed countries, such as Mexico and India, are in the process of granting citizens living abroad hitherto denied benefits such as the right to hold property and to vote via absentee ballot.

However, the diaspora approach is incomplete unless the benefits are balanced by some obligations, such as the taxation of citizens living abroad. The United States already employs this practice. This author first recommended this approach for developing countries during the 1960s, and the proposal has been revived today. Estimates made by the scholars Mihir Desai, Devesh Kapur, and John McHale demonstrate that even a slight tax on Indian nationals abroad would substantially raise Indian government revenues. The revenue potential is vast because the aggregate income of Indian-born residents in the United States is 10 percent of India's national income, even though such residents account for just 0.1 percent of the American population.

Unstoppable

The more developed countries need to go through a similar dramatic shift in the way they respond to the influx of illegal economic immigrants and asylum seekers. Inducements or punishments for immigrants' countries of origin are not working to stem the flows, nor are stiffer border-control measures, sanctions on employers, or harsher penalties for the illegals themselves.

Three sets of factors are behind this. First, civil-society organizations, such as Human Rights Watch, the ACLU, and the International Rescue Committee, have proliferated and gained in prominence and influence. They provide a serious constraint on all forms of restrictive action. For example, it is impossible to incarcerate migrants caught crossing borders illegally without raising an outcry over humane treatment. So authorities generally send these people back across the border, with the result that they cross again and again until they finally get in. More than 50 percent of illegals, however, now enter not by crossing the Rio Grande but by legal means, such as tourist visas, and then stay on illegally. Thus, enforcement has become more difficult without invading privacy through such measures as identity cards, which continue to draw strong protests from civil liberties groups. A notable example of both ineffectual policy and successful civil resistance is the 1986 Sanctuary movement that surfaced in response to evidence that U.S. authorities were returning desperate refugees from war-torn El Salvador and Guatemala to virtually certain death in their home countries. (They were turned back because they did not meet the internationally agreed upon definition for a refugee.) Sanctuary members, with the aid of hundreds of church groups, took the law into their own hands and organized an underground railroad to spirit endangered refugees to safe havens. Federal indictments and convictions followed, with five Sanctuary members given three- to five-year sentences. Yet, in response to a public outcry and an appeal from Senator Dennis DeConcini (D-Ariz.), the trial judge merely placed the defendants on probation.

Sanctions on employers, such as fines, do not fully work either. The General Accounting Office, during the debate over the 1986 immigration legislation that introduced employer sanctions, studied how they had worked in Switzerland and Germany. The measures there failed. Judges could not bring themselves to punish severely those employers whose violation consisted solely of giving jobs to illegal workers. The U.S. experience with employer sanctions has not been much different.

Finally, the sociology and politics of ethnicity also undercut enforcement efforts. Ethnic groups can provide protective cover to their members and allow illegals to disappear into their midst. The ultimate constraint, however, is political and results from expanding numbers. Fellow ethnics who are U.S. citizens, legal immigrants, or amnesty beneficiaries bring to bear growing political clout that precludes tough action against illegal immigrants. Nothing matters more than the vote in democratic societies. Thus the Bush administration, anxious to gain Hispanic votes, has embraced an amnesty confined solely to Mexican illegal immigrants, thereby discarding the principle of nondiscrimination enshrined in the 1965 Immigration and Nationality Act.

MINDING THE OPEN DOOR

If it is not possible to effectively restrict illegal immigration, then governments in the developed countries must turn to policies that will integrate migrants into their new homes in ways that will minimize the social costs and maximize the economic benefits. These policies should include children's education and grants of limited civic rights such as participation in school-board elections and parent-teacher associations. Governments should also assist immigrants in settling throughout a country, to avoid depressing wages in any one region. Greater development support should be extended to the illegal migrants' countries of origin to alleviate the poor economic conditions that propel emigration. And for the less developed countries, there is really no option but to shift toward a diaspora model.

Some nations will grasp this reality and creatively work with migrants and migration. Others will lag behind, still seeking restrictive measures to control and cut the level of migration. The future certainly belongs to the former. But to accelerate the progress of the laggards, new institutional architecture is needed at the international level. Because immigration restrictions are the flip side of sovereignty, there is no international organization today to oversee and monitor each nation's policies toward migrants, whether inward or outward bound.

The world badly needs enlightened immigration policies and best practices to be spread and codified. A World Migration Organization would begin to do that by juxtaposing each nation's entry, exit, and residence policies toward migrants, whether legal or illegal, economic or political, skilled or unskilled. Such a project is well worth putting at the center of policymakers' concerns.

*Jagdish Bhagwati is University Professor at Columbia University and Senior Fellow for International Economics at the Council on Foreign Relations.

Bhagwati, Jagdish. "Borders Beyond Control." *Foreign Affairs* 82, no. 1 (January/February 2003): 1–4.

Bringing Human Rights into the Migration and Development Debate

*by Stephen Castles**

International migration is a key aspect of global integration, yet migration is characterised by a global governance deficit: unlike such areas as finance and trade, there is a lack of international institutions to set standards and ensure conformity with international legal norms. State migration policies often fail or have unintended consequences, while for migrants the result may be high levels of risk and exploitation. The US has over 11 million irregular residents, and systematic use of irregular migrant labour can be found throughout the world. In recent years, however, there have been attempts to move towards global governance mechanisms in the migration field. At the same time, migrant associations have grown and linked up with international human rights organisations. The article examines these trends, paying special attention to the Global Forum on Migration and Development—an intergovernmental consultation process that has met annually since 2007—and the efforts of migrant associations and other civil society organisations to bring human rights into the debate. A final section discusses the initiative of a group of mainly Latin American academics to establish a new conceptual framework and set of strategic indicators to assess the links between migration, development and human rights.

Policy Implications
- Labour-importing countries can no longer pursue migration policies that ignore the interests, needs and rights of migrants and their communities of origin.
- It is important for government and international agencies to work together with civil society organisations and migrant associations to safeguard migrant rights and to improve outcomes for all concerned.
- Government policies on 'migration management' generally differentiate migrants into the highly skilled who are welcomed and offered legal entry and secure residency, and the low skilled who are treated as temporary migrants with limited rights or—even worse—as irregulars who are subject to criminalisation and high levels of risk and exploitation. Policies

of this kind often fail to achieve their objectives or have unintended consequences.

• Migration only benefits development if it is seen as part of a broader change process, which includes combating corruption, improving transport and communications infrastructure, upgrading education and health systems and improving rights and political participation. In other words, broadly based sustainable development comes first.

• Progress towards a more sustainable migration order that recognises the rights and needs of all involved must be based on the questioning of dominant assumptions and the development of new sets of indicators and new sources of data.

• Bringing human and worker rights into the migration and development debate is crucial for the establishment of fair and sustainable forms of global migration governance.

International migration is a key aspect of global integration. Just as multinational corporations and international financial institutions insist on the right to move capital and commodities around the world to ensure maximum efficiency (and profitability), they also promote the international deployment of labour. Over the last 30 years, a global labour market has emerged, in which processes of innovation, production and distribution are divided up all over the world, while remaining under the control of multinational corporations. The workforce is stratified not only according to possession of human capital (i.e. education, training and work experience) but also according to gender, ethnicity, race and legal status.

But there is a big difference between international migration and other forms of global integration. In such areas as finance, trade and intellectual property, international institutions have been set up to ensure a 'level playing field'. By contrast, international migration is marked by a global governance deficit: there is no international body with a mandate to set standards and to ensure that migrants receive protection and access to human rights. Migration policy has become highly politicised, and political leaders are at pains to claim that they are maintaining national sovereignty and protecting national interests through restrictive migration regimes. The result is that informal sectors (or shadow economies) have sprung up everywhere. Millions of migrants are forced into the legal limbo of irregular entry and employment, and suffer discrimination and marginalisation. The prime offender is the US, with over 11 million irregular migrants, who provided some 5 per cent of the labour force in 2008 (Passel and Cohn, 2009), but systematic use of irregular migrant labour is to be found throughout the world (Castles, 2010). The legitimating ideology for this system of inequality is the claim that migration will in the long run help to bring about economic and social development in the areas of origin.

Yet the apparent contradiction between enhanced global governance in most areas of international economic relations and the insistence on sovereignty with regard to people flows is not as irrational as it seems. It benefits many employers, who prefer to employ workers who can be forced to take low wages, and cannot complain to authorities or join trade unions (either because they are legally barred or because union activity would expose them to deportation). It benefits politicians who fear the electoral consequences of confronting racist and exclusionary discourses, and instead 'act tough on irregular migration' while actually turning a blind eye to employer practices. The governance deficit in migration is a powerful instrument in helping to stratify the global labour market.

How sustainable is this situation? Three main factors seem likely to bring about change. First, there is growing international competition to attract skilled migrants. Second, governments of immigration countries are having increasing difficulties in maintaining effective border control and regulating flows of lower-skilled workers. The result of these two factors is an emerging willingness for dialogue and cooperation with origin countries. Third, migrants cannot be seen just as passive objects of top-down policies of control and exclusion. Increasingly, they are building organisations to fight for worker and human rights, and are forging coalitions with civil society organisations at the national and international levels.

The top-down trend towards global governance and cooperation in migration and the bottom-up struggle for migrants' worker and human rights are closely linked in practice. This can be seen most clearly in the relationship between the Global Forum on Migration and Development (GMFD)—an annual intergovernmental consultation that includes both migrant-destination and origin countries[1]—and the People's Global Action on Migration, Development and Human Rights (PGA)—an international coalition of migrants' and human rights organisations set up to bring the human rights dimension into the migration and development debate, particularly by putting pressure on the GMFD.[2]

The key question to be addressed in this article is whether enhanced global governance will actually benefit migrant workers and their families, or whether it will instead lead to global migration management strategies that will actually reduce the rights of migrants and increase levels of exploitation of vulnerable migrant worker groups. A possible way of avoiding this, it will be argued, lies in linking migrant demands to broader struggles against inequality, impoverishment and exploitation in the Global South. To achieve this it is crucial to question dominant, neoliberal understandings of development and economic growth. An important mechanism is a proposed new set of strategic indicators for the relationship between migration, development and human rights, which will be discussed in the final section of the article.

THE REDISCOVERY OF MIGRATION AND DEVELOPMENT

During the 1950s and 1960s development economists believed that labour migration (both internal and international) was an integral part of modernisation (Harris and Todaro, 1970). They argued that the reduction of labour surpluses (and hence unemployment) in areas of origin and the inflow of capital through migrant remittances (money transfers home) could improve productivity and incomes. The governments of countries like Morocco, Turkey and the Philippines encouraged their nationals to migrate to Western Europe or the US—and later to Gulf oil economies—claiming that labour export would facilitate economic development at home. The authorities of immigration countries like Germany, France and the Netherlands enthusiastically supported this belief. However, the long-term results of labour recruitment schemes were often disappointing, with little economic benefit for the country of origin—as shown by a series of studies on Turkey (Abadan-Unat, 1988; Martin, 1991; Paine, 1974). The result was the general acceptance by the 1980s of the view that 'migration undermines the prospects for local economic development and yields a state of stagnation and dependency' (Massey et al., 1998, p. 272).

In the early 21st century, there has been a remarkable turnaround. After years of seeing South–North migrants as a problem for national identity and social cohesion, and more recently even as a threat to national security, politicians and officials now emphasise the potential of international migration to bring about economic and social development in the countries of origin (Dayton-Johnson and Katseli, 2006; IDC, 2004; Newland, 2007). Now, ideas on the positive effects of migration on development are at the centre of policy initiatives (e.g. DfID, 2007; GCIM, 2005; World Bank, 2006). In countries of origin like India, migrants are being redefined as 'heroes of development' (Khadria, 2008).

Why has this happened? Both researchers and policy makers have emphasised the importance of remittances—the money sent home by migrant workers, mainly to their families for local, regional and national development. In addition migration is said to bring several further benefits. Migrants are thought to transfer home skills and attitudes—known as 'social remittances'—which may support development (Levitt, 1998). Although skilled migration from poor to rich countries is growing, some researchers claim that 'brain drain' is being replaced by 'brain circulation' or 'brain gain', which can benefit both sending and receiving countries (Lowell et al., 2002). Migrant diasporas are increasingly regarded as a powerful force for development, through transfer of resources and ideas (De Haas, 2006; DFID, 2007).

All of these claims require careful analysis, and research evidence is mixed. There is no doubt that millions of families in origin countries have become dependent on remittances. Remittances in 2009 were estimated at US$414 billion by the World Bank, of which US$316 billion went to less developed countries. Remittances to such countries fell by 6 per cent from 2008 to 2009 due to the global economic crisis—the first drop after over 20 years of growth. The top four remittance-receiving countries were India (US$49 billion), China (US$47 billion), Mexico (US$22 billion) and the Philippines (US$20 billion) (IOM, 2010). Remittances are now the largest form of transfer from north to south, exceeding foreign aid, and even foreign direct investment. Remittances have helped millions of families to climb out of poverty, but detailed studies of origin countries show a diversity of experiences with regard to social and economic development (Castles and Delgado Wise, 2008; Delgado Wise and Guarnizo, 2007). Remittances do not automatically lead to beneficial changes. Indeed, they can lead to inefficient types of investment and economic dependence on continuing emigration, and sometimes even hide a reverse flow of funds to rich countries (Khadria, 2008).

Social remittances can also have varying effects (Levitt, 1998). The message coming back to home communities from emigrants can be that new ways of working, investing and running public affairs can bring prosperity, but it can also be that emigration is the only way out of a hopeless situation. The emergence of emigration as a 'rite of passage' for young people can lead to a loss not only of productive workers, but also to the absence of agents of change. Emigration of labour—whether skilled or less skilled—can lead to serious loss of potential growth for the country of emigration. The question is whether this loss can be outweighed in the long run by positive effects.

A key issue in the migration and development debate concerns *skilled migration* from the south. Migrant skills have become crucial in rich countries—for example, over 40 per cent of the employed migrants who arrived in Belgium, Luxembourg, Sweden and Denmark from 1995 to 2005 had tertiary education, while in France the figure was 35 per cent. Migrants often have higher skill profiles than local-born workers (OECD, 2007, pp. 67–68). Governments and international agencies now focus on changing what was previously seen as a damaging 'brain drain' into more positive forms of 'brain circulation' or 'brain gain'. Opinions vary on the consequences of taking the 'brightest and best' (Ellerman, 2003, p. 17) from the south. Loss of qualified personnel can harm health and education systems, and hold back development. In 2005 a quarter of all doctors in the US and a third in the UK were foreign trained (OECD, 2007, p. 181). Indian doctors and nurses from the Philippines were the largest sources for Organisation for Economic Cooperation and Development (OECD) countries. However, some experts argue that 'brain circulation' may help improve education systems in origin countries, and will in the long run lead to the return of enhanced skills to assist in development (Lowell et al., 2002).

Recognition of the role of diasporas in development does seem an important step forward. This new discourse in the international migration field follows changes of perceptions in emigration countries and the introduction of a range of measures and institutions to involve the diaspora in bringing about positive changes in the homeland (De Haas, 2006). However, collective remittances for community investment by 'hometown associations' and similar groups are still very modest compared with private flows (Orozco and Rouse, 2007). The development role of migrant associations is uneven and poorly understood (Portes et al., 2007).

In general, therefore, it seems that migration alone cannot remove structural constraints to economic growth, social change and greater democracy. There is a need for broadly based long-term approaches that link the potential benefits of migration with more general strategies to reduce inequality, red tape and corruption, and to improve economic infrastructure, social welfare and political governance. Policies to maximise the benefits of migration for countries of origin should thus be part of much broader strategies designed to reduce poverty and achieve development (UNDP, 2009).

In any case, policy discourses on linking migration to development seem to have been primarily motivated by the interests of labour-importing countries. Up to the 1970s, European policy makers and employers saw migrant labour as essential for expanding manufacturing in older core industrial areas. But after the 1973 'oil crisis' there was an important shift in both labour recruitment and capital investment strategies. Instead of investing in manufacturing in Western Europe, North America and Japan, corporations became multinationals, and moved labour-intensive production processes to low-wage areas of the south. Such shifts set the stage for a reassessment of ideas on the costs and benefits of labour migration epitomised in the title of an economic study of the time,

Trade in Place of Migration (Hiemenz and Schatz, 1979). Moreover, public opinion in destination countries turned against immigration due to the unexpected growth of minority groups who maintained their own languages, cultures and religions. At first official approaches focused on 'zero immigration', preventing family reunion and getting 'unwanted' workers to leave. When these policies failed, because the legal frameworks of European states had conferred welfare and family rights on immigrants, there was a new emphasis on community relations, integration and social cohesion. Immigration and diversity became highly politicised issues throughout Europe. From the 1990s asylum-seeker inflows emerged as central political issues. Governments sought to restrict the right to asylum through strict border control and 'offshore processing', but also through addressing the 'root causes' of flight—perceived as impoverishment and violence (Castles and Van Hear, 2011).

However, the early 2000s saw a new debate on Europe's 'demographic decline' and the long-term need for both highly skilled and less skilled workers. The European Commission argued that a system to recruit labour at all skilled levels was essential (CEC, 2005b), but the member states (especially the UK and Germany) were unwilling to grasp the nettle of legal recruitment of low-skilled workers, due to the hostile public climate. The result was an EU Policy Plan (CEC, 2005a) that concentrated on attracting the highly skilled from the rest of the world, while lower-skilled workers for specific sectors such as construction, agriculture and some areas of services and manufacturing were to be recruited through temporary migration schemes that severely limited migrants' rights to change jobs, bring in families and stay for the long term (see Castles, 2006). These 'circular migration schemes' explicitly traded worker and civil rights against larger migration numbers (Ruhs and Martin, 2008), but they were too limited to be adequately responsive to labour needs, thus essentially leaving low-skilled migration to market forces—that is to irregularity (Castles, 2010).

THE HIGH-LEVEL DIALOGUE AND THE GLOBAL FORUM ON MIGRATION AND DEVELOPMENT

Competition between developed economies to attract qualified and productive workers has intensified, while the emergence of new industrial and resource-based economies (in East and Southeast Asia, oil states and some parts of Africa and Latin America) has led to fears of future shortages. Even China, with its vast population, is now experiencing skill and labour bottlenecks. Labour-importing nations can no longer count on a limitless supply of willing workers for the foreseeable future. The result is the perceived need to cooperate with origin and transit countries to manage migration. This is all the more pressing in view of the frequent failure of efforts at border control by individual states or even regional organisations like the European Union.

In 1990, the UN General Assembly adopted the International Convention on the Protection of the Rights of All Migrant Workers and Members of Their Families. However, it took until 2003 for the necessary 20 states (out of the UN's 192 members) to ratify it, allowing the Convention to come into force. By November 2010, just 44 states had ratified the Convention—all of them migrant-origin states.[3] Similarly at the 1994 UN Population Conference in Cairo, a group of migrant-origin countries called for a global intergovernmental conference to find better ways of organising migration and protecting migrants. Labour-importing states ignored the demand, and the conference was never held.

But in 2003, then UN Secretary General Kofi Annan encouraged the creation of a Global Commission on International Migration, which reported two years later (GCIM, 2005). This report helped create the momentum for further dialogue. In 2006 the UN General Assembly at last convened a High-Level Dialogue consisting of ministers and senior officials to examine the relationship between migration and development and to seek better modes of cooperation. This was an important milestone, even though the High-Level Dialogue had no decision-making powers.

The High-Level Dialogue gave rise to the first Global Forum on Migration and Development, held in Brussels in 2007. This intergovernmental meeting attended by officials and sometimes by ministers was followed by annual meetings in Manila (2008), Athens (2009) and Puerto Vallarta, Mexico (2010). A fifth GMFD is planned for Switzerland in 2011. Like the High-Level Dialogue, the GMFD has no decision-making powers. Organisers claim that it has been influential in reshaping debates, and encouraging governments to take action. Critics say it is a toothless talking shop that merely legitimates continuing top-down strategies of migration control. Many international migrant associations and nongovernmental organisations take an in-between position: while critical of the GMFD, they believe it can provide opportunities for exerting civil society pressure on governments to take migrants' rights more seriously. The High-Level Dialogue will reconvene at the UN in 2013, but it remains to be seen whether it will take significant decisions on improving global cooperation and supporting migrants' human rights.

CIVIL SOCIETY AND MIGRANT RIGHTS

Throughout the history of migration, migrants have set up associations concerned with improving legal and social conditions, maintaining homeland cultures and combating discrimination (Moya, 2005). Governments have often been suspicious, with origin-country authorities seeking political control over associations, and destination-country authorities sometimes suppressing them as an illegitimate activity for non-citizens—for instance it was not until the early 1980s that migrants in France secured the right to form associations (Wihtol de Wenden and Leveau, 2001). Migrant associations have sometimes been limited to specific origin groups, but in recent years there have been trends toward establishment of roof organisations, linking diverse groups in their claims for improved rights. Immigration-country authorities have increasingly recognised the legitimacy of migrant associations and cooperated with them. Attempts by the British, French and German governments to work with moderate Islamic groups are examples of cooption strategies designed to control radicalisation.

The emergence of debates on global governance of international migration provides a new context for the internationalisation of struggles for migrant rights. Just as social movements concerned with civil liberties and the environment have become transnational (Tarrow, 2005), so too have movements established to combat exploitation of migrants and to improve their legal, political and social situation. Increasingly, migrant associations constituted at the national level are linking up first with host-country civil society organisations calling for the strengthening of citizenship and democratic rights, and then with transnational organisations.

Perhaps the largest of these is Migrants Rights International (MRI), which claims over 500 member organisations worldwide and has special consultative status with the UN Economic and Social Council. MRI defines itself as 'a nongovernmental organization and global alliance of migrant associations and migrant rights, human rights, labour, religious, and other organizations'.[4] MRI is at pains to portray itself as an (implicitly nonpolitical) human rights advocacy organisation, but other international migrant coalitions are linked to political, social or religious movements. Activists often move across such boundaries, and are involved in a range of associations and coalitions.

An example of a primarily political international movement is the World Social Forum on Migration—as the name implies, an offshoot of the World Social Forum, which has met annually since 2001. The World Social Forum brings together social movements and civil society organisations that are opposed to neoliberal globalisation, and that want to construct 'another possible world, a planetary society directed to a fruitful relationship between human beings and of human beings with the Earth, strengthening globalization based on solidarity'. The 4th World Social Forum on Migration (WSFM) that took place in Quito, Ecuador from 8 to 12 October 2010 defined itself as:

> not only an event but also a place where peoples on the move and social organizations fighting for universal citizenship, the right to freedom of movement, the right to settle, who are against migratory discrimination, and not being considered illegal, can converge together.[5]

One important feature of the WSFM meeting was its close links with Via Campesina, an international coalition of rural people's organisations meeting simultaneously in Quito. This allowed a more broad-based discussion of the needs of rural people, the meaning of development and the protection of the environment (formulated by a peasant leader as 'the rights of Mother Earth').

An example of an international coalition for migrant rights linked both to religious principles and to social action is to be found in the work of the Scalabrini Missionaries, a Catholic order originally set up in the late 19th century to provide assistance to Italian migrants. With the globalisation of international migration, the order has expanded to work with migrants everywhere, and now claims to be represented in some 25 countries.[6] The Scalabrinis have set up centres for social action, such as supporting migrants who experience human rights abuses when trying to cross the Mexico–US border, as well as for migration research. They publish specialised journals, including the influential *International Migration Review*. Interestingly, the order often takes on the role of advocating for migrant rights, which implies not only religious and social principles, but also political positions. This politicisation can be seen clearly in the proceedings and declarations of the Second International Forum on Migration and Peace held by the order in Bogota, Colombia, in September 2010.[7]

PEOPLE'S GLOBAL ACTION MEXICO 2010

Official international forums concerned with migration issues—especially the High-Level Dialogue and the GMFD—provide a focus for struggles for participation and influence by migrant associations and coalitions. At the same time, powerful international agencies that have long been involved in policy formation on migration are being challenged by these new international actors. Such agencies, which include the International Organization for Migration (IOM), the World Bank, the UN Department of Economic and Social Affairs (UNDESA), the UN Development Programme (UNDP) and the United Nations High Commissioner for Refugees (UNHCR), seek to work with international migrant organisations, and to secure their involvement in official policies on migration management and linking migration to development. The process of formation of international migrant rights organisations is taking place rapidly at present, and it is too early for a balanced assessment of the significance and scope of such trends.[8]

The GMFD was the result of the recognition by migrant destination-country governments of the necessity of building cooperative relationships with origin country governments. The legitimation of the process required some form of inclusion of migrant and civil society organisations. The approach taken was to provide 'civil society days' to document the formal inclusion of such groups, while setting these up in such a way that real debate and political initiatives could hardly emerge. The foundations entrusted with the organisation of the GMFD selected and invited a large number of NGOs, defined key themes, commissioned background papers and set the agenda for debates. At the first GMFD in Brussels in 2007, the hundreds of disparate organisations represented at the civil society days were expected to come up with a joint statement after just one day. This statement was then passed on to the intergovernmental meeting, which was the main focus of the GMFD, allowing government representatives to take as much or as little notice of its contents as they saw fit.

Civil society organisations were understandably critical of this process. Already at the 2006 High-Level Dialogue, such organisations had complained about lack of opportunities for participating in official debates. At the Brussels GMFD, a Global Community Forum on Migration, Development and Human Rights was convened by migrant associations as a parallel event of civil society 'to reintroduce the voice and concrete contribution of migrants, non-government organizations and civil society in the global debate'.[9] By 2008 in Manila the parallel event had grown in duration and scope, and had been renamed the People's Global Action on Migration, Development and Human Rights. A key idea of the PGA was that the technocratic debate on the links between migration and development could be turned on its head by bringing in the dimension of human rights, or more specifically issues of exploitation, human insecurity and inequality affecting migrants, their families and communities.

The mobilisation of civil society organisations continued with the Athens GMFD in 2009. Although the original single civil society day had been expanded to two days at Manila and Athens, the critique of the PGA remained that the whole process was tightly managed by the organisers, with no real interaction between civil society and government representatives, who largely ignored the ideas and wishes of the migrant associations and their nongovernmental partners. When the Mexican government agreed to host the 2010 Forum, it agreed to take dialogue with civil society more seriously than at previous GMFDs. The Mexican government officials responsible for convening the intergovernmental meeting were to liaise with the PGA and attend at least parts of its meetings, while PGA representatives were to be accorded specific roles in bringing civil society claims to the intergovernmental meeting.

A key problem for the PGA was the access to privileged knowledge and analytical capacities enjoyed by proponents of the dominant view on the benefits of migration for development. Knowledge on the relationship between migration and development has primarily been developed by destination-country governments and international agencies, and by the think tanks and academic researchers funded by these. Critics of dominant agendas in this area found it hard to obtain the data and analysis needed to formulate alternative approaches. The PGA sought to counter this deficit by finding ways of linking the everyday experience of migrants with the analyses of critical academics, particularly those of origin countries. A key innovative principle of the Mexico City PGA meeting was that the background papers and public presentation should, wherever possible, be the combined work of a civil society activist and a researcher. The meeting of the World Social Forum on Migration which had taken place just a few weeks earlier in Quito was also significant: many of the organisations represented at the PGA had also been present in Quito, and this had given them an opportunity for systematic preparation of strategies to counter migrants' lack of rights.

The climate at the 2010 PGA meeting was profoundly affected by two factors. The first was the positive influence of the trends towards democracy and critique of neoliberalism that has brought about major political changes in much of Latin America in recent years. The second—far more negative—was revulsion over the increased criminalisation of migrants and the growing violence towards them. This came to a head in August 2010 with the discovery in Tamaulipas state (Mexico) of the bodies of 72 Central and South American migrants murdered by drug gangs.[10] It became clear that the security agendas of migrant-destination states (notably the US) were denying human security to migrants by forcing them into perilous situations. Critical analyses of US border control policies have shown not only that increased restrictiveness has led to a high death rate, but also that it has had the unexpected result of turning temporary migrant workers into permanent settlers, due to the high risks of repeated border crossing (Cornelius, 2001; Delgado Wise, 2007; Massey et al., 2003).

The PGA meeting brought together some 800 representatives of migrant organisations, migrant support organisations, trade unions and faith and academic communities, from a wide range of regions and countries around the world. The fares and the costs of meeting in a historic convent in the middle of Mexico City were partly covered by US human rights foundations. Senior officials from the Mexican Foreign Ministry took part, along with the mayor and key officials of Mexico City. The proceedings were characterised by an open and participatory style, which sometimes led to long-winded discussions, but also ensured that people with varied experience and backgrounds could find ways of communicating with each other. Activists from all sorts of organisations from all over the world were present, including leaders of mass movements (such as the 2006 migrant demonstrations in the US), people engaged in day-to-day social assistance to marginalised groups, and political lobbyists seeking to achieve change in the European Union and other regional bodies.

The PGA meeting started with the presentation of a paper entitled 'Reframing the Debate on Migration, Development and Human Rights: Fundamental Elements' (Delgado Wise et al., 2010) prepared by Latin American analysts, which questioned key aspects of dominant discourses on migration and development, and examined the costs and disadvantages experienced by migrants and their communities of origin. Plenary themes included strategic indicators for migration development and human rights; human rights for migrants; labour rights; strengthening organisations and networks; environmental degradation, climate change, migration and development; and the role of migration in transforming knowledge systems. Round tables and workshops provided opportunities for activists from around the world to discuss networking, alliances and political strategies. The PGA concluded on 5 November 2010 by agreeing on a final statement containing a set of radical recommendations to the GMFD. These included: a human rights-centred approach to migration and development; measures to ensure the human security of migrants; recognition of the right to mobility; an end to the national security framing of migration and to the criminalisation of migrants; the right to decent work and the ending of social exclusion and discrimination based on immigration status, race, ethnicity, gender, class, religion and national origin; and inclusive research for a comprehensive approach to migration.

GMFD Puerto Vallarta 2010

The PGA appointed a number of participants—mostly representatives of migrant associations—as delegates to the GMFD, while many other PGA participants went on to Puerto Vallarta to join the official civil society days of the GMFD as representatives of their own organisations. The 2010 GMFD civil society days represented an advance on previous years, since the role of the PGA was officially recognised for the first time, and a 'common space' was created to allow some face-to-face interaction between civil society representatives and governments. Moreover, according to participants who had attended previous GMFDs, conservative voices among the officials and politicians were weaker than hitherto, and there seemed to be some genuine willingness to find more comprehensive solutions to pressing problems, like irregular migration, violence at borders and exploitation of migrants. Figure 1 gives an idea of the links between the discussions in the various meetings of October/November 2010.

Figure 1. Links between civil society and intergovernmental debates.

World Social Forum on Migration and Via Campesina meetings, Quito, 8–12 October 2010	People's Global Action meeting, Mexico City, 2–5 November 2010	Global Forum on Migration and Development, Puerto Vallarta, 8–11 November 2010
Ideas → Analyses → Strategies →	Ideas, analyses, demands → PGA delegates → Participants representing migrant associations and NGOS →	Civil society days including PGA delegates and invited representative of associations and NGOs, 8–9 November
		'Common space' meetings between government representatives, PGA delegates and other selected civil society participants, 9–10 November
		Intergovernmental meetings of representatives of governments of migrant-origin, transit and destination countries

Nonetheless, the civil society days at Puerto Vallarta remained a carefully stage-managed event in which the tone was set by the great and the good—including the president and first lady of Mexico, the governor of the state of Jalisco, the UN High Commissioner for Human Rights, Navy Pillay and the Special Representative of the Secretary General of the UN for Migration and Development, Sir Peter Sutherland. The themes and background papers were decided in advance by the organising body, the Bancomer Foundation (funded by one of Mexico's biggest banks), advised by a group of 'international experts', many of whom were linked to governments or intergovernmental organisations. The GMFD was thus a far cry from the radical democratic atmosphere of the PGA.

It came as little surprise then that the radical demands articulated in the PGA's statement were considerably watered down in the *Report of the GMFD Civil Society Days* (GMFD, 2010). Nonetheless, some of the civil society activists and critical academics who invested a great deal of effort in working with governments to improve the GMFD process argued that the Mexican event did represent a step forward, because civil society was given much greater recognition than in the past, making it possible to make the case for linking human rights to migration and development more strongly than ever before. By contrast, some critics of engagement with governments argued that the 2010 GMFD merely represented a new stage in the manipulation of dissent and the cooption of NGOs. It is hard to make a balanced assessment, because we lack objective yardsticks to judge whether the GMFD is bringing benefits for migrants and their communities, or whether it is merely helping to impose destination-country agendas on the rest of the world. When I asked GMFD organisers in the run-up to the Mexico meetings whether the process had so far brought about any changes, I was sent a spreadsheet of recommendations from previous forums, together with the measures taken (or proposed) by governments to respond to them. However, there is no similar spreadsheet to document the actual implementation of measures to improve migrants' rights and social situations. The intentions (or at least the rhetoric) of government may be good, but has there been real change? At this stage, it is difficult to know.

STRATEGIC INDICATORS FOR MIGRATION, DEVELOPMENT AND HUMAN RIGHTS

It is no coincidence that the international meetings of 2010 referred to in this article took place in Latin America. The trend towards democratisation and the opening to the left in the region in the early 21st century have created the space for new initiatives for active citizenship and for struggles against exploitation and inequality. With the election of left-wing governments in Brazil, Venezuela, Bolivia and Ecuador, Latin America has become a beacon for radical democratic movements worldwide. The publication in May 2010 by the UN Economic Commission for Latin America and the Caribbean (ECLAC) of the report *Time for Equality* (ECLAC, 2010) represented a seminal shift in economic and social understanding away from the neoliberal agenda that was dominant (and often enforced by US military and intelligence interventions) from the 1970s until recently. ECLAC argued that the claim that the neoliberal policies of the 1980s and 1990s would in the long run lead to economic growth and improved social outcomes could not be substantiated. In fact the neoliberal period—and in particular the structural adjustment policies imposed by the International Monetary Fund (IMF) and the World Bank—had led to a sharp growth in inequality and to impoverishment for millions. Growth rates were actually higher during the epoch of the much-maligned import-substitution policies of the 1970s.

In the light of these important findings, a group of mainly Latin American academics has put forward a proposal to establish a new conceptual framework and set of strategic indicators to assess the links between migration, development and human rights. The proposal was presented as a discussion paper (referred to here as the 'indicators paper') at the PGA (Puentes et al., 2010). The authors argued that the near monopoly of information and analysis on these issues by destination-country governments, think tanks and academics had led to a skewed debate that left out many of the effects of international migration on sending and receiving countries. The dominant discourse emphasises the costs of migration (especially of low-skilled workers) for destination countries in terms of threats to security and the undermining of national identity and social cohesion. It also claims that origin countries benefit considerably through remittances. This discourse generally says little about the big economic gains made by destination countries. Above all, the human costs to migrants, their families and their communities are often ignored.

The aim of the initiative was to initiate a discussion about a policy-oriented information system and a new set of strategic indicators, loosely modelled on the UNDP's Human Development Index (HDI). By shifting attention from narrow economic indicators of development—especially GDP per capita—to broader indicators of well-being including education, health, life expectancy, gender equality and democratic rights, the HDI has helped to change the way many people think about development. The authors of the discussion paper were aware that they lacked the organisational capacity to elaborate the new indicators or to collect the data needed for them. Instead, their aim was to seek the involvement of international agencies (especially UN bodies) and researchers in working out what indicators are needed and to what extent the data for them exist or could be collected.

The indicators paper (Puentes et al., 2010) argues that a comprehensive assessment of costs and benefits of international migration for all stakeholders requires a multidimensional analysis. The unit of analysis is the 'migration corridor': this concept (used increasingly by migration researchers) refers to the migration relationship between a specific origin area and a specific destination area (e.g. Mexico to the US, Somalia to the UK or Algeria to France). The idea is to look at all relevant linkages, including past colonisation, military intervention, economic dependence, labour recruitment, educational marketing and so on. The use of migration corridors may allow a finer-grained analysis than focusing on larger 'migration systems' that embrace whole regions. However, it is important not to separate migration corridors from their wider subregional, regional and global contexts.

The four *dimensions* of the analysis are:
- causes of migration;
- impacts on migrants and their families;
- impacts on countries of origin;
- impacts on countries of destination.

For each dimension, the paper suggests a set of key *factors* to be investigated. For example, for the dimension 'causes of migration' the factors to be studied are:
- economic asymmetries between origin and destination countries;
- social inequalities between sending and receiving countries;
- historical and geopolitical contexts;
- internal inequalities and size of countries;
- environmental degradation.

In turn, a set of *indicators* has to be established and data collected for each factor. For example, the following indicators are suggested for the factor 'social inequalities between sending and receiving countries':
- the Human Development Index data (itself already a composite index) for the origin and the destination country in a given migration corridor;
- the GINI coefficient (a standard indicator of relative inequality) for origin and destination country;
- gender inequality. Several indices are already available that estimate social and economic inequalities based on gender. The SIGI (Social

Institutions and Gender Index), developed by the OECD Development Centre, is a good example of a composite measure of gender discrimination that can be used for cross-country comparative studies (OECD Development Centre, 2009).

To examine the four dimensions proposed for each migration corridor requires a conceptual model that identifies the key factors and then a set of indicators for each of these. Then data for each of these indicators would have to be collected and analysed. Ideally, longitudinal as well as cross-sectional data are needed. To show how this could be done, the indicators paper (Puentes et al., 2010) attempts an analysis of the Latin America–US migration corridor. This is probably the most studied migration corridor in the world, with the best data availability, but even here much of the necessary data is not available. Nonetheless, the case study does show the explanatory potential of the strategic indicators approach. It is impossible to cover all the indicators used here, but a few examples follow to illustrate the type of information needed (all charts from Puentes et al., 2010, where detailed sources are given).

Figure 2 shows an *indicator* for *dimension* causes of migration, factor socioeconomic asymmetries between origin and destination country. Figure 3 shows an *indicator* for *dimension* impacts of migration on destination country, *factor* fiscal contributions by migrants. Figure 4 shows an *indicator* for *dimension* impacts of migration on migrants and their families, *factor* index of labour precariousness.

Clearly, the analysis outlined in the indicators paper is extremely complex: a large number of indicators can be identified for each dimension, and the suggestions given here are far from exhaustive. Much of the necessary data have never been collected. Because migration research has been dominated by the

Figure 2. Relative productivity index of Latin America vís-à-vís the US (1970 = 100) and emigration rate to the US (%of origin-region population) during the same period (1970-2007)

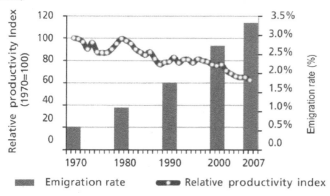

Figure 3. Ratio between taxes paid and benefits received from public social services in the US.

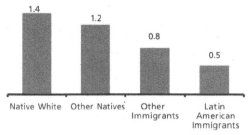

Figure 4. Level of labour precariousness in the US for migrant and native workers (2007).

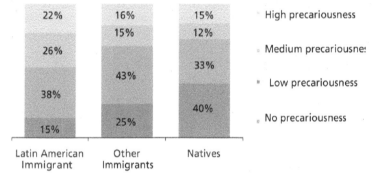

interests of labour-importing countries, there needs to be a major reorientation in conceptual frameworks and in data collection systems. This in turn would require a considerable shift in the priorities of national statistical offices and international agencies. The indicators paper initiative is designed to start an international discussion about the production of knowledge and the way it is used for policy planning in the migration field. Already, important agencies within the UN system have shown interest and have pledged to provide technical expertise for taking the project further. An international experts meeting is planned for late in 2011.

This initiative is at an early stage, but it could prove an important focus for questioning dominant views on the relationship between migration and development, and for bringing in issues of worker and human rights and the impacts of international migration on the origin areas, families and communities of the migrants. Whether this happens will depend not so much on the intellectual quality of the call for new strategic indicators, but on the ability of civil society groups and critical researchers to build a political coalition around such demands.

ENDNOTES

[...]

1. See: http://www.gfmd.org/
2. See: http://www.accionglobalmexico.org/iindex01.php
3. http://www.december18.net/present-status-ratification
4. See: http://www.migrantwatch.org
5. http://www.migration4development.org/content/4th-world-social- forum-migration-2010-quito-ecuador
6. http://www.scalabrini.asn.au/
7. http://www.forummigracionypaz.org/English/PressII1.html
8. This section and the two following are based on the author's participation in the meetings of the World Social Forum on Migration in Quito in October 2010, the People's Global Action on Migration, Development and Human Rights (PGA) in Mexico City and the GMFD in Puerto Vallarta, Mexico in November 2010.
9. See: http://globalcommunityforum.wordpress.com/program/
10. See: http://www.bbc.co.uk/news/world-latin-america-11090563

REFERENCES

Abadan-Unat, N. (1988) 'The Socio-Economic Aspects of Return Migration to Turkey', *Revue Européenne des Migrations Internationales*, 3, pp. 29–59.

Castles, S. (2006) 'Guestworkers in Europe: A Resurrection?' *International Migration Review*, 40 (4), pp. 741–766.

Castles, S. (2010) 'Background Paper: Joint Approaches to Address Irregular Migration of Vulnerable Groups'. Puerto Vallarta, Mexico: Global Forum on Migration and Development.

Castles, S. and Delgado Wise, R. (eds) (2008) *Migration and Development: Perspectives from the South*. Geneva: International Organization for Migration.

Castles, S. and Van Hear, N. (2011) 'Root Causes', in A. Betts (ed.), *Global Migration Governance*. Oxford: Oxford University Press, pp. 287–306.

CEC (2005a) 'Communication from the Commission: Policy Plan on Legal Migration', COM(2005)669 final. Brussels: Commission of the European Communities.

CEC (2005b) *Green Paper on an EU Approach to Managing Economic Migration*, COM(2004)811 final. Brussels: Commission of the European Communities.

Cornelius, W. A. (2001) 'Death at the Border: Efficacy and Unintended Consequences of US Immigration Control Policy', *Population and Development Review*, 27 (4), pp. 661–685.

Dayton-Johnson, J. and Katseli, L. T. (2006) *Migration, Aid and Trade: Policy Coherence for Development*. OECD Policy Brief 28. Paris: OECD.

De Haas, H. (2006) *Engaging Diasporas*. Oxford: International Migration Institute for Oxfam Novib.

Delgado Wise, R. (2007) 'The Reshaping of Mexican Labor Exports under NAFTA: Paradoxes and Challenges', *International Migration Review*, 41 (3), pp. 656–679.

Delgado Wise, R., Covarrubias, H. M. and Puentes, R. (2010) *Reframing the Debate on Migration, Development and Human Rights: Fundamental Elements*. Mexico City: People's Global Action on Migration, Development and Human Rights.

Delgado Wise, R. and Guarnizo, L. E. (2007) *Migration and Development: Lessons from the Mexican Experience*. Washington, DC: Migration Information Source. Available from: http://www.migrationinforamtion.org [Accessed 6 February 2011].

DfID (2007) *Moving Out of Poverty: Making Migration Work Better for Poor People*. London: Department for International Development.

ECLAC (2010) *Time for Equality: Closing Gaps, Opening Trails*. Santiago: Economic Commission for Latin America and the Caribbean. Available from: http://www.eclac.cl/publicaciones/xml/1/39711/100604_2010-115-SES-33-3-Time_for_equality_doc_completo.pdf [Accessed 6 February 2011].

Ellerman, D. (2003) 'Policy Research on Migration and Development'. Policy Research Working Paper 3117. Washington, DC: World Bank.

GCIM (2005) *Migration in an Interconnected World: New Directions for Action: Report of the Global Commission on International Migration*. Geneva: Global Commission on International Migration. Available from: http://www.gcim.org/en/finalreport.html [Accessed 25 May 2011].

GMFD (2010) *Report of the Global Forum on Migration and Development Mexico 2010*. Mexico City: Government of Mexico. Available from: http://www.gfmd.org/en/gfmd-meetings/mexico-2010.html [Accessed 25 May 2011].

Harris, J. R. and Todaro, M. P. (1970) 'Migration, Unemployment and Development: A Two-Sector Analysis', *American Economic Review*, 60 (1), pp. 126–142.

Hiemenz, U. and Schatz, K. W. (1979) *Trade in Place of Migration*. Geneva: International Labour Organization.

IDC (2004) *Migration and Development: How to Make Migration work for Poverty Reduction*. HC 79-II. London: House of Commons International Development Committee.

IOM (2010) *World Migration Report 2010*. Geneva: International Organization for Migration.

Khadria, B. (2008) 'India: Skilled Migration to Developed Countries, Labour Migration to the Gulf', in S. Castles and R. Delgado Wise (eds), *Migration and Development: Perspectives from the South*. Geneva: International Organization for Migration.

Levitt, P. (1998) 'Social Remittances: Migration Driven Local-Level Forms of Cultural Diffusion', *International Migration Review*, 32 (4), pp. 926–948.

Lowell, B. L., Findlay, A. M. and International Labour Office, International Migration Branch (2002) *Migration of Highly Skilled Persons from Developing Countries: Impact and Policy Responses: Synthesis Report International Migration Papers*, 44. Geneva: ILO.

Martin, P. L. (1991) *The Unfinished Story: Turkish Labour Migration to Western Europe*. Geneva: International Labour Office.

Massey, D. S., Arango, J., Hugo, G., Kouaouci, A., Pellegrino, A. and Taylor, J. E. (1998) *Worlds in Motion: Understanding International Migration at the End of the Millennium*. Oxford: Clarendon Press.

Massey, D. S., Durand, J. and Malone, N. J. (2003) *Beyond Smoke and Mirrors: Mexican Immigration in an Era of Economic Integration*. New York: Russell Sage Foundation.

Moya, J. C. (2005) 'Immigrants and Associations: A Global and Historical Perspective', *Journal of Ethnic and Migration Studies*, 31 (5), pp. 833–864.

Newland, K. (2007) *A New Surge of Interest in Migration and Development*. Washington, DC: Migration Information Source. Available from: http://www.migrationinformation.org [Accessed 6 February 2007].

OECD (2007) *International Migration Outlook: Annual Report 2007*. Paris: OECD. Available from: http://www.oecdbookshop.org/oecd/display.asp?K=5L4RW7MZQN46&lang=EN&sf1=RegularIdentifier&st1=REG-81011P1 &sort=sort_date/d&ds=International%20Migration%20Outlook&m=4&dc=5&plang=en [Accessed 23 September 2007].

OECD Development Centre (2009) *OECD Tracks Gender Inequality in Developing Countries*. Paris: OECD. Available from: http://www. oecd.org/document/55/0,3343, en_2649_33935_42278391_1_1_1,00.html [Accessed 26 May 2011].

Orozco, M. and Rouse, R. (2007) *Migrant Hometown Associations and Opportunities for Development: A Global Perspective.* Washington, DC: Migration Information Source. Available from: http:// migrationinformation.org [Accessed 6 February 2007].

Paine, S. (1974) *Exporting Workers: The Turkish Case.* Cambridge: Cambridge University Press.

Passel, J. S. and Cohn, D. V. (2009) *A Portrait of Unauthorized Immigrants in the United States.* Washington, DC: Pew Hispanic Center. Available from: http://pewhispanic.org/files/reports/107.pdf [Accessed 10 September 2010].

Portes, A., Escobar, C. and Radford, A. W. (2007) 'Immigrant Transnational Organizations and Development: A Comparative Study', *International Migration Review*, 41 (1), pp. 242–282.

Puentes, R., Canales, A., Rodríguez, H., Delgado-Wise, R. and Castles, S. (2010) *Towards an Assessment of Migration, Development and Human Rights Links: Conceptual Framework and New Strategic Indicators.* Mexico City: People's Global Action on Migration, Development and Human Rights. Available from: http://rimd. reduaz.mx/documentos_miembros/7081PuentesCanal esetal29102010.pdf [Accessed 6 February 2011].

Ruhs, M. and Martin, P. (2008) 'Numbers vs Rights: Trade-Offs and Guest Worker Programs', *International Migration Review*, 42 (1), pp. 249–265.

Tarrow, S. G. (2005) *The New Transnational Activism.* Cambridge: Cambridge University Press.

UNDP (2009) *Human Development Report 2009: Overcoming Barriers: Human Mobility and Development.* New York: United Nations Development Programme. Available from: http://hdr.undp. org/ en/reports/global/hdr2009/ [Accessed 5 March 2010].

Wihtol de Wenden, C. and Leveau, R. (2001) *La beurgeoisie: les trois ages de la vie associative issue de l'immigration.* Paris: CNRS Editions.

World Bank (2006) *Global Economic Prospects 2006: Economic Implications of Remittances and Migration.* Washington, DC: World Bank.

*Stephen Castles is research chair in sociology at the University of Sydney. Castles is a sociologist and political economist, and works on international migration dynamics, global governance, multiculturalism, transnationalism, migration and development, and regional migration trends in Africa, Asia, and Europe.

Castles, Stephen. "Bringing Human Rights into the Migration and Development Debate." *Global Policy* 2, no. 3 (2011): 248–258.

Global Policy by London School of Economics and Political Science. Reproduced with permission of John Wiley & Sons.

Part 2: Perspectives on Migration and Development

Part 2 examines the relationship between migration and development. "Development" refers to more than improvements in economic prosperity. It is also measured in how people live their lives, from the health and education services that are available to them, to the rights and freedoms they are able to enjoy. The notion of migration being a tool for development is a very recent one. The purpose of Part 2 is to examine how that can happen; what the possible obstacles and pitfalls may be; and how different countries with very different interests view the development–migration relationship.

Part 2 commences with an extract from the conclusions of the 2006 United Nations General Assembly High-Level Dialogue on International Migration and Development. This event brought together senior representatives from 127 UN Member States as well as representatives of UN agencies, intergovernmental organizations, civil society, and the private sector. This document is important because it confirms broad-based political support for many of the key messages of the present anthology: for example, that international migration can be a positive force for development in both countries of origin and countries of destination; that laws and policies around migration should seek to ensure people migrate out of choice and not out of necessity or desperation; that migration, development, and human rights are intrinsically connected; and that respect for the human rights of migrants is essential for reaping the full benefits of international migration.

The second piece in this section, a short extract by Christina Boswell and Jeff Crisp, considers the causes and impact of migration from the perspective of source countries. Boswell and Crisp challenge the forced/voluntary dichotomy that is so often used to characterize migration flows, noting that the distinction is frequently blurred in practice. They emphasize that triggers for migration are typically multiple and overlapping, comprising a complex mix of higher-level political, social, and economic factors as well as individual family, social, and psychological considerations. When reflecting on development impact, the authors focus on those who are left behind, discussing the effect of remittances (usually, but not always positive) and the outflow of skilled workers (almost always negative).

The next piece is a 2010 note produced by the Secretariat of the United Nations Conference on Trade and Development titled "Maximizing the Development Impact of Remittances." The note outlines the different contributions made by remittances to both sending and receiving countries. It confirms that migrant remittances help to promote development and reduce poverty in countries of origin, many of which are developing countries, and that such positive impacts can be enhanced through strategies to promote saving of remittances as well as investment in infrastructure and productive capacity. The note urges governments in countries of origin to be more proactive and creative in promoting the productive use of remittances and also to consider how diaspora networks could contribute to development. Working at bilateral, regional, and multilateral levels, countries must also address barriers to migration and to remittance transfers, thereby improving the capacity of remittances to promote development and reduce poverty.

A companion piece by Boswell and Crisp, this time considering the impact of migration on receiving countries, provides the fourth contribution to this part.[1] It is often difficult to identify and untangle impacts of migration on receiving countries, not least because discussion and research may be influenced by underlying policy positions on migration itself. The authors point out, for example, that while costs are often cited as a negative impact, migration control policies (detention, restrictions on employment) can themselves be a major determinant of costs. Security concerns associated with immigration are often difficult to substantiate but nevertheless feed into public anxieties that in turn affect the political response. Apart from a growing recognition of the economic benefits of high-skilled labor migration, discussions on the benefits of immigration have tended to receive much less attention. For example, there is little consideration for the "wider and less tangible contribution of immigrant communities to the cultural and social life of receiving societies."[2]

The next article, by Delancey Gustin and Astrid Ziebarth, outlines the key findings of a major study into public opinion around migration conducted in Canada, France, Germany, Italy, the Netherlands, Spain, the United Kingdom, and United States during 2008–9. General findings across all countries included a widespread willingness to be involved in the resettlement of migrants displaced by climate change. However, at the individual country level, there were significant differences in how migration was perceived. In the United States, for example, the study found that the most prominent issue driving the American immigration debate was illegal immigration. There was particular concern over a perceived connection between illegal immigration and criminality. However, this concern did not necessarily translate into a rejection of irregular migrants:

Half of all those surveyed favored granting undocumented migrants a right to remain. A majority supported increased border security as a measure to address migration problems. While both Americans and Canadians generally agreed that migration had enriched the national culture, public opinion about immigration in Canada was found to be much more positive—Canadians were the least likely of all nationalities surveyed to say that there were too many migrants. The authors note that Canada has been able to exercise more control than other countries in selecting immigrants based on labor market needs and national priorities; the most controversial issue over the past few years has been fraudulent asylum claims and the length of asylum proceedings.

The final contribution to Part 2—a background paper prepared for a 2011 roundtable organized by the Global Forum on Migration and Development—addresses irregular migration and development. The paper affirms the need for all countries to take account of the development-related causes and implications of irregular migration, as well as the human rights and special vulnerability of migrant children, women, and men in an irregular situation. It then examines the complex and controversial cause-and-effect relationship between irregular migration and development, pointing out that certain assumptions (e.g., that development reduces irregular migration) need to be tested. The (typically negative but occasionally positive) impacts of irregular migration on countries of origin, transit, and destination are examined in detail, along with the development strategies commonly proposed to address irregular migration. The paper concludes that the effects of irregular migration are negative for involved countries as well as for migrants who are exposed to insecurity and vulnerability. It acknowledges, however, that more stringent efforts to reduce such migration have largely been ineffective and often directly counterproductive. The authors do not make specific recommendations for addressing these immediate problems. Rather they propose a broader conception of the migration-development nexus: one that addresses all stages of the migration cycle and seeks to enhance development outcomes for migrants and their countries of origin.

As you read the articles in this part, consider the following questions:
• The development–migration link is very new. Why did it not emerge earlier? Do you think it offers more benefits to some countries than to others?
• How can governments in countries of origin encourage more productive use of remittances? Are collective remittances for community investment (perhaps organized through the involvement of diasporas) a viable option?
• Why are people so concerned about irregular migration? Does ir-

regular migration dilute or even take away the development benefits of migration?

• Do you agree that more stringent controls of irregular migration have created negative consequences, such as markets for smugglers and traffickers? Is there a way to avoid such impacts short of moving away from immigration controls?

Notes

1. The authors note that while the term "receiving country" technically covers any country hosting immigrants or refugees, it is typically used in a more narrow sense to refer to the most frequent destination countries for migrants and refugees of Western Europe, North America, and Australia. This usage obscures the reality of international migration flows that are increasingly directed toward countries in Asia, the Middle East, South America, Central and East Europe, and Southern Africa.

2. Christina Boswell and Jeff Crisp, *Poverty, International Migration and Asylum—A Policy Brief* (Helsinki: United Nations University World Institute for Development Economics Research, 2004), 20.

Summary of the High-Level Dialogue on International Migration and Development

by the President of the United Nations General Assembly

I. Format and Participation

1. In accordance with paragraph 11 of General Assembly resolution 60/227 of 23 December 2005, the President of the sixty-first session of the General Assembly has the honour to transmit herewith the summary of the first High-level Dialogue on International Migration and Development that the General Assembly conducted on 14 and 15 September 2006 at United Nations Headquarters.

[. . .]

II. Key Issues

6. The High-level Dialogue on International Migration and Development demonstrated the strong commitment of Member States, United Nations entities, observers, non-governmental organizations, civil society and the private sector to examining the relationship and synergies between international migration and development. There was general consensus that the High-level Dialogue presented a unique opportunity to identify ways and means to maximize the developmental benefits of international migration and to reduce its negative impacts.

7. Participants stressed the global character of international migration. They affirmed that international migration was a growing phenomenon, both in scope and in complexity, affecting virtually all countries in the world. They agreed that international migration could be a positive force for development in both countries of origin and countries of destination, provided that it was supported by the right set of policies.

8. Participants noted that international migrants contributed to development in both developing and developed countries. In some countries, migrants were essential in meeting labour shortages. A number of participants also underscored the social and cultural contributions of migrants. Some countries reported on their long experience in receiving and integrating international migrants. Other countries had only recently become migrant receiving coun-

tries. Many participants mentioned how their countries had benefited from the emigration of their citizens and from the financial and other contributions that migrant communities had made to the development of their countries. The role of migrant entrepreneurs in reinvigorating urban areas was mentioned.

9. Participants felt that it was essential to address the root causes of international migration to ensure that people migrated out of choice rather than necessity. They observed that people often had to migrate because of poverty, conflict, human rights violations, poor governance or lack of employment. There was widespread support for incorporating international migration issues in national development plans, including poverty reduction strategies. Participants noted that international migration could contribute to the achievement of the internationally agreed development goals, including the Millennium Development Goals, but cautioned against viewing international migration by itself as a long-term development strategy. The need to generate jobs with decent working conditions and to ensure that sustainable livelihoods were possible in all countries was emphasized.

10. Participants recognized that international migration, development and human rights were intrinsically interconnected. Respect for the fundamental rights and freedoms of all migrants was considered essential for reaping the full benefits of international migration. Many noted that some vulnerable groups, such as migrant women and children, needed special protection. Governments were called upon to ratify and implement the core human rights conventions and other relevant international instruments, including the International Convention on the Protection of the Rights of All Migrant Workers and Members of Their Families. Participants underlined the need for concerted efforts on the part of Governments to combat xenophobia, discrimination, racism and the social exclusion of migrant populations.

11. Participants emphasized that the social consequences of international migration deserved urgent attention. The integration of international migrants in receiving countries required mutual adaptation and acceptance by both the host society and the migrants themselves. It was important to combat all types of intolerance. Information campaigns about the positive contribution of international migrants to the host society and about the rights and responsibilities of international migrants were deemed useful.

12. Participants acknowledged that remittances were the most tangible benefit of international migration for countries of origin. They noted that the volume of remittances had increased markedly in recent years. While remittances benefited millions of families of migrants, participants believed that their devel-

opment potential could be enhanced by appropriate measures. These encompassed increasing competition among money-transfer companies and banks to reduce transfer fees, improving the access to banking services, including credit, of migrants and their families and expanding financial literacy in countries of origin. There was consensus that remittances were private flows and should not be considered a substitute for official development assistance, direct foreign investment or debt relief. Some participants warned about the potentially negative consequences of remittances, including the culture of dependency that they might foster at both the household and national levels.

13. Participants agreed that migrant communities had significant potential to contribute to the development of their countries of origin. A number of countries had taken measures to strengthen ties with their nationals abroad and to encourage highly skilled workers in the direction of return and circular migration. Several participants noted that, through co-development projects, migrant entrepreneurs had been agents of development in their countries of origin. The role of international migrants in transferring know-how, skills, technology, expertise and new ways of thinking to their countries of origin was also underscored.

14. Participants also focused on ways of minimizing the negative consequences of highly skilled emigration from developing countries. The outflow of highly skilled workers from the health and education sectors was of particular concern, since it compromised the delivery of services in countries of origin. Participants urged the implementation of measures to retain highly skilled workers by, among other things, ensuring equitable pay and decent working conditions. The promotion of return, even on a temporary basis, of skilled workers to their countries of origin was also recommended. Some participants noted that their countries had adopted or were about to adopt codes of conduct barring the active recruitment of health workers from developing countries affected by labour shortages in the health and education sectors. A number of participants suggested that cooperative arrangements could be made to train skilled workers in developing countries and others argued for different mechanisms for compensation.

15. Participants remarked that labour migration was crucial for the world economy. In some countries, the labour market was highly dependent on foreign workers. In others, temporary labour migration allowed for the filling of specific labour needs. Participants noted that the relatively high participation of women in labour migration had prompted some countries to re-examine their labour migration regulations and procedures to ensure that they were gender sensitive and that they offered adequate protection for female migrants.

16. Participants noted that about half of all international migrants were fe-

male. Women, like men, migrated in order to improve their livelihoods. For many women migration was a means of empowerment. The entrepreneurial potential of female migrants deserved support, and the contribution of migrant women to development in both countries of origin and those of destination had to be recognized. However, migration also entailed risks that were often more serious for women than for men, especially when women were relegated to undesirable low-paying jobs. It was important, therefore, to adopt policies that addressed the particular circumstances and experiences of female migrants and reduced their vulnerability to exploitation and abuse. Women and girls who were victims of trafficking were entitled to special protection.

17. Participants expressed concern about the increase in irregular migration and the exploitation and abuse of migrants in an irregular situation. There was general consensus that trafficking in persons and the smuggling of migrants, especially women and children, should be combated with urgency at the national, bilateral, regional and global levels. Some participants noted that restrictive migration policies contributed to an increase in irregular migration and argued for an increase in legal avenues for migration and for the regularization of migrants in an irregular situation. Participants suggested that information campaigns highlighting the dangers involved in migrating without authorization could help in reducing irregular flows. Although effective border control was considered necessary by many participants, there was recognition that security and control measures alone would not eliminate irregular migration. Hence, there was a call for migration policies that could produce a better balance between unmet labour demand and the inflows of workers from abroad. Participants also underscored that measures to control irregular migration should not prevent persons fleeing persecution and other vulnerable populations from seeking international protection.

18. Most participants considered that national strategies to address the impact of international migration on development should be complemented by strengthened bilateral, regional and multilateral cooperation. They considered that such cooperation was needed to promote legal, safe and orderly migration, reduce irregular migration and improve the chances of reaping the full benefits of international migration. The proliferation of regional consultative processes was seen by participants as proof that cooperation was particularly effective at the regional level. Many participants provided examples of regional mechanisms that, through improved dialogue and better mutual understanding, had led to practical measures to address migration issues.

19. Participants also recognized the usefulness of bilateral agreements and

cited examples of those addressing labour migration, the portability of pensions, the readmission of nationals or the fight against trafficking in persons and the smuggling of migrants. Many participants considered that regional and bilateral initiatives had to be complemented by initiatives at the global level, noting that the United Nations was a natural venue for such initiatives. Participants also mentioned the work of the Global Commission on International Migration, whose report provided useful guidance, the International Agenda for Migration Management, produced by the Berne Initiative, and the annual dialogue on migration policy sponsored by IOM.

[. . .]

United Nations General Assembly, *Summary of the High-Level Dialogue on International Migration and Development: Note by the President of the General Assembly*, 61st session, Agenda Item 55(b), UN Doc A/61/515, 13 October 2006, paragraphs 1 and 6–18. © United Nations 2006.

Used by permission.

Source Countries: Causes and Impact of Emigration

*by Christina Boswell and Jeff Crisp**

The literature on the causes of emigration usually distinguishes between refugee flows and voluntary economic migration. In practice, such a distinction is often difficult to sustain. The factors triggering migration usually comprise a complex mix of political, social and economic conditions, as well as individual psychological factors, and in many cases it makes little sense to ask if movement is voluntary or coerced. Moreover, many of those who leave for predominantly economic reasons may attempt to secure residence in destination countries through applying for asylum, producing what has been coined 'asylum migration'—a phenomenon which further complicates the distinction between forced and voluntary movement.

Nonetheless, when analysing 'push' factors in countries of origin one can distinguish between those related to political and security conditions—including human rights violations, persecution of minority groups, armed conflict and generalized violence; and those related to socio-economic conditions, including poverty, lack of employment opportunities, inadequate welfare, education or social services, environmental degradation, or demographic growth creating a surplus of labour.

Much research has been devoted to the causes of economic migration, and in particular attempts to delineate the general social and economic 'macro' variables that induce migration. Yet most scholars are now in agreement that income and employment variables alone cannot explain patterns and levels of emigration. In fact, most economic migration does not occur from least developed countries (LDCs), but from middle income countries or those undergoing a phase of transition.

There are two main reasons for this. One is the so-called 'poverty constraint', which prevents the poorest sections of the population or those from LDCs from raising the financial resources necessary to move.[7] The poverty constraint has become more important in shaping migration decisions as international movement has become more expensive, often requiring substantial resources to pay smuggling or trafficking agents. Thus many of the poorest either do not move, or if they do, move internally or to neighbouring countries.

The second reason why more migration occurs from relatively developed countries and not LDCs is that development processes themselves can be an important trigger for emigration. Economic restructuring can upset traditional livelihoods and labour patterns, with substantial repercussions for traditional family and social structures. A typical scenario is where restructuring or trade liberalization pushes people from rural areas to towns, which in turn are saturated with labour, creating pressures for a further outlet through international migration.

Within sending countries a number of factors will determine which social groups move. In many societies young single males are the most mobile group. But research on regions such as the Caribbean also points to the growing frustration of young women who are exposed to notions of gender equality which are not being realized in places of origin.[8] In cases where emigration is motivated by a combination of political and economic factors, ethnic minority groups facing systematic discrimination may well be more likely to move.[9]

Other scholars have focused on the 'micro' level of explaining decision-making on migration. Recent research has emphasized that emigration is often not an individual decision, but may be a collective family strategy for enhancing incomes. This has been referred to as a form of 'portfolio diversification': an attempt to manage the costs and risks involved in migration through selecting one family member to move.[10] Another typical strategy is for the male head of the family to move first to secure a job or legal status in the country of destination before being joined by the rest of his family. In some cases it is judged more effective to send a child or a female member, because of the perceived higher prospects for being granted asylum.

Thus far we have largely focused on 'macro'-theories of the general conditions creating migration pressures, and 'micro'-theories of individual or family decision-making processes. But the so-called 'meso'-level of migration theory is also crucial in explaining who moves, and their choice of destination.

Of central importance here are migrant networks, which provide a source of information, financial assistance and support for those considering moving, and which can provide economic, social and psychological support on arrival. Such networks can mean that migration flows between particular places become self-perpetuating, encouraging the chain migration of people, despite changes in macro-conditions in the place of origin.

Migration has a number of implications for those left behind. In a positive sense, it can provide an invaluable source of remittances for families in source countries, who are often able to purchase accommodation or land, invest in education, machinery or businesses, or increase consumption with money from relatives abroad. For governments, remittances can provide crucial foreign currency to help balance current accounts. In many sending countries the level of remittances far outweighs total inflows from development assistance and foreign direct investment—a recent estimate put total flows in 2000 at as much as US$ 100 billion.[11]

Levels of remittances will depend on a number of factors, including if migration is temporary or long-term, how secure the migrant's status is in the country of destination, how much he or she can earn, if he or she has moved alone or with a family, and how strong ties remain with his/her family or places of origin. For example, some research suggests that migrants entering through selective programmes for the highly skilled are likely to remit less because their relatively stable legal status allows family reunion, thus severing ties with those at home.[12]

Others have suggested that so-called 'wider diaspora' in regions further afield will be able to send more resources than 'near diaspora' in poorer neighbouring countries.[13] It should be pointed out that there is some debate as to whether such remittances are always positive, with some scholars arguing they increase inequalities between families with relatives abroad and those without, and that the increased spending on consumption may fuel inflation.

A second major impact for sending countries concerns the outflow of skilled workers. Migration research has consistently shown that emigration is self-selective, that is to say it is usually the brightest, most skilled or enterprising who move. While this thesis may be somewhat overstated—many are also compelled to migrate because of a real lack of alternatives, rather than above-average prospects—the emigration of skilled and talented people is clearly immensely costly for sending countries. In some cases the departure of skilled doctors, nurses, teachers, or ICT specialists may start with a brain outflow of surplus skilled labour.[14]

But as this outflow leads to a deterioration in education, research or business opportunities, or a decline in standards of social services, it may well generate a brain drain of middle-class, qualified nationals. Examples of this phenomenon include Zambia, Pakistan and Romania, where brain drains have led to a serious deterioration in health and education services, public administration, and the private sector. Moreover, the loss to sending countries is not simply a function of the absence of skills, but also results from the huge costs of investing in education and training for those who subsequently move.

Some scholars have argued that the mere possibility of being able to participate in such a skilled migration programme encourages more people to invest in education, potentially benefiting those who end up staying at home. But other scholars have questioned this more optimistic thesis, pointing out that enrolment in tertiary education does not seem to be higher in high-skilled migrant sending countries.[15] The problem of brain drain is likely to be reinforced by selective entry policies in receiving states. And it represents an unresolved tension in developed states' migration policies: recruiting high qualified migrants may seriously undermine efforts at development, in turn creating additional migration pressures.

ENDNOTES

[. . .]

7. Timothy J. Hatton and Jeffrey G. Williamson, 'What Fundamentals Drive World Migration?', UNU-WIDER conference paper.

8. Susan Mains, 'Mobility and Exclusion: Towards an Understanding of Migration in the Context of Jamaica', UNU-WIDER conference paper.

9. On the example of Iraqi emigrants, see Géraldine Chatelard, 'Iraqi Forced Migration in Jordan: Conditions, Religious Networks, and the Smuggling Process', UNU-WIDER conference paper.

10. Claude Sumata, 'Risk Aversion, International Migration and Remittances: Congolese Refugees and Asylum Seekers in Western Countries', UNU-WIDER conference paper.

11. The figures are from Philip Martin, cited in Khalid Koser and Nick Van Hear, 'Asylum Migration: Implications for Countries of Origin', UNU-WIDER conference paper.

12. Riccardo Faini, 'Migration, Remittances and Growth', UNU-WIDER conference paper.

13. Koser and Van Hear (supra, 11).

14. Arno Tanner, 'Country of Origin and Democratic Responsibility. Argumentation in National Labour Immigration Policy—Brain Drain and Domestic Racism Focused', UNU-WIDER conference paper.

15. Faini (supra, 12); and Margo Alofs, 'Legal Migration Probabilities, Illegal Migration and the Brain Drain', UNU-WIDER conference paper.

*Christina Boswell is professor of politics, and deputy dean of research in the College of Humanities and Social Science, at the University of Edinburgh.

Jeff Crisp is head of the policy development and evaluation service at the United Nations High Commissioner for Refugees and has worked on refugee, humanitarian, and migration issues for almost 30 years.

Boswell, Christina, and Jeff Crisp. Poverty, International Migration and Asylum—A Policy Brief. Helsinki: United Nations University World Institute for Development Economics Research (UNU-WIDER), 2004: 9–12.

Used by permission.

Maximizing the Development Impact of Remittances

by The United Nations Conference on Trade and Development Secretariat*

Executive summary

Migrants make important economic, developmental and cultural contributions to sending and receiving countries. Remittances from migrants have positive impacts on poverty reduction and development in originating countries, mostly developing ones, substantially contributing to the achievement of the Millennium Development Goals. These positive impacts become greater when remittances can be saved and invested in infrastructures and productive capacity. Government policy measures could induce such use. Significant barriers to migration and remittance transfers need to be addressed in order to harness opportunities for development and poverty reduction, including through easing financial transfers, setting appropriate incentives, improving policy coherence in migration and remittances policies, and facilitating the temporary movement of people.

I. INTRODUCTION

1. Recent evidence points to a significant and growing contribution of migration to economic and social development throughout the world. Migrants form part of a diverse but highly engaged workforce that not only provides required labour inputs and brings new developmental and cultural resources to receiving countries, but also contributes to poverty reduction and development finance, as well as domestic demand, knowledge and skills transfer, and trade and commercial networks in both sending and receiving countries.

2. Remittances have attracted increasing interest at the national and international level. Drawing linkages between migration, remittances, trade, investment and development is complex and multifaceted. For the purposes of this note, a wide definition of "remittances" is used, encompassing private monetary transfers that a migrant makes to the country of origin, and including investments made by migrants in their home countries, as such funds significantly contribute to development and pov-

erty reduction. A stricter statistical definition made by the International Monetary Fund (IMF) includes workers' remittances, compensation of employees and migrant transfers. Migration, remittances and development issues were addressed in 2009 at the Ad Hoc Expert Meeting on the Contribution of Migrants to Development: Trade, Investment and Development Linkages.[1] The present note seeks to respond to paragraph 170 of the Accra Accord and to the United Nations General Assembly resolution passed in 2010 on international migration and development,[2] and also to provide input to the informal thematic debate in 2011 on international migration and development in preparation for the second United Nations high-level dialogue on migration and development to be held in 2013.

II. CURRENT MIGRATION TRENDS

3. People have continuously moved, seeking better economic opportunities, family reunion, and humanitarian relief. Globalization, modern communications and transportation have greatly facilitated such movement. The United Nations Department of Economic and Social Affairs (DESA) estimates that the total migrant stock increased from about 195 million to 215 million between 2005 and 2010 at 1.8 per cent annually on average, while the share of migrants in the total population remained stable in the same period (only moving from 3.0 to 3.1 per cent). Compared to the 2000–2005 period, the growth in the number of migrants in developed countries decelerated between 2005 and 2010. Migrant workers, who are the main source of remittances to their home countries, numbered about 86 million by 2009. The stock of international migrants is expected to rise to 405 million by 2050.

4. South–North migration through traditional corridors remains important, accounting for 43 per cent of migrant stock from the South, which suggests that South–South migration has become larger. The latter accounts for 73 per cent in sub-Saharan Africa, reflecting that most migration occurs within regions.[3] The prosperity of certain countries attracts large numbers of migrants, explaining why Saudi Arabia, the United Arab Emirates and Singapore are favoured destinations.

5. The number of migrants varies considerably across regions (see fig. 1). Most migrants live in Europe, Asia and North America, with growth rates in 2005–2010 in North America and Europe standing at about 10 and 8 per cent respectively. Growth is expected to continue but at lower

rate in those two regions. The top migrant destinations in 2009 were the United States, the Russian Federation, Germany, Saudi Arabia and Canada. As a share of total population, the top receiving countries were Qatar (87 per cent), the United Arab Emirates (70 per cent) and Kuwait (69 per cent), whose popularity as destinations has increased owing to their more resilient labour markets as has been revealed during the recent economic crisis.

Figure 1. Estimated number of migrants at mid year (2005–2010)

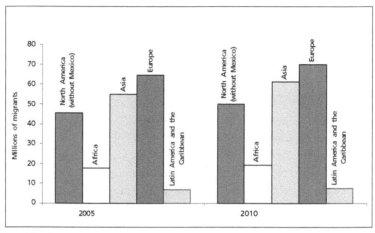

Source: DESA (2009).

6. Female migrants constitute a significant proportion of international migrants, though their numbers have remained relatively stable, going from 49.2 per cent in 2005 to 49 per cent in 2010. Migrant women are in many cases the only contributor to family finances. Many fundamental aspects relating to them need to be addressed, including rights-related issues and equal labour opportunities.

7. In terms of sectoral distribution, migrants are concentrated in key sectors such as construction, tourism, manufacturing and agriculture, accounting for 29, 23, 17 and 16 per cent respectively (see fig. 2).

8. The crisis has severely impacted on sectors that absorb large amounts of labour (e.g. construction, tourism, and financial services). Demand for labour has fallen substantially. The number of unemployed people worldwide reached nearly 212 million in 2009, adding 19 million more jobless to the 2008 total.[4] Disproportionately more jobs have been lost among immigrant youth, in particular among men. In 2009, the unemployment

Figure 2. Share of migrant workers in total sector employment

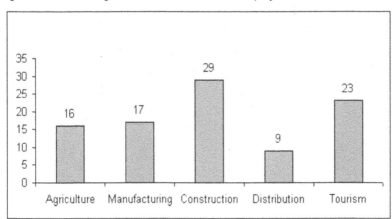

Source: UNCTAD, based on data from the International Labour Organization (ILO) (2010).

rate of the foreign born between 15 and 24 years old reached 15 per cent in the United States, 20 per cent in Canada and 24 per cent on average in the European Union (EU). Consequently, migration to OECD countries fell by about 6 per cent in 2008 to about 4.4 million people, reversing a continuously upward growth trend[5] (see fig. 3). Unemployment is projected to continue to rise, at 10 per cent on average in 2010. More than 57 million people will be unemployed compared with 37.2 million at the end of 2008, which makes OECD labour markets less appealing for new migrants and difficult for existing migrants. Globally, according to DESA, the number of international migrants continues to increase despite the crisis.

• 9. Some countries responded to the crisis by restricting the inflow of migrant workers, often under public pressure to keep jobs for nationals, with the attendant effect on remittance flows. Such measures have included lowering numerical limits (quotas and caps); tightening labour market tests; inserting "hire nationals" provisions in stimulus packages; limiting the possibilities for migrants to change status and renew permits; and promoting return migration. The changes in visa regulations and/or restrictions on work permits that have been introduced in some countries, such as Canada, India, Japan, Malaysia, Thailand, Singapore, the United Kingdom and the United States, have impacted on migrants, including highly skilled migrants.[6]

Figure 3. Evolution of international migration flows from 2003–2008

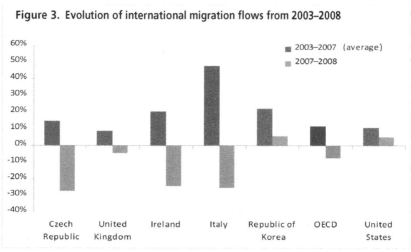

Source: OECD (2010).

10. The number of migrants may increase as post-crisis economic prospects improve. Some longer-term trends have not yet been reversed, necessitating future migration. Labour demand will continue to exist in the Organization for Economic Cooperation and Development (OECD) countries, due to ageing population trends and continuous demand for certain jobs in domestic, healthcare, and education services. Emerging developing countries are expected to attract higher migration flows as the amount of labour force in developed countries is projected to remain stable at about 600 million until 2050, whereas in emerging developing countries it is expected to increase from 2.4 billion in 2005 to 3.6 billion in 2040.

11. Climate change and natural disasters are increasingly relevant to migration flows. Environmental changes such as rising sea levels, extreme weather events, decreased or increased rainfall, and shifts in disease patterns could trigger population displacement. At least 20 million people were estimated to have been displaced (in many cases temporarily) by climate-related disasters in 2008, and about 200 million people may be displaced by 2050.[7] On the other hand, measures to mitigate the impacts of climate change and to promote environmental sustainability are creating green jobs, for example solar/wind power engineers and technicians and repair and maintenance specialists. It is estimated that 2.1 million jobs will be created in wind energy, 6.3 million in solar photovoltaic energy, and 12 million in biofuels by 2030.[8]

III. TRENDS IN REMITTANCES

12. Data clearly indicate the increasing importance of workers' remittances to developing countries. Asia is the biggest remittance-receiving region, followed by Latin America and Africa (table 1). From 1990 to 2008, Asia experienced the fastest annual remittance growth (17 per cent), followed by Latin America (14.3 per cent) and Africa (10.2 per cent). A rapid increase in workers' remittances to Asia is evident. In 1990, workers' remittances to Asia were roughly 20 per cent less than to Africa and 47 per cent greater than to Latin America. In 2008, they were roughly 2.3 and 2.4 times the size of inflows to Africa and Latin America respectively.

Table 1
Top five receiving countries, by region (in billions of dollars, 1990–2008)[1]

	1990	2000	2008	Average growth rate (1990–2008)
Asia[2]	5.5	21.5	93.2	17.0
Latin America[3]	3.8	12.2	41.4	14.3
Africa[4]	6.9	7.8	39.5	10.2

[1] Credit of workers' remittances.
[2] Bangladesh, China, India, Pakistan and the Philippines.
[3] Colombia. the Dominican Republic, El Salvador, Guatemala and Mexico.
[4] Egypt, Morocco, Nigeria, Sudan and Tunisia.
Source: UNCTAD (2010), based on IMF BOP statistics.

13. The level of remittances fell during the crises due to decreased migration flows, in particular to OECD countries, and due to the reduced income of migrants. In 2009, remittances to developing countries reached $316 billion, down 6 per cent from $336 billion in 2008. They are expected to increase by 6 per cent in 2010, 6.2 per cent in 2011 and 8.1 per cent in 2012, to reach $374 billion by 2012.[9] The crises have generated different effects in key migration corridors. Remittances to Latin America and the Caribbean, Central Asia, and the Middle East and North Africa fell more deeply than the world average, by 15 per cent, 21 per cent and 8 per cent respectively, whereas overall remittances to South Asia continued to grow at 6 per cent, adding to the resilience of domestic demand in this region.[10] Flows to East Asia and the Pacific region remained flat, while they fell by 3 per cent in sub-Saharan Africa.[11] The growth of remittances in Asia and modest falls in sub-Saharan Africa can be explained by higher diversity in destination countries including other developing countries. For example, India received 27 per cent of all its remittances from Saudi Arabia, the United Arab Emirates and Qatar in 2009.

14. China, India, Mexico and the Philippines remained the top recipients in 2009 (fig. 4). It is worth noting that remittances are not only of value to developing countries. In 2009, developed countries such as France, Germany and Spain were among the top recipients. Spain has been a major recipient since the 1960s. The United States is the largest source of remittances, with $46 billion in recorded outward flows in 2008, followed by the Russian Federation, Switzerland and Saudi Arabia.

Figure 4. Top remittance recipient countries (2009)

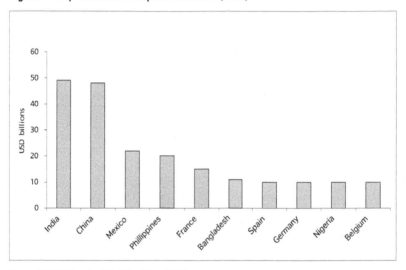

Source: UNCTAD, based on World Bank data (2008).

15. In 2009, remittances accounted for 1.9 per cent of the gross domestic product (GDP) of developing countries and LDCs. In terms of share of GDP, smaller countries such as Tajikistan, Tonga and the Republic of Moldova, and a few LDCs including Lesotho and Samoa, were the largest recipients in 2008 (see fig. 5), suggesting the greater role of remittances in these countries' economic and social development. The impact of remittances on LDCs can be even higher. Remittances account for more than 5 per cent of gross national income (GNI) in almost a third of the LDCs.[12] The share is more than 10 per cent in some LDCs such as Cape Verde, Gambia, Haiti and Lesotho. For Cape Verde, it ranged from 12 to 17 per cent during 2000 and 2006 (a relevant period for the LDC graduation evaluation) and remittances were the second largest source of foreign exchange.[13] Remittance inflows are considered to be one of the contributors to LDC graduation, for example in the case of Cape Verde's graduation from LDC status in 2007.

Figure 5. Top ten countries in terms of remittances as a % of GDP (2008)

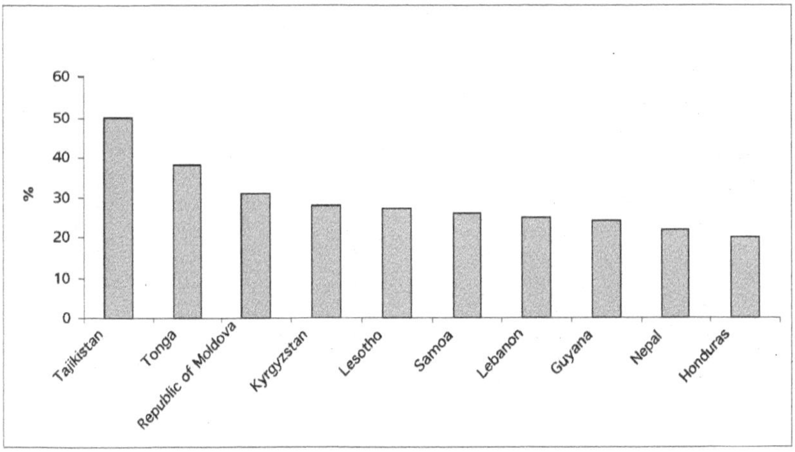

Source: UNCTAD based on data from World Bank (2008).

16. Remittance inflows have proved to be resilient relative to foreign direct investment (FDI) and are an important component of financing for development. Figure 6 shows the evolution of FDI inflows versus remittances in developing countries between 2005 and 2009. FDI tends to be higher in developing countries' balance of payments. However, the gap is getting smaller as a consequence of the crises. FDI fell by about 40 per cent from $598 billion in 2008 to $358 billion in 2009. It is not expected to return to the pre-crisis level until more solid economic recovery driven by output levels and trade recovery gains momentum. Remittances became an even more important source of external financing during the crisis and in the recovery phase. The reasons for the resilience of remittance flows include the value-driven nature of remittances, some level of stability of many resident migrants in host countries, and continued demand for many of the services performed by migrants even during the crisis because the services are not performed by locals either due to demographic change or the unwillingness of locals to do them. As economic conditions improve in migrant receiving countries, remittance flows to developing countries are projected to increase by 6.2 per cent in 2010 and 7.1 per cent in 2011, partly offsetting the weak recovery in other financial flows to developing countries.

Figure 6. FDI and remittances inflows to developing countries

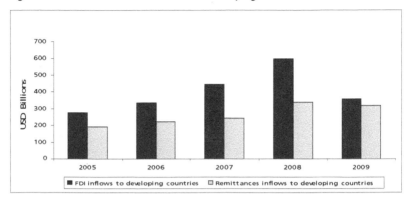

Source: UNCTAD and World Bank data (2010)

IV. REMITTANCES, DEVELOPMENT AND POVERTY REDUCTION

17. Remittances are expected to reduce poverty, as they are, in many cases, directly received by the poor, augmenting their income and alleviating their poverty. In some countries, remittances may make up over 50 per cent of the recipient's total household income. They also represent a more stable source of poverty reduction than other capital flows. Flows can last for one generation or more, and usually go to more or less the same family members.

18. While there are concerns about brain drain, remittance-dependence, and the negative impact of remittances on small countries' export competitiveness due to pressure on currency appreciation, in general, remittances have contributed positively to advancement of the Millennium Development Goals (MDGs). In Nepal, for example, remittances, together with urbanization and higher wages, have resulted in a decline of the incidence of poverty of about one percentage point annually since the mid-1990s (from 42 to 31 per cent).[14] The Asian Development Bank estimates that 4.3 million people in the Philippines remain above the poverty threshold simply because of remittances. Studies in El Salvador and Sri Lanka find that children of remittance-receiving households have a lower school dropout rate.[15] Qualitative studies in Ecuador, Mexico, the Philippines and Thailand[16] have demonstrated that migration also allows rural women to gain autonomy by taking paid work in urban areas or abroad. Finally, remittances contribute to improving child and maternal health by allowing the purchase of food and medicines. In

Guatemala, Mexico, Nicaragua and Sri Lanka, children in remittance-receiving households have higher birth weights and better health indicators than children in other households.[17]

19. Recent analysis demonstrates that an increase in international migration is positively linked to a decline in the number of people in poverty. Various studies indicate that a 10 per cent increase in the share of remittances in a country's GDP leads to, on average, a decline from 1.6 to 3.5 per cent in the proportion of people in poverty. Despite heterogeneous effects across countries, remittances have reduced the incidence and depth of poverty at the household level in sub-Saharan Africa, Latin America,[18] Asia and the South Pacific.[19] Recent evidence indicates that the effect on reducing the poverty gap could in some cases be more important than the effect on the poverty rate.[20]

20. A recent study by UNCTAD (see box 1) provides additional evidence on the linkage between remittances and poverty reduction in developing countries. For larger countries such as India, the impact of remittances is perceived as less notable, however remittances do form an important part of the country's economic and financial variables.

Box 1.

India: Remittances and poverty reduction

Using the panel data for 77 developing countries (1980–2008), the study finds that remittances significantly reduce poverty in recipient countries, but that results are more reliable for countries where remittances make up 5 per cent or more of GDP. In these countries, on average, for the given level of GDP, a 10 per cent rise in remittances leads to a reduction of 3.9 per cent in the poverty headcount ratio and to approximately a 3–3.5 per cent reduction in the poverty gap. With respect to India, empirical estimates show that a 10 per cent rise in remittances as a share of GDP leads to a 1.7 per cent reduction in the poverty ratio. At the regional level, the province of Kerala, which receives about 20 per cent of total remittances in India, has experienced higher levels of average per capita consumption than the rest of India. Between 1988 and 2008, it witnessed an increase in annual average per capita net state domestic product by 5.8 per cent, against a 14.7 per cent increase in per capita remittances. Empirical causal tests undertaken in the Kerala region indicate that higher remittance levels have led to higher per capita income and higher levels of investment, which are considered key variables affecting poverty reduction.

Source: UNCTAD (2010). *Impact of Remittances on Poverty in Developing Countries.*

21. The way in which remittances are used can produce wide multiplier effects in the economy and for development. While there are differences among countries on how remittances are spent, evidence shows some similarities in the order of priorities that recipient families and sending migrants give to their use (fig. 7). Household consumption represents 70 per cent of the amounts transferred.

Figure 7.

22. The multiplier effect can be felt in the purchase of essential goods and services, home appliances, and medical and education services. Most of the goods and services consumed (mostly utilities and financial services) are produced locally, except for home comfort goods with a high level of imported component. Such consumption increases the local demand, particularly in poor or rural areas, thereby driving domestic production. To avoid remittance-dependence, investment in education becomes particularly relevant for long-term human development, as professional prospects of the next generation improve, generating less dependency on remittances in the future.

23. When a share of remittances is used for small business investments, the multiplier effect becomes larger and more sustainable as they create income stream. On average, around 10 per cent of remittances are found to be saved and invested.[21] Evidence shows that remittances help to increase the level of small business activities in the recipient developing countries. For example, in Ghana and Guatemala, about one third of remittances are used for starting small businesses and house construction.

Remittances are key sources of finance for investment in farming, or for underwriting risks in new agricultural ventures. Providing financial counselling to remittance recipients helps to mobilize their savings into the financial sector, which could then be utilized for credit to enhance the country's productive base. It has been reported by DynaMicrofinance in Senegal that 20 per cent of its remittance clients have acquired a savings or loan product, in part due to its efforts to systematically offer savings accounts and other financial products to remittance recipients and to explain how they work.[22]

24. Remittances can help local entrepreneurs bypass inefficient or non-existent local credit markets, especially in rural areas, and to start productive activities. El Salvador[23] implemented a pilot programme (2008–2009), together with a non-profit organization from the United States (TechnoServe), to help small-scale entrepreneurs leverage remittances to access credit and grow their businesses, including hotel and restaurant services.

25. Remittances can also play an essential role in responding to devastating natural disasters. Reconstruction can be supported by international aid and assistance and also by private philanthropic support during the initial phase, however this aid can not be long- lasting. Remittances and other supports from migrants abroad could play a more effective role in the post-disaster recovery and rehabilitation (box 2).

Box 2.

> **Remittances and post-earthquake reconstruction in Haiti**
>
> Officially recorded remittance flows to Haiti were $1.4 billion in 2008, but the true figure could be near $2 billion. Haitian diasporas have played a key role in the reconstruction and rehabilitation of Haiti. In 2009, they sent $1.64 billion to Haiti, constituting 26 per cent of the country's GDP. Some 300 Haitian hometown associations in the United States and Canada also donated $10,000 each to their communities for social projects. The temporary protected status granted by the United States after the earthquake for a period of 18 months to Haitians already in the United States enabled over 200,000 Haitians without proper documents to work in the United States legally. This allowed more money to be sent through formal channels.
>
> *Source: Mobilize the Diaspora for the Reconstruction of Haiti by Ratha (2009).*

26. Remittances and other diaspora funds (including investment) can be channelled as a source of development finance by home countries to support development and poverty reduction, including the building of local infrastructure and productive capacity. To create opportunities for development-oriented investment from migrants, as stated in the United Nations Doha Declaration on Financing for Development, several tools have been utilized by developing countries.

27. Diaspora bonds could be used as an innovative tool for development financing by tapping into the wealth of a diaspora population and opening new marketing channels. India was the first developing countries to issue diaspora bonds during the economic crisis in 1991, when it experienced a large trade and fiscal deficit, high inflation and devaluation of the Indian rupee. The Indian Development Bonds targeted at Indian diasporas enabled India to raise $1.6 billion in a short period of time, which was critical to India's recovery from the crisis. In 2000, the Indian Government sold Resurgent India Bonds to non-resident Indians.[24] Since then, it has been selling diaspora bonds to support the budget and keep the Indian diaspora engaged by using national values as a key component of the marketing strategy. It is estimated to have raised a total of $11 billion from diaspora bonds.[25] Foreign banks were allowed to sell the bonds, as they were considered better located to serve the Indian diaspora. Tax and credit incentives could make diaspora bonds more attractive. The Philippines has also used this type of bond to finance social housing projects. Greece is also planning to issue diaspora bonds to alleviate the country's debt problem.

28. Steady flows of remittances and other funds from migrants can have important stabilizing effects on the balance of payments. Despite chronic trade deficits, the current account balance of Bangladesh, Nepal and the Philippines has turned positive with the rise of remittances.[26] Such funds also improve a country's creditworthiness for external borrowing (box 3).

29. Many migrants, in time, become important investors by setting up businesses in home countries. Starting from 1978, businessmen from Hong Kong SAR, Macao SAR and Taiwan Province of China, as well as members of the Chinese diaspora living in South-East Asia, became the first investors to seize the opportunity of China's open-door policy combined with various tax incentives. Most of them started their businesses in China by investing in their regions of origin. They made important contributions to China's trade and development, especially in the early

Box 3.

Turkey: Attracting expatriates' funds to strengthen international reserves

Turkey has allowed its expatriates to open foreign currency deposit accounts at the Central Bank since 1976, when it had difficulty in financing increasing current account deficits due to the oil crisis. Because the Turkish lira was not convertible until 1989, these account enabled Turkish expatriates to hold their savings in foreign currency with attractive returns. In order to facilitate the efficient transfer of savings, Turkey signed special agreements with the European central banks, the German postal services, and financial institutions from Europe and the United States, and from Turkey. During the financial crisis in 1994, which led to a sudden capital outflow, the Turkish Government launched a new instrument (Super Foreign Exchange Accounts), offering longer-term and higher interest rates to Turkish expatriates. The two special accounts now account for roughly half of Turkey's international reserves, which can be used as safeguard against swift capital reversals and can help to reduce interest premiums on external borrowing.

Source: Atalay A. (2005). *Almanya'daki İşçi Tasarruflarının Değerlendirilmesi: Kredi Mektuplu Döviz Tevdiat ve Süper Döviz Hesapları Örneğinde Bir Makro Analiz.*

years of China's economic take-off. As their investment is concentrated in the manufacturing sector, they have promoted China's exports in manufactures through their networks in foreign countries, and have introduced new technology and management expertise, thus helping this sector's development. Their success encouraged multinational companies to invest directly in China a decade later. The Indian diaspora has played a well-known key role in the growth of India's ICT outsourcing services through direct investment and by facilitating commercial relations between United States & European firms and Indian firms.

30. Government assistance, including credit provision and incentives, can induce migrants and diasporas to invest in home countries. Supported by the Inter-American Development Bank, Brazil established a Mutual Fund for Investment in Emerging Enterprises (the "Dekassegui Fund") in the early 2000s, aimed at channelling a small portion of regularly transferred remittances to more productive uses. The fund offers support to Brazilians abroad (principally those in Japan) hoping to open small businesses in Brazil. This support includes selection and training

of potential entrepreneurs in Japan; integration and business training in Brazil; and start-up and growth of new businesses. The results seem to be encouraging, with more than 11,000 entrepreneurs supported, 1,000 training activities, and 3,500 consultancies undertaken to assist Brazilian returnees from Japan between 2005 and 2008. The funds also provide microcredits for start-up businesses, for example in restaurants, food processing, and agribusiness. In Morocco, the Groupe Banques Populaires is a state-owned bank with branches in several European countries. Receiving about 60 per cent of all remittances to Morocco, it provides subsidized credit for real estate and entrepreneurial investments in Morocco. Bangladesh has announced the creation of an expatriate welfare bank to provide collateral free loans, in particular to returnees, as well as support for investment in productive sectors of the economy.

31. Diasporas can play an important role in supporting the development of local infrastructure and public services such as roads, hospitals and schools. The Indian Government is presenting an ambitious $500 billion national infrastructure project to overseas Indians in more than 50 countries.[27] Indian diasporas will participate through public–private partnerships that will include knowledge and financial contributions from them.[28] If successful, this model could open a new way to finance significant infrastructure projects by diasporas interested in promoting development and higher standards of living in their countries of origin. In addition to family remittances, Somali diasporas have built flexible social support networks to gather resources to finance infrastructure, equip schools and hospitals, pay health and educational service providers, and train professionals in Somalia. Members of the Somali diaspora in the Netherlands were assisted by the Diaspora Partnership Programme (DPP) established in 2008 by a non-governmental organization, CARE. DPP strengthens diasporas' capacities to deal with a wide range of local partners to undertake joint development projects. Mexico is also well known for its active efforts in seeking diaspora contributions in local development projects by providing matching funds (the "3x1" citizens' initiative). The programme's budget went from $5 million in 2002 to $42 million by 2009, and more than 12,000 projects had been implemented by 2010.[29]

32. Diaspora spending can attract trade in goods and services (such as nostalgic goods and nostalgic tourism) from countries of origin. Nostalgic goods include traditional exports such as tortillas, tea and curry, which tend to be labour-intensive and artisanal. In this way, the export earnings

are more likely to benefit the local population. Nostalgic tourism usually refers to the circular flow of tourists for holidays and other personal purposes. ILO has estimated that a significant percentage of migrants visit their home countries as tourists. A study on Oaxaca in Mexico shows a positive correlation between nostalgic tourism and local development.[30]

33. The level of coherence and coordination of policies, regulations and institutions relating to migration and the use of remittances varies among countries. A comprehensive approach that seeks to: (a) set clear and aligned policy goals and priorities; (b) strengthen regulatory and institutional capacity; (c) assess labour market needs; and (d) provide pre- departure and return reintegration training of migrants, as well as multi-stakeholder consultations processes, could facilitate remittance flows for development and rights-based managed migration. Cooperation and trade agreements at bilateral, regional and international levels can also contribute to ensuring benefits from migration and facilitated remittance flows.

34. An institutional mechanism, as set up by Ecuador in 2007, could facilitate such coherence in countries of origin. The Secretaría Nacional del Migrante (SENAMI) is in charge of all policies related to migration and remittances, with competence at the national and international level. It has signed cooperation agreements with local institutions, including tax authorities, banks, the post office, the national civil register, and universities, to provide tax incentives (e.g. tariff exemptions for returning migrants' housing and working equipment) and services of interest to migrants. SENAMI has introduced facilitated migrant return programmes that provide business plan design, training, and seed capital provision. A bank for migrants to provide low-cost transfers and soft credits is also planned. SENAMI has also signed agreements with public and private institutions abroad to protect migrants' rights, promote circular migration, and facilitate transfers of remittances and mutual recognition of social security. Sri Lanka has created a multi-stakeholder committee to formulate and implement a comprehensive national migration strategy to develop a vision for the role of labour migration in the economy, improve protection of migrants' rights, and enhance benefits from migration including remittances.[31] This policy was adopted by the cabinet of Sri Lanka in 2009. Some destination countries are deploying efforts to improve coherence. More specifically on remittances, Albania has developed a comprehensive action plan which includes expansion of banking services, development of partnerships between national banks in main destination

countries, and strengthening of microfinance institutions. In destination countries, the EU's Global Approach to Migration aims to create partnership agreements with non-EU countries and to address all migration and asylum issues.[32] It guides several policy areas including development, foreign affairs, employment and social affairs. An example is the EU–Africa Partnership on Migration, Mobility and Employment (2007) which includes specific EU measures such as encouraging the use of one services provider in the EU for remittance transactions, and supporting diaspora groups engaged in development-related activities and country initiatives to safeguard skills for development.

V. Addressing Barriers and Harnessing Opportunities

35. Significant barriers exist in harnessing the positive roles of remittances in development and poverty reduction. There are barriers that increase the risk or cost of sending home remittances, and barriers that impede new flows of remittances. The former can be found in both home and host countries; they include lack of safe, reliable, affordable and accessible transfer systems for remittances, taxation, information asymmetries regarding the nature of the services, prices and competition. The latter include migration policies and trade-related barriers including market access limitations related to the temporary movement of natural persons. Remittance flows could benefit from lower transaction costs and facilitated movement of people. Strengthening the financial services sector will be key in reducing cost and channelling remittances into productive sectors.

A. Addressing Cost-Related Barriers

36. Several policy options can be identified to ensure safety and security in transactions, ensure affordability and accessibility, promote competition in remittance- related services, increase remittance flows via tax exemptions, and improve transparency and information flows.

37. Regarding safety and reliability, banks, money transfer organizations (MTOs) and post offices offer the highest levels of security and larger geographical reach through their branch networks. It is generally agreed that remittances transferred through formal rather than informal systems are more likely to be leveraged for development. Many migrants have felt obliged to use informal channels as a consequence of being undocument-

ed. Consular ID cards, such as those as issued by the Mexican Government, could address their needs to access formal financial services. Such cards have been accepted by mainstream financial institutions in the United States.[33] Formal transfers can also reduce the risk that migrants and recipients will be exploited by money-laundering networks. To facilitate access to bank accounts in EU countries, the European Investment Bank and Mediterranean developing countries signed an arrangement to allow migrants access to simplified banking facilities upon presentation of identity or consular registration cards.[34]

38. Affordability is one of the most important barriers to remittance flows, as the transfer fee is a key cost component of sending remittances. The lower the transaction cost is, the greater the benefits and opportunities are for receiving families and countries to capture development gains and reduce poverty. The volume of remittances from destination countries and the average total cost are closely correlated. The global average total cost fell to 8.7 per cent in 2010, but it remains high.[35] Generally, it is more expensive to send money through commercial banks, with a global average cost of 12.3 per cent in Q1 2010. Post Offices and MTOs were the cheapest, at 6.7 and 7.1 per cent respectively.

39. Latin America and South Asia have recorded the lowest regional average total cost for remittances. While transfer cost in Latin America was 5 per cent in 2010,[36] South Asia has seen a consistent drop in average total cost since 2008, from 7.8 per cent in 2008 to below 6 per cent in Q1 2010. Lower costs are the consequence of high transfer volumes and high levels of competition among service providers in both host and home countries. Africa has the highest average cost—between 10 and 14 per cent in the 2008–2010 period—mainly due to lower volume and to lack of competition in the provision of financial services in home countries, for example, owing to exclusivity contracts between MTOs and their agents. South–South transfers are expensive too, with an average cost of 12.3 per cent in Q1 2010.

40. There are solutions to reduce the cost of remittance transfers. Turkish banks, which receive half of workers' remittances transferred, have been using a cost-effective "passing trade system" and collective accounts. The easier and faster passing trade system is similar to a post office transfer and does not need either the sender or the recipient to open an account at the bank concerned. The cash remittance takes place simply on presentation of identity documents valid in the country of residence

for the sender and in Turkey for the recipient. The money is transferred to Turkey on the same day, at a lower cost than other financial institutions.[37] The "collective accounts" system has been set up among banks to overcome the constraints caused by the inadequate network of Turkish branches abroad. The Turkish expatriate deposits the money to be transferred at a Turkish bank abroad, which passes the money to the collective account of the recipient's bank in Turkey. The transaction can take less than four days; the only cost is the transferral fee between different banks, as in the case of the passing trade system.

41. Costs involved in the migration cycle can impact on the amount of remittances sent home. The upfront costs tend to rise inversely against migrants' skill levels. Employers often cover these costs for more skilled migrants, but lower-skilled migrants frequently have to pay themselves, due to lack of information and bargaining power vis-à-vis recruiters and employers. For instance, Asian migrants moving to Qatar, Saudi Arabia and the United Arab Emirates often pay 25–35 per cent of what they expect to earn over two to three years as recruitment-related fees.[38] Responsibility for reducing the costs of migration lies with both origin and destination countries. Some countries have enacted relevant legislation. For example, Canada and the United States require employers to cover the recruitment and travel costs of migrant workers, and the Philippines has set ceilings on what migrant workers should pay to recruitment agents.[39]

42. Partnerships between non-governmental organizations (NGOs) and banks could also be considered in addressing this issue. In 2009, the Global Forum on Migration and Development commissioned a study on the feasibility of providing low-cost loans to Bangladeshi migrants, who typically spend a third of their expected earnings over three years on recruitment, travel, and related fees. The study[40] proposes that low-cost loans be provided early in the recruitment process via NGOs already operating microfinance schemes in villages, in partnership with banks. The NGOs would also check the validity and terms of the contracts. The loans would be repaid via remittances sent through the banks. Such partnerships could be launched with donor funds, and should become self-financing over time.

43. Widespread retail payment networks in home countries have proved to be a relevant factor for ensuring accessibility, particularly in rural or poor areas where such networks do not exist or are not well developed.

Some countries have taken steps to expand networks of remittance services. Mexico has invested significantly in improving the retail payment infrastructure to promote safe and efficient receipt of remittances. It has more collection points than the African continent.[41] To increase the financial services available in Mexico, particularly to low-income Mexicans, the Banco de Servicios Financieros has created the second-largest network in Mexico of popular banks, microfinance institutions and credit unions to act as remittance distributors. It received about $580 million of remittances in 2008. In El Salvador, 40 per cent of remittances go to rural areas where there are few commercial banks. The Federation of Salvadorean Savings and Credit Cooperatives (FEDECASES) and other microfinance operators has played an important role in expanding networks, by establishing branches in low-income and rural areas. The success of FEDECASES has attracted support from the IADB to strengthen its financial and administrative capabilities in providing such remittance services. Remittances transferred by FEDECASES went from $1.2 million in 2001 to $88 million in 2004.[42] At the regional level, under the ASEAN framework on transport and communications cooperation, inter-country remittance services were provided between Brunei Darussalam, Malaysia and Singapore through postal and money orders.

44. New smartphone-based products and services can help increase both affordability and accessibility. In many parts of Asia and Africa, mobile phone companies are developing ways of transferring money to remote parts of the country. Under the money transfer arrangement between Vodafone Qatar and Philippines-based Globe Telecom, 200,000 Filipinos working in Qatar will be able to send money to the Philippines.[43] Safaricom, a United Kingdom telecom operator in Kenya, has launched broad financial mobile services to facilitate the transfer of workers' remittances.[44] It has more than 7 million subscribers, generating more than $88.5 million worth of transactions daily. Efforts are also being deployed by France and French-speaking Africa in identifying regulatory challenges to allow remittance transfers via the internet and mobile phones.[45] To facilitate such transactions, there is a need to legalize related operations, harmonize certain technical standards, and take specific measures to address security and consumer protection issues. Joint cooperative mechanisms among central banks, associations of financial institutions, and telecommunication providers in home and host countries could help address some of these challenges. Such cooperation could also serve as

a platform to respond to concerns regarding intermediaries and unfair competition practices among service providers.

45. Allowing non-bank institutions such as microfinance institutions to transfer remittances under proper oversight could facilitate distribution and lower transaction costs, in particular when anticompetitive practices are prevalent. Abusive exclusivity agreements between international MTOs and local banks are reported to exist especially in Africa, where 60 per cent of funds are transferred by banks.[46] Such agreements and internal regulations authorizing only banks to operate impede the ability of microfinance institutions to engage in remittance payouts. Development cooperation agencies, international and regional institutions could support the enhancement of regulatory and institutional capacity, especially in Africa where the highest transfer costs are found.

46. Taxes on remittances could raise transaction costs, incentivize informal transfers, and reduce resources that in many cases go to the poor. Most developing countries offer tax incentives to attract remittances, but a few countries still worry about tax evasion.[47] On the destination countries' side, recently in the United States, the states of Oklahoma and Kansas have imposed taxes on remittances. Oklahoma introduced a $5 tax on each remittance transaction or wire transfer, plus an added 1 per cent charge on amounts over $500, generating concerns in Mexico. Both home and host countries need to maintain due restraint on taxes on remittances in order to maintain remittance flows and ensure that they benefit those in need.

47. Improving transparency and information flows could help to address information asymmetries and make senders aware of the best transfer options. Centralized information centres and training services in both home and host countries could be particularly useful for low-skill workers. Information provided could include safe and reliable suppliers of remittance services, means of transfer, and fee comparisons. For example, Mexico and the Philippines (in their overseas workers resource centres) have sought to improve transparency by maintaining a price database that provides competitive price information to consumers. Countries could establish a similar database by using the World Bank's *World Remittances Prices Database*, which covers prices in the main migration corridors, and country-to-country information. Development aid could play a useful role in helping developing countries to maintain information services, which require human and financial resources.

B. Addressing Barriers Impeding Flows of Remittances

48. Barriers to migration in general, and more specifically to the temporary movement of natural persons (mode 4), can impede temporary and circular migration processes (temporary workers going back home and returning to host countries upon new contracts) and potential growth in remittance flows. The migration policies of destination countries can have important implications for remittance flows. There has been found to be a correlation between the level of integration of migrants and their preponderance to remit. Legal status, for example, is an important variable in determining the extent to which migrants make contributions to their country of origin.[48] Introducing stricter requirements for visas and work permits without providing facilitated options for temporary migration in sectors where demand for foreign labour is high is counterproductive. Experiences in Eastern Europe have shown that strict migration policies exacerbate human trafficking, pushing would-be immigrants into irregularity and fostering irregular migration.[49] One compelling argument for migrants not leaving the host countries is the prospect of being unable to return due to increasingly strict and burdensome regulations on migration. The more predictable, transparent and open the regular channels are, the fewer incentives there would be for irregular migration. Some migrant workers' programmes have understood this paradox. For example, the return programmes of the Spanish Government for Ecuadorian workers provide cash incentives plus priority consideration in applying for new contracts for workers who have chosen to return home.

49. By and large, temporary migration is facilitated in highly skilled professions, whereas it is more restricted for lower-skilled labour. Trade agreements can partially address these barriers through the World Trade Organization (WTO) services negotiations in the context of Doha Development Agenda (DDA). Barriers to mode 4 found in key markets include quotas, economic needs tests, burdensome visa procedures, and the lack of mutual recognition of qualifications. Fewer commitments have been made by WTO members in mode 4 than in other modes of supply. Commitments during the Uruguay Round have been low and limited to the higher-skilled categories (managers, executives and specialists), with approximately one half relating explicitly to intra-corporate transferees. While mode 4 technically covers all skill levels, only about 17 per cent of horizontal commitments cover low-skilled personnel, and only 10 countries have allowed some form of restricted entry to "other level" personnel. Existing mode 4 commitments have not produced the

expected results for developing countries and LDCs. This imbalance was supposed to be corrected in the DDA, nevertheless offers in mode 4 remain limited. Commercially meaningful commitments in mode 4 could bring important development gains for developing countries estimated at between $150 billion and $300 billion, without including other benefits such as development and poverty reduction impacts. A great part of these benefits will take the form of remittances. A coherent trade liberalization policy that not only liberalizes movement of goods and capital but also provides real market access in mode 4 will contribute positively to economic integration, poverty reduction, facilitating managed migration flows, and increased remittances.

50. A special arrangement on mode 4, including market access and regulatory issues, could be explored. It could contain elements such as a stand-still clause on restrictions; focused request and offer sessions with special consideration for LDCs in the WTO Council for Trade in Services (e.g. providing objective criteria for economic needs/labour market tests or progressively expanding quotas); and specific regulatory principles applicable to mode 4 in the domestic regulation negotiations (e.g. balancing requirements for experience vs. academic qualifications, and non-discrimination in relation to the origin of service providers). An early harvest on the most-favoured-nation waiver for LDCs enabling unilateral openings in mode 4 could address some of the barriers in areas of interest to both destination countries and LDCs. Positive outcomes in these areas could become a deal-maker in the General Agreement on Trade in Services (GATS) and other negotiations under the DDA. It could also facilitate continuous flows of remittances, and incentivize circular migration.

51. Bilateral arrangements accompanying mode 4 commitments could dissipate concerns about making binding commitments in WTO. These arrangements could be similar to the existing bilateral labour agreements, which cover, among other things, areas such as short-term employment, recognition of qualifications, and technical and cultural exchanges. By ensuring that migration takes place in accordance with agreed principles and procedures, they would help to guide the migration process towards meeting economic, social and development objectives. Deeper engagement, implementation and monitoring of partnerships under the Global Forum on Migration and Development could also assist in optimizing mutual benefits. These arrangements, such as Canada's guest worker programmes with several countries in Central America and the Carib-

bean, enable circular migration, create a steady flow of remittances, and reduce the incidence of brain-drain. Another example is the 2009 agreement on temporary contractual employment between the United Arab Emirates, India and the Philippines, which provides for a framework for worker selection, orientation, training, contract validation, and return and reintegration.

52. Regional trade and cooperation agreements, such as the Caribbean Community, the Andean Community, and the Association of Southeast Asian Nations, can be useful avenues for addressing barriers to the flow of people, including mode 4, as they imply wider and deeper political agreement and trade-offs between Parties that could facilitate some openings in this mode. North–South integration agreements could also offer a facilitated framework; for example, the EU economic partnership agreement negotiations with the African, Caribbean and Pacific Group of States could provide commercially meaningful access on mode 4.

53. Lack of access to social benefits such as pensions, and their non-portability, affects migrants and reduces their potential to contribute to development through remittances. In the case of lack of access to the social benefits system in destination countries, originating countries could explore facilitating registration and direct payments to the social security system by migrants. Some countries, such as Mexico and the Philippines, allow migrants to contribute to the national pension and healthcare schemes regardless of their access in destination countries.[50] Many migrants consider returning home after some time, or at retirement age. Encouraging coverage and payments to the social security system to workers abroad could incentivize social investment in pension and health insurance, with benefits upon retirement. Non-portability of contributory pensions not only discourages return and circular migration due to the impossibility of accumulating benefits, but also reduces the amount of remittance money that can be sent home. Solutions to address the portability issue[51] include unilaterally allowing full or partial portability, and bilateral agreements seeking to avoid double contribution of social benefits in both origin and destination countries.

VI. Conclusions

54. Migration is a win-win pro-development opportunity for origin and destination countries. Empirical evidence indicates a positive correlation between remittances, development, and poverty reduction. Remittances

have, if properly harnessed, multiplier effects on economic and social development. Proactive policy measures could induce the productive use of remittances and capitalize on diaspora networks for developmental purposes. There is a need for a comprehensive and coherent policy—a regulatory and institutional framework at the national level with the involvement of all stakeholders.

55. Expanding networks to transfer and distribute remittances, strengthening the capacity of the financial services sector to channel remittances into productive activities, using new technology, and improving information flows can facilitate the efficient transfer and use of remittances. To enable temporary and circular migration and steady remittance flows, there is a need to remove barriers to the movement of people, including through GATS mode 4 commitments. Managing migration and facilitating the flow of remittances also requires increased efforts toward a higher level of policy coherence and cooperation at bilateral, regional and multilateral levels.

ENDNOTES

1. See UNCTAD/DITC/TNCD/2009/2, and the Report of the Ad Hoc Expert Meeting on Contribution of Migrants to Development: Trade, Investment and Development Linkages.

2. A/C.2/65/L.69.

3. World Bank (2010a). *Migration and Remittances Factbook 2011*.

4. ILO (2010). *Global Employment Trends*.

5. OECD (2010a). Economy: Migration key to long-term economic growth.

6. International Organization for Migration (2010a). *World Migration Report*; and WTO (2010). WT/TPR/OV/W/3.

7. International Organization for Migration (2008a). *Migration, Environment and Climate Change*.

8. United Nations Environment Programme, International Labour Organization, International Organization of Employers, and International Trade Union Confederation (2008). *Green Jobs: Towards Decent Work in a Sustainable, Low-Carbon World*.

9. World Bank (2010a).

10. UNCTAD (2010). *Trade and Development Report*.

11. World Bank (2010c). *Migration and Development Briefs, 12*.

12. UNCTAD (2008). *Least Developed Countries Report 2008*.

13. African Development Bank (2009). *Republic of Cape Verde: Country Strategy Paper 2009–2012*.

14. UNDP (2010). *MDGs: Nepal*.

15. Migration Policy Institute (2007). *Leveraging Remittances for Development*.

16. IOM (2010c). *Migration and the MDGs.*

17. World Bank (2007). *Increasing the Macroeconomic Impact of Remittances on Development.*

18. Fajnzylber and Lopez (2006). *Close to Home: The Development Impact of Remittances in Latin America.*

19. Brown (2010). *Assessing the Impact of Remittances on Poverty using Household Survey Data.*

20. ADB (2009). *Remittances in Asia: Implications for the Fight against Poverty and the Pursuit of Economic Growth.*

21. UNDP (2005). *International Financial Flows and Worker Remittances: Best Practices.*

22. ILO (2010). *Remittance Transfers in Senegal.*

23. Hudson Institute (2010). *The Index of Global Philanthropy and Remittances.*

24. Inter-American Dialogue (2003). *Worker Remittances in an International Scope.*

25. World Bank (2007). *Development finance via diaspora bonds: Track record and potential.*

26. GFMD (2010). *Key Trends and Challenges on International Migration and Development in Asia and the Pacific.*

27. Ministry of Overseas Indian Affairs and Confederation of Indian Industry (2010). *Engaging the Global Indian.*

28. One India. *Prez woos diaspora to invest in India.* 11 January 2010.

29. Secretaría de Desarrollo Social (México) (2010).

30. Reyes, Mata, Gijón, Cruz and López (2009).

31. ILO (2008).

32. EU Commission. COM(2008) 611.

33. MPI (2003). *Consular ID cards: Mexico and Beyond.*

34. EIB (2006). Study on improving the efficiency of workers' remittances in Mediterranean countries.

35. World Bank and IFC (2010). *Remittance Prices Worldwide.*

36. Inter-American Dialogue (2010). A scoreboard in the market of money transfers.

37. OECD (2005). *Principal Channels and Costs of Remittances: The Case of Turkey.*

38. UNDP (2009). *Human Development Report.*

39. GFMD Mexico (2010).

40. Philip Martin (2009). *Reducing the Cost Burden for Migrant Workers: A Market-Based Approach.*

41. World Bank and IFC (2010).

42. Institute for Inter-American Integration (2006). *Levering efforts on remittances and financial intermediation.*

43. Vodafone enables mobile money transfers between Qatar and Philippines. *Cellular News.* 10 November 2010.

44. Greenwood (2009). Africa's mobile banking revolution.

45. République Française, AFD, UBM, BAD, and CDBCA (2009). *Transfert de fonds des migrants au Mahgreb et en Zone Franc.*

46. IFAD (2009). *Sending money home to Africa*.

47. MPI (2007).

48. IOM (2010).

49. Journal of Comparative Economics (2010). *The Economics of Human Trafficking and Labour Migration: Micro-Evidence from Eastern Europe*.

50. Holzmann (2010). *Portability of Pension, Health, and Other Social Benefits: Facts, Concepts, Issues*.

51. Ibid.

*The United Nations Conference on Trade and Development (UNCTAD) promotes the development-friendly integration of developing countries into the world economy. Established in 1964, UNCTAD has progressively evolved into an authoritative knowledge-based institution whose work aims to help shape current policy debates and thinking on development, with a particular focus on ensuring that domestic policies and international action are mutually supportive in bringing about sustainable development.

United Nations Conference on Trade and Development. "Maximizing the Development Impact of Remittances." Expert Meeting on Maximizing the Development Impact of Remittances. Geneva, 14–15 February 2011.

Used by permission.

Impact on Receiving Countries

by Christina Boswell and Jeff Crisp*

The term 'receiving countries'—in its strict sense—denotes any country hosting immigrants or refugees, or a country to which flows are directed. In fact, this definition would cover just about every country in the world. In much of the literature on international migration, the term is used in a more narrow sense to refer to the most frequent destination countries for migrants and refugees, particularly developed western countries: Western Europe, North America and Australia.

These are of course not the only countries to receive large numbers of immigrants, and indeed a number of countries in Asia, the Middle East, South America, Central and East Europe and South Africa are increasingly becoming the preferred destination for migrants. Moreover, most refugees in fact choose to or are compelled to stay in countries closer to home. But these Western states remain the first choice destination for many immigrants from the south, a trend which has become more pronounced since the 1980s.[26] They have also generally been the most outspoken in their opposition to and attempts to control immigration and refugee intake since the early to mid-1970s. Hence much of the discussion of the impact of migration on 'receiving countries' has focused on these western industrialized states.

The major patterns of migration flows to Western countries since the 1970s have been well covered in the literature, and can be relatively quickly summarized.[27] Until the 1970s most western states received considerable numbers of immigrants through legal migration schemes and as refugees. A number of factors combined to produce more restrictive policies from around 1972–3: the oil crisis and ensuing economic recession; growing concerns about integration and inter-ethnic relations; and growing levels of south-north migration and refugee flows.

After initial attempts to restrict these flows through limiting legal migration channels in the 1970s, many immigrants began to use alternative channels for entering the west: family reunion, or asylum systems. This triggered in turn a series of measures to restrict numbers of asylum-seekers and possibilities for family reunion. One result of this was to shift flows into more nefarious channels, in particular illegal migration through illegal entry or overstay, and the increased use of smugglers and traffickers. Illegal migration appears to be still on the rise, although it is difficult to obtain reliable statistics. Asylum also remains a popular route for entering western countries. After a decline in applications in the second half of the 1990s, numbers have again risen in most western receiving states.

In looking at how these flows have affected receiving countries, we need to be careful to disentangle different types of impacts. Many sections of the population and political parties have been highly vocal in their resistance to immigration, emphasizing numerous negative impacts of migration. Some of these are fairly concrete financial or social costs, which may be possible to measure. For example, there have been estimates of the costs of reception and application processing for asylum seekers.[28] There have also been some studies on the fiscal and economic impact of labour migrants, although less on the impact of employed asylum seekers and refugees. Other measurable social impacts of immigrants, asylum seekers and refugees may be derived from statistics on criminality or the performance of schools in areas of high immigration.

But such estimates of the costs or benefits of migration should also be treated with caution. One reason is that migration and asylum policies themselves can be a major determinant of costs. Thus, for example, the extensive use of accommodation centres or detention for asylum seekers can substantially increase reception costs, while denying access to labour markets can increase fiscal costs.

Other costs relate to more abstract anxieties about the impact of immigration on identity or security. Here it is extremely difficult to ascertain how far such concerns are actually caused by immigration as such. On the one hand, immigration since the second world war has clearly had a major impact on society and identity in western European countries, and it is not surprising that this would have major repercussions. This is especially likely where immigrant communities are concentrated in areas of social deprivation, or where problems with language, cultural norms or discrimination impede integration. The rise in illegal immigration has also been viewed as a security threat, as have fears about immigrants active in international terrorist networks, especially in the wake of 11 September 2001.

But on the other hand, fears about cultural identity are clearly also located in a number of other socio-economic and political changes. Some authors have linked concerns about immigration to processes of globalization and modernization, which have eroded traditional categories of identity in developed countries—be these based on class, ideology, extended family, religion or the nation-state.

It has been argued that this has generated a search for new categories of membership, including those which differentiate between nationals and foreigners, or residents versus newcomers. Another, not incompatible thesis, is that pressures of globalization and EU integration have brought about significant changes in the role and competence of nation-states. These changes, it has been argued, also generate insecurity about the capacity of states to protect citizens from security threats, or to protect their privileged socio-economic status from competition from outsiders. According to these accounts, immigration simply provides a symbolic issue on which to pin these anxieties.

Whether or not one understands these concerns as a function of migration flows or as a 'construct', the fact remains that public concerns are very real, and certainly cannot be ignored by political parties and governments seeking legitimacy and electoral support.

Discussions on the benefits of immigration have tended to be much less prominent. One exception is the clear and growing recognition of the economic benefits of high-skilled labour migration. But there is less explicit acceptance of the benefits of low-skilled labour—an oversight that many see as hypocritical, given the structural dependence of most industrialized states on cheap flexible labour.

Nor is much said about the cultural gains of immigration. There have been attempts by some to emphasize the contribution of immigrants to receiving societies, often highlighting the achievements of sports players, artists or entrepreneurs. But this overlooks the wider and less tangible contribution of immigrant communities to the cultural and social life of receiving societies—for example how far immigration contributes to the dynamism of multi-cultural cities like London, New York, Berlin or Amsterdam.

Perhaps a more balanced discussion on the costs and benefits of migration will emerge as demographic pressures increase the demand for labour migration in developed countries. Governments may feel increasingly pressured to make a more positive case for immigration as the need for immigration becomes more urgent.

ENDNOTES

[. . .]

26. Stocks of migrants in US, France, Germany, Canada, Australia and the UK rose by 25 per cent in 1986/7–1996/7; see Susan F. Martin, Andrew I. Schoenholtz and David Fisher, 'Impact of Asylum on Receiving Countries', UNU-WIDER conference paper.

27. Brief overviews are provided in Stephen Castles and Sean Loughna, 'Trends in Asylum Migration to Industrialized Countries 1990–2001'; Matthew Gibney and Randall Hansen, 'Asylum Policy in the West: Past Trends, Future Possibilities'; and Christina Boswell, 'Explaining Public Policy Responses to Asylum and Migration'. All three were presented at the UNU-WIDER Conference.

28. Martin, Schoenholtz and Fisher (*supra*, 26).

*Christina Boswell is professor of politics, and deputy dean of research in the College of Humanities and Social Science, at the University of Edinburgh.

Jeff Crisp is head of the policy development and evaluation service at the United Nations High Commissioner for Refugees and has worked on refugee, humanitarian, and migration issues for almost 30 years.

Boswell, Christina, and Jeff Crisp. *Poverty, International Migration and Asylum—A Policy Brief*. Helsinki: United Nations University World Institute for Development Economics Research (UNU-WIDER), 2004: 18–20.

Used by permission.

Transatlantic Opinion on Immigration: Greater Worries and Outlier Optimism

*by Delancey Gustin and Astrid Ziebarth**

This article outlines some of the key findings of the 2008 and 2009 *Transatlantic Trends: Immigration*[1] public opinion study. The countries surveyed include the United States, the United Kingdom, France, Germany, Italy, the Netherlands, and, for 2009 only, Spain and Canada.[2] Some of the findings are highlighted in this article, including the limited effect of the economic crisis on attitudes; approval ratings of governments' migration management; political support for U.S. immigration reform components; Canada's outlier optimism; increasing Dutch skepticism; and support for the resettlement of migrants displaced by the effects of worldwide climate change.

SURVEY OVERVIEW

Transatlantic Trends: Immigration (TTI) is designed to gauge public opinion on immigration and integration policies in Western Europe and North America on a longitudinal basis, and the survey covers a range of issues relevant to the large migrant-receiving countries in these regions. There are presently other surveys, such as the Eurobarometer and European Social Survey in Europe and various one-off or ad-hoc surveys in the United States and Canada, which focus on or include questions about immigration. TTI distinguishes itself from these other surveys in that it compares opinion on this issue across the Atlantic on an annual basis. All countries included in TTI have large immigrant populations, but each has a unique history and national experience with immigration and integration. By systematically addressing pertinent issues in all of these countries, stakeholders in national immigration debates can get a sense of their country's opinions vis-à-vis other large migrant-receiving countries.

Transatlantic Trends: Immigration General Key Findings

One of the most anticipated issues in comparing the 2008 and 2009 TTI surveys was the potential effect of the economic crisis on attitudes about immigration. The first edition of the survey gathered opinion in early September 2008, before the financial crisis that triggered the global recession. As the 2009 survey fieldwork was conducted 1 year later, many questions were designed to measure the effects of a worsening economic outlook on attitudes about migration. Initial findings seemed to point to a more negative attitude; topline data for 2008 and 2009 revealed that more respondents in every country were more skeptical about immigration in the second year of the survey (*see* Figure 1). The European average of respondents claiming that immigration was more of a problem than an opportunity for their countries went up from 43 percent in 2008 to 50 percent in 2009. The United States also saw a 4 percent jump in skepticism, from 50 percent to 54 percent saying that immigration was more of a problem for the United States.

Initial explorations of the survey data attempted to tie this growth in skepticism to the economic crisis, but very little evidence has yet been found. The only conclusive finding was that respondents whose household financial situation got worse in the last 12 months were slightly more worried about legal immigration. However, this finding only held true for Canada and the European countries in the survey—the American data showed no effect. Though the increase in negative views of immigration might be tied to the economic crisis, the TTI data does not provide conclusive evidence that this is the case.

Immigration Management Approval Levels

Moving from the economy to politics, TTI 2009 asked respondents to assess the steps that their national governments had taken to manage immigration.

Figure 1. Increase in Skepticism: Immigration Seen as More a Problem than an Opportunity in 2009.

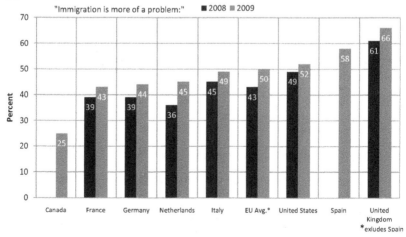

The results were strikingly disparate across countries. Whereas Germans (71 percent), Canadians (63 percent), the Dutch (53 percent), and the French (50 percent) thought that their governments were doing either a good or fair job at immigration management, the British (71 percent), the Spanish (64 percent), Americans (63 percent), and Italians (53 percent) thought that their governments were doing either a poor or very poor job. There are many explanations for these diverse findings, including approval of the governments in general, but the findings do provide some sense of respondents' views of their governments' competence in managing immigration. In the next three sections, three national case studies will be examined: the United States, Canada, and the Netherlands. More specific questions about policy preferences and perception in these countries will be placed in the context of ongoing national immigration debates.

UNITED STATES

Public Opinion and U.S. Comprehensive Immigration Reform

Though immigration reform has been one of the most contentious domestic policy issues for the past 5 years, most of the components of eventual reform are clear. They would include increased border security, increased internal enforcement efforts involving employers and local law enforcement, an expansion of temporary labor programs at the expense of family reunification quotas, and some form of legalization for many of the estimated 11 million undocumented immigrants currently living in the United States. TTI addressed all of these issues in 2008 and 2009, thereby shining some light on the thinking of the American public on these components of reform. In particular, the results lay bare the deep divisions between self-described Democrats, Independents, and Republicans in their support for these policies.

Illegal Immigration and Declining Support for Legalization

The most contentious issue driving the American immigration debate is the problem of illegal immigration, a phenomenon that gained momentum in the economically healthy years of the 1990s and early 2000s. At present, estimates of the undocumented immigrant population in the United States range from 10 to 12 million individuals. TTI data shows that levels of anxiety about this problem vary across the political spectrum. While percentages of Americans worried about *legal* immigration are relatively stable across party affiliation (Democrat 17 percent, Independent 18 percent, Republican 19 percent), anxiety levels about *illegal* immigration vary wildly. A full 76 percent of self-identified Republicans are "worried about illegal immigration," compared with 59 percent of Independents and 48 percent of Democrats. Republicans and Independents seem to be particularly concerned with the connection between illegal immigration and criminality—69 percent and 64 percent of them, respectively—say that illegal immigrants increase crime in society, compared with 50 percent of Democrats.

One of the most critical questions, then, is what to do with migrants who are already in the country illegally. In 2008, 50 percent of Americans were in favor of giving the undocumented "an opportunity to obtain legal status that allows them to stay in the United States." Unsurprisingly, Democrats were the most likely to be in favor of this policy, at 61 percent support, whereas only 47 percent of Independents and 40 percent of Republicans agreed. In 2009, TTI measured a decline in support for the legalization of undocumented migrants, with an overall 46 percent—now a clear minority of Americans—favoring legalization. The 4 percent drop in support is due to declining support across all three political groups in the sample. However, the greatest decline was actually among Democrats. Their support for legalization dropped 8 percentage points, from 61 percent in 2008 to 53 percent in 2009. Republicans—dropping from 40 percent to 35 percent—and Independents—from 47 percent to 45 percent—showed more modest drops in support. This decline seems to indicate that political will for a legalization or "amnesty" measure is growing weaker among Democrats, even as Democratic elected officials strive to push the policy forward.

Support for Increased Border Security and Employer Sanctions

While Democrats have made legalizing the undocumented immigrant population a priority, Republicans in Washington have been focusing on border security. In TTI, Americans were asked whether they supported or opposed strengthening border controls as a means of controlling illegal immigration. A full 91 percent of Republicans said that they supported reinforcing border controls (with 75 percent saying they *strongly* supported the policy), whereas a lower majority of Democrats (77 percent) answered that they supported it (51 percent strongly). This data is remarkably similar to the findings of 2008, when Republicans also strongly supported increasing border controls. In 2009, Republicans also picked border security out of a host of options as the policy most *effective* policy to control illegal immigration to the United States. They chose this option over employer sanctions, development aid, and increased avenues of legal immigration. Democrats and Independents were more ambivalent about the most effective means of reducing illegal immigration.

Another policy of enforcement, punishing employers who hire illegal immigrants was also addressed in TTI. In 2009, the Obama administration continued to develop and fine-tune E-Verify, a system that employers can use to check the immigration status of their employees. Additionally, the administration eschewed George Bush's policy of high-profile workplace raids in favor of more discrete, but more widespread, audits of employers suspected of hiring the undocumented. The program resulted in millions of dollars in fines levied to businesses found to be violating immigration laws. Across political affiliations, Americans were found to be in favor of this policy. Seventy-two percent of them support punishing employers as a means of controlling illegal immigration to the country.

Temporary Versus Permanent Labor Programs

Turning to legal immigration schemes, Americans on average were in favor of allowing labor migrants to immigrate to the United States permanently, rather than on a temporary basis. At present, several temporary visas such as the H-1B for highly-skilled migrants are actually stepping stones to permanent residence in the United States. As 71 percent of Americans favored permanent over temporary labor migration (including majorities across all political parties), it seems that Americans would be in favor of a continuation or expansion of these "stepping stone" visa policies. It should be noted that the question only specified that the migrants would be legal, not necessarily high- or low-skilled. Nevertheless, policymakers should consider expanded permanent or "stepping stone" labor migration schemes as they discuss the expansion of foreign worker programs.

A Future of Political Compromises

Though political support for legalization among Democrats is declining, a majority of 53 percent still support the policy. In contrast, Republicans oppose legalization but are emphatic in their support for border security. As Americans across the political spectrum support employer sanctions and permanent labor programs for legal migrants, TTI data supports the commonly-held view that a legalization-for-border-security compromise could be the grand tradeoff that allows U.S. Comprehensive Immigration Reform to move ahead.

CANADA

Canada and Optimism About Immigration

In Canada, where one in five persons is an immigrant, and several of the largest cities can claim that half of the population was born abroad, public opinion about immigration is largely positive. The country was polled in TTI for the first time in 2009, quickly distinguishing itself as an outlier on a number of issues covered in the survey. Though its immigrant-to-native ratio is by far the highest among the countries surveyed, Canadians were the least likely of any country, at 24 percent, to say that there are "too many" immigrants in their country. Also, when asked whether immigration was more of a problem or more of an opportunity for Canada, a full 68 percent of Canadians said that it was more of an opportunity. To put this optimism in perspective, an average of only 40 percent of Americans and Europeans in the survey said that immigration was an opportunity for their countries.

Explanations for Canadian positivity abound. Unlike the United States, where the problem of illegal immigration has made the debate increasingly contentious, Canada's geographic isolation has prevented illegal immigration from becoming a substantial issue. Instead, Canada is able to select its immigrants based on labor markets and national priorities, such as family reunification and acceptance of refugees. In the past few years, as other countries have grappled with a perceived failure of integration or large numbers of undocumented immigrants, the most controversial issue in Canada has been fraudulent asylum claims and the length of asylum proceedings. Economic and family migration to Canada has been largely free of contentious debate, and Canada's expedited system of naturalization ensures that many immigrants become citizens in as little as 3 years. Perhaps as a result of the millions of naturalized immigrants, or New Canadians, who have the right to vote, there are no serious anti-immigrant agenda items on any of Canada's political party platforms. In short, Canada is seen in many ways an immigration success story.

Perception of Immigration's Effects: Canada Versus the United States

Given that the United States and Canada have similar histories in that their populations, cultures, and economies have been shaped by immigration, the survey data from the United States puts that of Canada into perspective. In TTI 2009, for instance, Canadians (65 percent) and Americans (66 percent) shared the opinion that immigration enriches, rather than negatively affects, national culture. This finding is in keeping with a traditional absorption of foreign cultural elements—such as music, sport, and cuisine—into Canadian and American life.

Though they share a view on immigration's cultural benefits, it is clear that the two countries think differently about the labor market effects of immigration. Whereas 50 percent of Americans thought that immigrants take jobs away from the native born, only 30 percent of Canadians agreed. Likewise, a plurality of Americans (48 percent) believed that immigrants bring down the wages of native born workers; only 25 percent of Canadians thought the same about immigrants' effects on Canadian wages. Overall, it seems that threat perception of immigrants in the labor market is much greater in the United States than it is in Canada, which might explain some of the relative skepticism in the United States about immigrations' benefits.

Another question aimed at labor market effects had to do with the immigrants' entrepreneurial spirit. Since a quarter of new U.S. patent applications were filed by at least one foreign-born person (Wadhwa, 2009), a majority of Americans (57 percent) recognized that immigrants *create* jobs as they set up new businesses. However, an even bigger majority (75 percent) of Canadians said that immigrants create jobs in Canada. Canada's points-based immigration system focuses on skills and education, so it seems that Canadians recognize the innovative and growth creating abilities of highly-skilled migrants. To emphasize the point, when asked whether highly-skilled immigrant numbers to Canada should be reduced, 70 percent of Canadians were in opposition.

The fact that Canada emphasizes the immigration of highly-qualified individuals is one of the most likely reasons for the optimism seen in TTI. Tellingly, 88 percent of Canadians perceived legal immigrants to be hard workers, and they undoubtedly see this work ethic and its fruits as windfalls for Canada. As the highly-skilled generate economic growth and are also traditionally considered to be easier to integrate into the host society, some of Canadians' positivity could be explained by the perceived benefits of highly-skilled immigration.

Federal-Provincial Relations and Immigration

Though the national policy of Canada is to emphasize the acceptance of highly-qualified migrants, a program exists which allows *provinces* to set their own immigration priorities. The Provincial Nomination Program (PNP) allows provinces to sponsor individuals who wish to immigrate to a particular Canadian province, thereby putting them on a fast-track to permanent residence and Canadian citizenship. In 2009, PNP-sponsored immigrants and their families accounted for 14 percent of the new economic and family-based permanent residents of Canada (Citizenship and Immigration Canada, 2009). The PNP has its foundations in the French-speaking province of Québec, where the admission of French-speaking migrants to Canada has long been a priority. Québec was granted the ability to select such migrants under its own program, but the PNP policy was subsequently established for all other Canadian provinces and two territories, all of whom select immigrants according to local priorities and labor markets.

To gauge support for such devolution of immigration policymaking, TTI asked Canadians whether they thought decisions about immigration issues should be made by provincial and local authorizes or by national government authorities. Overall, 74 percent of Canadians were in favor of *national* jurisdiction on this issue. Given their traditional leanings toward autonomy, however, only 57 percent of the Québécois supported national government control, while 39 percent preferred for provincial and local (in this case, probably Québécois) authorities to make immigration policy decisions. This finding in Québec compares to other big Canadian provinces such as Ontario, British Columbia, and Alberta, all of whom had 80 percent or higher majorities favoring national government control over immigration decision making.

Canadian Immigration Policies Moving Forward

Among the countries surveyed in TTI, Canada is an anomaly in that it has a comparatively high immigration rate and a markedly more positive attitude about immigration in general. The survey found that in 2009, 76 percent of Canadians supported a policy already in place in Canada, namely accepting immigrants permanently rather than temporarily. This and other pro-immigration policies, among a generally pro-immigrant population, undoubtedly contribute to the 59 percent majority opinion that the Canadian government is doing either a good or a fair job at managing immigration. The findings of TTI indicate that Canadians are largely in favor of continued large-scale immigration and increasing diversity in their country.

THE NETHERLANDS

Increase in Skepticism About Immigration

In the Netherlands, discussions about immigration and integration have become increasingly heated in the policy sphere and public debate in the past decade. This trend continues despite low immigration levels, relatively high levels of naturalization, and low unemployment rates in the general Dutch population. In fact, the stock of foreign-born persons living in the Netherlands has remained relatively stable, at around 10 percent, for the past several years. Nevertheless, the Dutch public is becoming increasingly skeptical about immigration and integration, a phenomenon that is also reflected in TTI survey from 2008 and 2009.

Whereas most countries polled in TTI saw only a moderate increase in skepticism year-on-year, Dutch respondents were much more negative in 2009 than 2008. This result was striking, considering that the Netherlands was the most optimistic on immigration issues in 2008, with only 36 percent of the population claiming that immigration was more of a problem. In 2009, by contrast, 45 percent answered that immigration was a problem for the Netherlands. Though the Dutch were not the *most* likely to say that immigration was more of a problem for their country (comparatively, 66 percent of the British and 58 percent of the Spanish think that immigration is more of a problem), this unrivaled 9 percent jump warrants a closer look at the Netherlands' TTI data.

Explaining public opinion on immigration is highly complex, but perceived economic and cultural threats of immigration are considered to have considerable impact on individuals' attitudes towards immigration (Citrin and Sides, 2008; Coenders et al., 2008; OECD, 2010). With the strong rise of right-wing anti-immigrant and anti-Islam parties such as the Pim Fortuijn List (PFL) in the early 2000s and, most recently, Geert Wilders' Freedom Party (PVV), assessing respondents' perceived cultural effects of immigration could be a telling factor to contextualize the jump. Thus, shedding more light on economic and cultural perceptions of the Dutch respondents might help to understand the increase in concern about immigration.

Non-Perception of Economic Threat

In light of the economic crisis, one might suspect that perceptions of immigrants as economic threats might explain the increasing negativity in the Netherlands. However, most Dutch respondents in TTI did *not* believe that immigrants bring down wages or take jobs away from native-born workers. There was even a slight downward trend among respondents in the Netherlands who believed that immigrants take jobs away from native-born, down from 27 percent in 2008 to 23 percent in 2009. To put the Netherlands' attitudes in perspective, the United States and the United Kingdom both had majorities agreeing that immigrants take jobs away from natives (50 percent and 57 percent, respectively). From these results, it is clear that the Dutch do not consider immigration to be a threat to the native labor market.

The fact that the Dutch are unconcerned with immigrants' taking their jobs or lowering their wages might be due to an increasingly positive economic outlook in general. In the fall of 2009, the Eurobarometer survey found that the Netherlands, among all 27 EU countries, had the most increased positive outlook on the economic situation of the EU, the world, their own country, and the domestic labor market when compared to the data of 2008 (European Commission, 2009).

Despite the absence of economic anxieties related to migration, the Dutch public still supports stricter admission controls. TTI inquired as to whether it should be made easier to come to the Netherlands to work and study. The approval rating for this measure dropped from 64 percent in 2008 to 55 percent in 2009 among Dutch respondents. Perhaps related to this changing public sentiment, within the same time period the Dutch government continued to discuss more selective labor migration policies under the "Modern Migration Policy" bill, proposed in 2008. As economic concerns do not seem to be driving this increasingly restrictive mood in the Netherlands, cultural considerations might serve as a better answer.

Immigration and Cultural Perceptions

In the Netherlands, immigrant groups of Turkish and Moroccan origin are commonly at the center of attention when discussing integration and cultural identity challenges. These groups are, on average, in a disadvantaged position within Dutch society, with poor labor market outcomes, high unemployment, and high welfare dependency rates. Given this situation, it is possible that Dutch respondents rationally perceive that they are not competing for the same jobs as immigrant groups. However, poor labor market integration and welfare dependency are seen by some to be a failure of cultural integration. In general, beliefs about immigrants' effects on the receiving society's culture and social fabric have frequently been related to attitudes about immigrants (Citrin and Sides, 2008; Coenders et al., 2008; OECD 2010).

The discussions about ethnic and religious relations within Dutch society have become heavily politicized in the past 10 years. In the 1980s and 1990s, the Netherlands had a multicultural model of immigration and integration, with "technocratic" discussions about these issues steering clear of any sensitive cultural discussions. In the early 2000s, particularly after 9/11, a so-called "democratic" and politicizing phase began, involving wider parts of the Dutch public in discussions of cultural and integration issues (Bruquetas-Callejo et al., 2007; Boswell, 2009). Competing political parties and mass media took up the topic of integration, claiming that the multiculturalist policies of the 1980s and 1990s had failed to keep Dutch society together as they allowed groups to maintain their own culture and institutions. They further claimed that new assimilationist approaches were needed to regain social cohesion (Bruquetas-Callejo et al., 2007; Coenders et al., 2008).

Heightened concerns among the public about immigration and integration are mirrored in the rise of far right-wing parties in the past few years, such as the List Pim Fortuijns (LPF) and Freedom Party (PVV) referenced earlier. The latter has a clearly-stated anti-immigrant and anti-Islam agenda, such as a proposed policy to ban the Koran. These parties have reshaped the political landscape in the Netherlands, forcing other political parties to adopted restrictionist immigration policies for fear of losing voters.

Interestingly, TTI data does not fully support the notion that the Dutch public unduly fears negative impacts on their culture due to immigration. In 2008, the Netherlands had the highest percentage of respondents among all countries polled (72 percent) who agreed that immigration in general will improve their culture with new ideas and customs. Likewise, in 2009, a clear majority (60 percent) of the Dutch respondents thought that immigration enriches Dutch culture. However, of the Dutch respondents who view immigration as more of a problem (again, 45 percent of the Dutch sample), 58 percent thought that immigration negatively affects Dutch culture. This seems to indicate that those who view immigration in the Netherlands negatively have cultural considerations as at least one factor contributing to their skepticism.

Furthermore, TTI 2009 aimed to find out if preference for admission should be given to immigrants who will fit in smoothly with the national culture or to immigrants who have a better chance of finding employment. In general, respondents indicated that it is not enough for immigrants to be able to integrate only culturally or only economically—they must do both. Dutch respondents, however, put a larger emphasis on cultural adaptation than did other survey respondents. When asked what the greatest barrier to immigrant integration in Dutch society, a majority (54 percent) thought it is the unwillingness of immigrants to integrate rather than discrimination by society. This finding was also seen across the political spectrum, as pluralities or majorities among Dutch respondents self-identifying on the political left, center, and right, claimed that the lack of integration had more to do with the immigrants' unwillingness than societal discrimination. This sentiment was also supported across all age groups and even 55 percent of college graduates shared this opinion. As age and education are typically correlated with more positive attitudes about immigration, with the younger and higher educated being more favorable towards immigrants (OECD, 2010), the fact that the Dutch across age and education groups agree on the greatest barrier to integration is telling. Overall there seems to be consensus that the greatest barrier to integration in the Netherlands is *immigrants'* unwillingness, rather societal discrimination.

Dutch Society and Islam

With the rise of anti-Islamic parties such as Geert Wilders' PVV, it is also important to look into the data of TTI 2008, which gauged public opinion on attitudes towards immigrants of a Muslim background and Muslim culture in general. According to 2006 data of the Central Statistical Bureau of the Netherlands, the religious makeup of the Dutch public is as follows: 29 percent Roman Catholic; 19 percent Protestant; 5 percent Muslim, 5 percent Other, and 42 percent not religious (Central Statistical Bureau 2008). It should be noted that, though not all Muslims in the Netherlands are immigrants or from immigrant families, the majority are.

When asked in TTI whether Muslim immigrants have a lot to offer Dutch culture, only a minority (41 percent) among Dutch respondents agreed. This finding might be compared against the question discussed above, in which respondents were asked whether immigration *in general* would improve their culture with new customs and ideas, to which 72 percent of the Dutch answered in the affirmative. Though these two questions are not directly comparable, it is notable that, among all countries surveyed, the gap of 31 percentage points (72 percent positive about immigration's cultural benefits versus 41 percent positive about Muslim immigrants' cultural benefits) was the largest in the TTI survey. Though this issue needs to be researched further, it seems to indicate that dissatisfaction with immigrants' cultural integration cannot be divorced from the debate about Islam in the Netherlands.

Dutch respondents were also asked whether Western European and Muslim ways of life are reconcilable, and a slight majority of 53 percent agreed that they were. The Dutch public is largely in line with most other countries on these sentiments; however, only the U.S. and France had more favorable views of Muslims and Muslim culture. Asked whether most Muslims respect other cultures the Dutch public was divided with a plurality agreeing (49 percent) and a slightly lesser sample of respondents disagreeing (43 percent). The same split can be seen for the question whether most Muslims coming to the Netherlands want to integrate into the Dutch culture: 47 percent supported this sentiment and 44 percent disagreed. These ambivalent findings are in line with findings from most other European countries, though France was more clearly positive about Muslim immigrants' cultural effects. This similarity to other Europeans suggests that the Dutch public is not an outlier in their sentiments about Muslim immigrants and culture.

Overall, however, the increase in Dutch respondents saying that "immigration is more of a problem" in 2009 may be partially due to the explicitly anti-Islamic PVV party's rise to prominence between the two survey years. In July 2009, Geert Wilders requested from all ministries a cost-benefit analysis of immigration, claiming that the government had spent an enormous amount of money that could have been put to better use, for example, on the pension system for native Dutch. Shortly thereafter, Mr. Wilders also proposed taxing Muslim headgear, a measure that was not acted upon. Though there is no data on Muslim immigrants specifically in 2009, these political developments might partially explain the more negative view of immigration that the Dutch expressed in the 2009 survey overall (Traynor, 2010).

In conclusion, neither perceived economic or cultural threats alone account for the jump in Dutch skepticism seen in TTI. Ongoing debates in the political, public, and media spheres in the summer and fall of 2009 about the costs and benefits of immigration are a more ready explanation as to what might have influenced Dutch attitudes.

ENVIRONMENTAL MIGRATION

Support for the Resettlement of Environmental Migrants in the West

In 2009, TTI turned its attention to an issue that could affect all countries included in the survey and the international community overall. Environmental deterioration, including natural disasters, rising sea levels, and more frequent droughts affecting agricultural production, could cause an unprecedented number of people to leave their homes in the coming decades. While population movements due to environmental factors have occurred in the past, they were also spurred by a combination of environmental and economic factors. Researchers are currently trying to establish a link between migration movements and climate change, arguing that global warming will lead to an increase in extreme weather situations which could, in turn, lead to greater numbers of people being permanently displaced. However, a definitive causal relationship between climate change and migration has not yet been established. As a subject that has only recently appeared on the radar screen of the general public and policymakers alike, actionable policy options are hard to come by. Despite the lack of scientific certainty, some argue that environmental migration is already underway and that policies need to be shaped to deal with its consequences.

Both academics and policymakers are trying to assess the evidence, in initiatives such as the Study Team on Climate Induced Migration of the German Marshall Fund, the Climate Change, Environment and Migration Alliance (CCEMA), or the Foresight Project on Global Environmental Migration of the UK government, in order to explore potential routes of action. Most research currently implies that if increased environmental migration were to occur, it would most likely result first and foremost in internal migration within affected countries, such that policy options focusing on affected areas would be the most practical. The likelihood of environmental migration movements across continents, for example, from Africa to Europe, is considered marginal. However, some researchers caution that movements across continents could occur if the effects of climate change are not adequately addressed. They stress that governments and societies should be prepared to admit and resettle environmental migrants.

Transatlantic Trends: Immigration presents the first attempt to gauge public opinion on this complex matter. Although exact numbers of expected environmental migrants are hard to come by and estimates range from around 50,000 to up to one billion potential migrants, most respondents surveyed expressed support for allowing the settlement of environmental migrants in their respective countries. Canada (75 percent) and Spain (80 percent) showed the most support for such measures; European countries polled averaged 68 percent support; and 59 percent of Americans also supported allowing environmental migrants to settle in their country. Even in the United Kingdom, the country in the survey with the highest proportion of respondents claiming that immigration is more of a problem, a majority (57 percent) supported the admission of environmental migrants. It should be noted that the question asked to respondents mentioned two "slow onset" environmental changes—sea level rise and more frequent drought—that might induce people to move away from their homes. These are the types of events which might cause the most people to move, but also those which are often difficult to separate from economic incentives to emigrate.

While a wide range of support for allowing environmental migrants to settle in respondents' countries was expected, the scale of the support was not. Public opinion research on immigration attests that the public is on average more favorable towards refugees than to other immigrants (Mayda, 2006; O'Rourke and Sinnot, 2006). Potentially, the coupling of concern about climate change and assessing a refugee situation in the posed question might have contributed to the high affirmation rates: in 2009, GMF's *Transatlantic Trends* found that large pluralities in Europe, with the exception of the Netherlands, are *very concerned* about climate change (Germany 59 percent; Italy 54 percent; France 47 percent; UK 47 percent; Spain 47 percent; the Netherlands 23 percent); a plurality in the United States (40 percent) said the same. Even among those respondents of TTI who thought that there were currently *too many* immigrants in their country, a majority (53 percent) would nevertheless allow environmental migrants to settle in their country in the future. Furthermore, majorities of respondents who self-identified as being on the political left, center, or right all supported the measure, and respondents were in favor of the policy regardless of their level of educational attainment.

One overall caveat of the TTI data on environmental migration is that it can be safely assumed that the majority of the survey respondents had not heard of or developed a personal opinion about environmental migration before the survey. As this issue is only beginning to get media and policymaker attention, the general public has not been exposed to debate about the benefits and drawbacks that such a policy might entail. As such, the TTI data on this question should be taken as a benchmark for future public opinion research on this topic, as the public becomes better informed. Nonetheless, as the policy arena slowly moves toward concrete policy recommendations about environmental migration, TTI data suggests that the policy option of resettlement would be an accepted option among the general public on both sides of the Atlantic.

CONCLUSION

The TTI survey questionnaire in both 2008 and 2009 included around 30 substantive questions and numerous socio-demographic questions to respondents in all countries. Given the wealth of data generated from these two editions, this article was only able to address a small percentage of the findings. The survey is designed to foster transatlantic comparison, and many parallels can be drawn between several of the countries in the survey. This piece was designed to highlight some issues that might be of interest to researchers, but the authors highly encourage interested parties to visit <http://www.transatlantictrends.org> for complete topline data and the official Key Findings Reports for both 2008 and 2009. The third edition of the survey, TTI 2010, will include some of the same questions covered in this article, alongside new questions focusing on second-generation immigrant integration, immigration and population aging, and preconditions for citizenship acquisition. It will be released in December 2010.

ENDNOTES

1. *Transatlantic Trends: Immigration* (TTI) has been conducted since 2008 by the German Marshall Fund of the United States, in cooperation with its partners, the Lynde and Harry Bradley Foundation, the Compagnia di San Paolo, the Barrow Cadbury Trust, and the Fundación BBVA.

2. Methodological Note: Findings are based on nationally representative samples in all eight countries. In each country, a random sample of approximately 1,000 persons, aged 18 and older, was interviewed by telephone. The maximum sampling error is ±3 percentage points, at a 95 percent confidence level. National samples are weighted by age, gender, education, and region, and the U.S. sample is also weighted for race. The results for the European average are calculated using a weight for each country according to population size. For more details on the methodology used in this survey or to request access to the data, please visit <http://www.transatlantictrends.org>.

REFERENCES

Boswell, C.
2009 "Knowledge, Legitimation and the Politics of Risk: The Functions of Research in Public Debates on Migration." *Political Studies* 57:165–186.

Bruquetas-Callejo, M., B. Garces-Mascarenas, R. Penninx and P. Scholten
2007 *Policymaking Related to Immigration and Integration. The Dutch Case.* IMISCOE Working Paper 15. Retrieved from the IMISCOE website: <http://library.imiscoe.org/en/record/234827> (accessed September 9, 2010).

Central Statistical Bureau (CBS), The Netherlands
2008 *Only a few Dutch People Go to Church or Mosque Regularly.* Retrieved from the Central Statistical Bureau website: <http://www.cbs.nl/en-GB/menu/themas/vrije-tijd-cultuur/publicaties/artikelen/archief/2008/2008-2476-wm.htm> on September 9, 2010.

Citizenship and Immigration Canada
2009 *Facts and Figures 2009: Summary Tables—Permanent and Temporary Residents.* Retrieved from the Citizenship and Immigration Canada website: <http://www.cic.gc.ca/english/resources/statistics/facts2009-summary/index.asp> on August 27, 2010.

Citrin, J. and J. Sides
2008 "Immigration and the Imagined Community in Europe and the United States." *Political Studies* 56:33–56.

Coenders, M., M. Lubbers, P. Scheepers and M. Verkuyten
2008 "More than Two Decades of Changing Ethnic Attitudes in the Netherlands." *Journal of Social Issues* 64(2):269–285.

European Commission
2009 *Standard Eurobarometer 72.* Retrieved from the European Commission website: <http://ec.europa.eu/public_opinion/archives/eb/eb72/eb72_first_en.pdf> on August 20, 2010.

Mayda, A. M.
2006 "Who Is Against Immigration? A Cross-Country Investigation of Individual Attitudes Towards Immigrants." *The Review of Economics and Statistics* 88:510–530.

OECD
2010 "Public Opinion and Immigration: Individual Attitudes, Interest Groups and the Media." In *International Migration Outlook: SOPEMI 2010*. Eds. Garson, J.-P., J.-C. Dumont, G. Lemaitre, 115–155. Paris: OECD.

O'Rourke, K. H. and R. Sinnot
2006 "The Determinants of Individual Attitudes Towards Immigration." *European Journal of Political Economy* 22:838–861.

Traynor, I.
2010 "Geert Wilders's Party Wins Seat in Dutch Elections—Early Results." Retrieved from The Guardian website: <http://www.guardian.co.uk/world/2010/mar/04/ geert-wilders-dutch-elections-results> on August 28, 2010.

Wadhwa, V.
2009 "A Reverse Brain Drain." *Issues in Science and Technology* 45–52. Spring. Retrieved from: <http:// papers.ssrn.com/sol3/papers.cfm?abstract_id=1358382> on September 6, 2010.

*Delancey Gustin is a policy analyst in the Office of Citizenship at the United States Citizenship and Immigration Services, and a former associate of the Immigration and Integration Program at the German Marshall Fund of the United States.

Astrid Ziebarth is the director of the Immigration and Integration Program at the German Marshall Fund of the United States. She is responsible for the Transatlantic Forum on Migration and Integration, and Transatlantic Trends on Immigration, an annual public opinion survey.

Gustin, Delancey, and Astrid Ziebarth. "Transatlantic Opinion on Immigration: Greater Worries and Outlier Optimism." IMR: *International Migration Review* 44, no. 4 (Winter 2010): 974–991.

Addressing Irregular Migration Through Coherent Migration and Development Strategies: Istanbul Thematic Meeting, Background Paper

*by The International Centre for Migration Policy Development**

1. BACKGROUND AND CONTEXT[1]

The issue of irregular migration first appeared on the agenda of the GFMD in Manila in 2008. The focus of discussion was on minimizing the negative impacts of irregular migration, emphasizing the migrant vulnerability and protection. The issue of irregular migration appeared again in Mexico in 2010 within the framework of Roundtable 1, intensifying discussions on joint strategies to address irregular migration. Whilst it was agreed that the issue of irregular migration must remain on the agenda of the Global Forum, the main conclusions of the 2010 Roundtable were:

1. The importance of establishing joint mechanisms for international cooperation at multilateral, regional and bilateral levels based on the principle of shared responsibility between countries of origin, transit and destination.

2. The need for a greater focus on irregular migration that prioritizes the protection of the most vulnerable groups, specifically irregular migrants, victims of trafficking, women and unaccompanied children.

In the Swiss Chair's programme for 2011, the issue of irregular migration is elaborated under cluster II, which addresses irregular migration through coherent migration and development strategies. The emphasis of the Chair's programme under this cluster is put on national practices, models and polices for inter-state cooperation between countries of origin, transit and destination, in managing irregular migration, taking account of i) the development-related causes and implications of irregular migration, and ii) the human rights and special vulnerability of migrant children, women and men in an irregular situation.

In order to deepen and intensify the discussion on irregular migration under the perspective illustrated above, the thematic meeting in Turkey on 13–14 October addresses practices, models and policies for cooperation between countries of origin, transit and destination in managing irregular migration with a view to address the development-related causes and implications. The Istanbul meeting follows directly the El Salvador meeting of 4–5 October 2011 on irregular migration, which focuses on increasing the human and economic development potential of migration, reducing the vulnerability of migrants in an irregular situation, upholding the human rights and protection of migrants and promoting legal and labour migration. Thus the two meetings will be of complementary nature, addressing the priorities identified by the Swiss Chair under cluster II.

2. DEFINING THE RELATIONSHIP BETWEEN IRREGULAR MIGRATION AND DEVELOPMENT: CONCEPTS AND PRACTICAL CHALLENGES

2.1. Concepts and Definitions

"Irregular migration" describes a number of different migration phenomena including migrants who enter or remain in a country of which they are not citizens without authorization, people who are smuggled or trafficked across international borders, refused asylum seekers who stay in the country, visitors who are overstaying visas or people who managed to circumvent immigration controls through the arrangement of 'bogus marriages'. For these various forms of irregular migration different terms such as undocumented, unauthorized or illegal migration are used. There are ongoing controversial debates on the adequacy of these concepts and we suggest, in accordance with the Global Commission on International Migration, to use the term 'migrants with irregular status', as an individual person should not be referred to as 'irregular' or 'illegal'.[2] There are also significant regional differences in the criteria to define irregular migration.

Although no accurate data on stocks and flows of irregular migration exists, estimates suggest that in 2004 between 10 and 15 per cent of world's immigrant stock are in an irregular situation.[3] The majority of the migrant population therefore has a regular status.

Irregular migration is of special concern because it exposes migrants to insecurity, vulnerability and exploitation. It sometimes allows migrants to access better jobs than at home, but they lack access to basic services, although they often pay taxes like local residents with regular status. The outcomes in terms of human development are lower compared to migrants with legal status.[4] Regardless of the status, migrants with irregular status contribute to the development of the host country as well as to the development of their home countries, although human development outcomes might be limited compared with migrants having regular status.

"Development" can be described by the concept of human development that defines the expansion of people's freedom to live their lives as they choose. This concept, which is also known as the capabilities approach inspired by Amartya Sen, puts emphasis on the freedom to achieve vital 'beings and doings'. It is therefore about creating an environment in which people can develop and make use of their potential. Economic growth is only one factor which contributes to the creation of a supportive environment. Access to knowledge, better nutrition and health services, human security, participation and freedom are equally important.

According to Martha Nussbaum, mobility is one of the basic human functional capacities individuals can use to realise their plan of life. This freedom to choose the place of living is part of development and is referred to as human mobility.[5] The act of movement itself is the exercise of this freedom. The distinction of capabilities and actions is therefore crucial. Human mobility should be understood as a positive freedom, i.e. the absence of formal restrictions to movement is not sufficient if circumstances such as political persecution or environmental degradation restrict the scope of people's freedom to decide where to live.

2.2. The Relationship Between Irregular Migration and Development

The cause-effect relationship between irregular migration and development is complex and controversially discussed, as the relationship of migration and development in general.[6] Frequently mentioned push factors include economic differentials between countries or disempowering social, economic and political conditions in the home country.

Migration, however, cannot exclusively be explained by these factors. Environmental factors play an increasing role in contributing to various patterns of migration on the continuum of forced and voluntary migration. Migrant networks developed from previous migration movements are also determining the volume and direction of migration flows.[7] Moreover, conditions in destination countries have a major role in attracting migrants. The growth of the informal sector in 'developed countries' is one of the outcomes of neoliberal approaches and economic deregulation and some authors argue that this created a major pull factor for irregular migration flows. Irregular migration is vital for the survival of certain industries in advanced economies because it contributes to increasing competitiveness and flexibility.[8]

The demand for labour results in two conflicting immigration policies: On the one hand the official restrictive immigration policy which satisfies anti-immigration constituencies, while on the other hand the actual policy tolerates a steady inflow of migrants to satisfy the demand for cheap labour.[9] Migrants with irregular status fill gaps in the labour market that natives are unable or unwilling to fill. Although the effects of irregular migrant workers on the entire economy cannot be estimated, government's lack of attention to irregular entries shows that influential groups may view irregular migrant workers as economically efficient.[10]

Although the assumption that development reduces migration is being repeated by policy makers, migration researchers question this simple causal linkage and underline that development is likely to initially lead to increased emigration.[11] One concept used to explain this relationship is the 'migration hump'. It shows that emigration is increasing as economic growth takes off, followed by flattening curve and decline in the long run, as a developed industrial economy emerges. This can be explained by the fact that migration requires resources.[12] Poor people mainly migrate if they are forced by conflicts, war or disasters but remain in the neighboring countries or provinces. However, every emigration country needs to be considered in detail as the relationship between migration and development is too complex for generalizations. The high level of migration between developed countries shows that the decrease of migration in a 'mature' stage of development should not be taken as granted. Researchers highlighted that relative deprivation rather than absolute or chronicle poverty is the key driver of human movement.[13]

Questions for discussion: Does irregular migration take place when legal channels do not exist/are exhausted or is it also a distinct form of migration? Can irregular migration be characterised as a crisis caused by uneven development, impoverishment of certain groups and gross inequality? Can irregular migration be considered as an indirect effect of state policies targeting the restriction of migration?

3. Impacts of Irregular Migration on Countries of Origin, Transit and Destination

Irregular migration can have a number of negative outcomes while the positive outcomes for the countries of origin, transit and destination as well as for the migrants themselves should not be underestimated.

For the country of destination irregular migration may, in particular when it receives great media attention, undermine the public confidence in the effectiveness of state's migration and asylum policies. At the same time migrants with irregular status fill gaps in the labour market and contribute to the growth of certain sectors of the economy. However, the impacts of irregular migration on development in the destination country can only be briefly touched upon as very few studies explore this complex relationship.

As regards irregular migrants themselves, people who migrate in an irregular manner face higher risks while trying to cross land or sea borders. More generally, people who remain in a country without authorization are often confronted with adverse working conditions and lack of social protection. In many cases they are unable to make full use of their skills, qualifications and experience. Women might additionally be confronted with gender-based discrimination, have often the most menial jobs in the informal sector and face specific health-related risks.[14] Migrants with irregular status are often less willing to seek redress from authorities because they fear deportation and arrest. Even where public services are to some extend available for migrants with irregular status, they do not always make use of these services such as emergency health care. It might be also difficult for migrants with irregular status to access education for their children.[15] The ability of migrants, however, to contribute to their own and their families' welfare, to their home communities, but also to the national economy through social security and tax contributions is directly related to their conditions of work and living.[16]

Nevertheless, also irregular migration may have relatively positive outcomes for the migrants concerned compared to the situation in the home country and migrants on average achieve positive increases in income and assets through the migration experience. In some cases, migrating irregularly is also a way to ensure a higher income compared to a migrant with regular status. Prohibitive transaction costs play a key role to choose unauthorized migration routes. One example in this regard is that Burmese migrants have to register with the Burmese authorities before leaving the country which subjects them to a 10 per cent tax on their income earned abroad.[17]

For countries of origin the impacts are similar to those discussed in the migration and development discourse which may be positive or negative depending on the context and viewpoint. Migrants contribute through remittances to the income diversification of households whereas access to formal transfer channels might be limited. The government of Mexico addressed this issue in close co-operation with the U.S. government by introducing the 'Matricula Consular', an identity document, which allows Mexican citizens residing irregularly in the U.S. to open U.S. bank accounts.[18] The possible loss of labour potential might have a negative effect for the country of origin whereas the brain drain phenomenon applies more to regular migration.[19] The other scenario is that a labour surplus exists, which implies that departing workers can be replaced at low wages and migration therefore contributes to the reduction of pressure on those left behind in the home labour market.[20] At the same time the outflow of people through informal channels also affects migration decisions of other potential migrants to take irregular ways to migrate.

Questions for discussion: What are the impacts of irregular migration on countries of origin, transit and destination? Are there positive impacts? What are the impacts on the migrants concerned?

4. DEVELOPMENT STRATEGIES ADDRESSING IRREGULAR MIGRATION AND IDENTIFICATION OF FORMS OF DEVELOPMENT COOPERATION THAT CAN OFFER PEOPLE VIABLE ALTERNATIVES TO IRREGULAR MIGRATION

Rising unemployment in countries of origin might encourage more people to leave to seek for employment opportunities outside their home country, irrespective of conditions in destination countries.[21] Structural imbalances in terms of political, social and economic development are the main drivers of international migration. Well known push factors such as low salaries, limited access to education and health care services as well as a low level of availability of jobs are often used to explain migration patterns. It appears clearly that a single strategy is not sufficient to overcome development constraints contributing to migration movements. Only a combination of coherent investment, trade, governance, education etc. policies may contribute to reduce (irregular) migration.[22]

Therefore, migration and development actors advocate for mainstreaming migration into national development strategies.[23] Some developing countries integrated migration into their Poverty Reduction Strategy Papers (PRSPs) and emphasize the connection between lack of economic opportunities and migration. Although more attention is given to internal migration, some causes would also apply to international migration. The actions addressing the causes of migration vary from country to country. India as an example introduced the National Rural Employment Guarantee Programme to increase incomes of the rural poor, create crop insurance and ensure more secure land tenure rights. This approach reflects the view on migration as risk management and adaption strategy to external shocks.[24] Climate and environmental change plays an increasingly important role as an exacerbating trigger of migration movements.

According to the research literature on migration and development, the approach to address the root causes of irregular migration will not lead to a significant decrease of irregular migration movements if no channels to migrate regularly exist. Efforts to reduce irregular migration have to consider the complex forces driving irregular migration which include not only the root causes in the country of origin but also the self-sustaining nature of migratory processes and the demand for migrant workers in countries of destination.[25] It is therefore suggested by migration specialists to allow different channels for migration such as temporary migration schemes or seasonal migration. Migration has been identified as a proactive action by people to diversify income which allows family members to remain in their original place of residence. Migration policies can support this form of risk diversification and adaptation to worsening conditions in countries of origin through creating legal migration opportunities.

Questions for discussion: *Which good practices of finding viable alternatives to irregular migration exist? Is allowing different channels and forms of migration such as circular migration, temporary migration schemes, seasonal migration, etc. the right answer/alternative to irregular migration?*

4.1. Partnerships to Jointly Address Various Causes of Irregular Migration

Multilateral or bilateral partnerships and agreements are important instruments to address irregular migration during the whole migration cycle. Measures which can be jointly developed by countries of destination and origin can for example include pre-departure trainings and information about conditions in destination countries and existing regular migration channels as well as awareness-raising measures in mass media and information campaigns to draw attention on the dangers of irregular migration. Government agencies can inform migrants about channels to report abuse and to receive legal assistance.[26] Countries, in which refugees and asylum seekers initially arrive, can also be supported in strengthening the protection capacities in order to prevent irregular secondary movements. To assist migrants upon return, governments implement reintegration programmes to facilitate access to the labour market.

At regional level the international or regional dialogues on migration provide a good option to enhance consultations between governments which are affected by similar migration issues. Another advantage is their informality because it fosters exchange of information. At the same time it is also a disadvantage that their recommendations and conclusions are non-binding.[27] One example is the Budapest Process, which comprises around 50 governments and aims to at developing comprehensive and sustainable systems for orderly migration. Through dialogue and follow-up activities the Budapest Process contributes to the transfer of good practices and the common understanding of migration and in particular on the prevention of irregular migration.[28] The main dialogues in Africa involve the countries of Eastern, Middle and Southern Africa (MIDSA) and the countries of Western Africa (MIDWA) while different migration dialogue platforms connect Europe and the African continent (dialogue on Mediterranean Transit Migration (MTM), Rabat Process as well as the Africa-EU Partnership on Migration, Mobility and Employment. The Asia-Pacific consultations on Refugees, Displaced persons and Migrants (APC) and the Manila Process for countries of Eastern and South-Eastern Asia led to the adoption of the Bangkok Declaration on Irregular Migration which underlines that *"migration, particularly irregular migration, should be addressed in a comprehensive and balanced manner, considering its causes, manifestations and effects, both positive and negative, in the countries of origin, transit and destination".*[29]

4.2. Joint Knowledge Base of Irregular Migration, Its Patterns and Actors

Migration profiles are a valuable instrument to enhance knowledge about (irregular) migration and development and have the potential to contribute to the development of coherent and evidence based policies. Besides the original purpose of creating an instrument to gather and provide concise information on migration and migratory movements in a standardized form, there has been a move towards preparing what is called Extended Migration Profiles. Extended migration profiles cover a wider range of issues, such as labour market conditions, income levels, and socio-economic indicators. Migration profiles could therefore contribute to the identification of underlying factors that contribute to migration and could be addressed through development strategies. Besides the extended migration profiles, the i-Map concept, an online interactive platform serving governments, provides an instrument for exchange of information on migration matters.

An additional method to create a stronger knowledge base on the linkage between (irregular) migration and development is to monitor and evaluate the impacts of development actions on (irregular) migration. Qualitative studies on the motives for migrating irregularly, the routes and the reasons for staying in destination countries with an irregular status provide another possibility to elucidate the complex relationship between supply and demand for migrant workers with irregular status.

5. SUMMARY

Irregular migration poses real challenges for states as well as exposing migrants to insecurity and vulnerability. The forces driving irregular migration are very complex, powerful and difficult to modify such as the disparities in the level of prosperity, human rights and security in different parts of the world. While there has been much talk of improving economic and security conditions in source countries with a view to alleviate migration pressures, the emphasis was more on policies aimed at curbing immigration at the destination end so far. However, from an economic perspective destination countries may have an interest in irregular migration and therefore efforts to govern irregular migration are not likely to succeed if its economic rationale is not properly understood.

Thus, despite tighter immigration systems in the destination countries and increased security enforcement of the last decades, it must be acknowledged that efforts to reduce irregular migration have not always been efficient. Certainly a perspective focused primarily on irregular migration obscures the broader picture and fails to address irregular migration through more comprehensive, coherent and effective approaches. When tightening of immigration policies is the only response, though it is a legitimate response by States to irregular migration, the effect may be to push more people into the hands of smugglers and traffickers, thereby increasing irregular modes of migration, vulnerability and exploitation. This undermines security due to links with organized crime, violence, and corruption. Furthermore, the concentration and assets dedicated to the fight against irregular migration may also outweigh its quantitative significance.

It is generally accepted that poverty and differences in the level of development, security and human rights among countries and regions remain important causes of irregular migration. Over the last decades, the link between migration and development has featured high on the global international policy agenda. However, at the same time the international debate registered a gap between rhetoric and action. This can also be explained by a conflict of interest of various actors both within and between countries of origin and destination. Besides the restrictive approach, there are actors focusing on finding ways to make migration contribute to development. This is a positive step, but the migration and development nexus should be understand as a broader concept. The linkage between migration and development needs to be considered at all stages of the cycle of (irregular) migration: reducing the reasons for people to migrate in an irregular manner, making migration a free and legal choice as well as creating safe living conditions for migrants in countries of destination would contribute to enhance the development outcomes for both migrants and countries of origin.

In the recent past a lot of emphasis has been put on the joint responsibility of countries of destination, transit and origin in addressing irregular migration. Therefore, bilateral cooperation between countries of origin, transit and destination, cooperation through regional dialogues and other forums as well as understanding of migration patterns would be needed to jointly develop comprehensive strategies and programmes addressing irregular migration.

ENDNOTES

1. This Background paper has been prepared by the International Centre for Migration Policy Development (ICMPD) in close collaboration with the Turkish Ministry of Foreign Affairs and the Government of Switzerland (Federal Office for Migration). The paper is based on open sources and does not aim to be exhaustive. The sole objective of this document is to inform and facilitate discussion of the thematic meeting "Addressing Irregular Migration through Coherent Migration and Development Strategies". The document does not necessarily reflect the views of the GFMD organizers or the governments or organizations involved in this workshop. Any reproduction, partial or whole, of this document should cite the source.

2. See GCIM (2005): Migration in an interconnected world: New directions for action. Report of the Global Commission on International Migration. Available at: http://www.gcim.org/attachements/gcim-complete-report-2005.pdf

3. See IOM (2010): World Migration Report 2010—The Future of Migration: Building Capacities for Change. Geneva: IOM, available at: http://publications.iom.int/bookstore/free/WMR_2010_ENGLISH.pdf, and Khalid Koser (2010): Dimensions and dynamics of irregular migration. In: Population, Space and Place 16, pp. 181–193

4. See Rachel Sabates-Wheeler (2009): The Impact of Irregular Status on Human Development Outcomes for Migrants. Human Development Research Paper. UNDP

5. See UNDP (2009): Overcoming barriers: Human mobility and development. Human Development Report 2009. New York: UNDP

6. As one dimension the category of irregular migration, the vulnerability to trafficking may increase as a result of economic underdevelopment as studies by IOM, UNICEF, OSCE, ILO and others indicate. See UNDP 2009, op. cit.

7. See GFMD (2009): Addressing the root causes of migration through development, specifically in light of the current global economic crisis. Available at: http://www.gfmdathens2009.org/fileadmin/material/docs/workp/working_paper_1_3.pdf

8. See Stephen Castles and Mark Miller (2009): The Age of Migration. International Population Movements in the Modern World. (4th edition). New York: Palgrave Macmillan

9. See Castles, Miller 2009, op. cit.

10. See Castles, Miller 2009, op. cit.

11. See Castles, Miller 2009, op. cit.

12. See Castles, Miller 2009, op. cit.

13. See Hein de Haas (2008): Migration and Development. A theoretical perspective. University of Oxford: International Migration Institute

14. See GCIM 2005, op. cit.

15. See Sabates-Wheeler 2009, op. cit.

16. See Office of the United Nations High Commissioner for Human Rights: Migration and Development. A Human Rights-Based Approach. Available at: http://www2.ohchr.org/english/bodies/cmw/docs/HLMigration/MigrationDevelopmentHC'spaper.pdf

17. See Sabates-Wheeler 2009, op. cit.

18. See Kevin O'Neil (2003): Consular ID Cards: Mexico and Beyond. MPI, available at: http://www.migrationinformation.org/feature/display.cfm?ID=115, and Monica Christine DeHart (2010): Ethnic entrepreneurs: identity and development politics in Latin America. Stanford: Stanford University Press

19. See GFMD (2010): Joint Strategies to address irregular migration. Roundtable 1: Partnerships for migration human development: shared prosperity—shared responsibility. Available at: http://www.gfmd.org/en/component/simpledownload/

20. See Louka T. Katseli, Robert E.B. Lucas and Theodora Xenogiani (2006): Effects of Migration on Sending Countries: What do we know? Paris: OECD

21. See GFMD (2009): Addressing the root causes of migration through development, specifically in light of the current global economic crisis.

22. See Susan Martin (2008): Policy and Institutional Coherence. At the Civil Society Days of the GFMD. Available at: http://www.migrationanddevelopment.net/research-publications/policy-and-institutional-coherence/at_download/file

23. Mainstreaming means to integrate the interconnections between migration and development at all stages of development planning, comprising design, implementation and monitoring and evaluation. See Global Migration Group (2010): Mainstreaming Migration into Development Planning. A handbook for policy-makers and practitioners.

24. See Martin 2008, op. cit.

25. See Stephen Castles (2004): Why migration policies fail. In: Ethnic and Racial Studies, Vol. 27, pp. 205–227

26. See International Council on Human Rights Policy (2010): Irregular Migration, Migrant Smuggling and Human Rights: Towards Coherence. Geneva: ICHRP, and BSR (2008): International Labor Migration: A Responsible Role for Business, available at: http://www.bsr.org/reports/BSR_LaborMigrationRoleforBusiness.pdf

27. See Khalid Koser (2005): Irregular migration, state security and human security. Paper prepared for the Policy Analysis and Research Programme of the Global Commission on International Migration. London: University College

28. See ICMPD (2011): Budapest Process, available at: http://www.icmpd.org/Budapest-Process.1528.0.html

29. See Bangkok Declaration on Irregular Migration, available at: http://www.smc.org.ph/rights/bangkok.htm

*The International Centre for Migration Policy Development, established in 1993 by Austria and Switzerland, is an international organization that provides its 15 member states and numerous partners with in-depth knowledge and expertise in dealing with the phenomena of migration.

The Global Forum on Migration and Development is a voluntary, informal, nonbinding, and government-led process open to all member states and observers of the United Nations. The Forum aims to advance understanding and cooperation on the mutually reinforcing relationship between migration and development and to foster practical and action-oriented outcomes.

International Centre for Migration Policy Development. Addressing Irregular Migration Through Coherent Migration and Development Strategies: Background Paper. 2011 Istanbul Thematic Meeting, Global Forum on Migration and Development (October 2011), 1–9.

Used by permission.

Part 3: Human Rights in Migration

The purpose of Part 3 is twofold: first, to situate the issue of migration rights within the broader legal and policy framework around human rights; and second, to introduce the key thematic human rights issues relevant to migration, such as refugee protection, the rights of migrant workers, and special protections for child migrants. A further objective of the chapter is to affirm the important links between development and human rights by identifying the ways in which respect for human rights can reinforce the positive impacts of migration on individuals and communities.

The first article in this section, "International Legal Protection of Migrants and Refugees: Ghetto or Incremental Protection? Some Preliminary Comments," by Vincent Chetail, provides a general introduction to the legal system for protection of migrant rights. As Chetail points out, it is important to acknowledge, upfront, the carefully guarded sovereign right of states to control aliens' admission into—and expulsion from—their territory. In other words, states do indeed have a right to control their own borders. International law—most particularly human rights law—has evolved to place constraints on this general rule but has certainly not displaced it. Chetail then explains the structure of the legal framework around migrant rights, focusing particularly on two categories of migrants: refugees and migrant workers. In relation to refugees, the most important restriction on the sovereign right of states to control their borders is imposed by the principle of *non-refoulement*: States may not return a person to a situation where that person risks persecution. Human rights law has extended this principle beyond refugees to prohibit return where there is a serious risk of torture or inhumane treatment. Chetail reminds the reader that, in common with all aliens (including refugees and asylum seekers), migrant workers are entitled to protection of their basic human rights. However, it has proved to be very difficult to extend those protections substantially, particularly in the case of migrant workers who are in an irregular situation. Chetail notes a trend toward the development of protection regimes for certain categories of migrants and certain vulnerable groups (such as trafficked persons) and away from an engagement in more comprehensive regulation. He concludes his analysis by affirming the central role of international human rights in guaranteeing a general framework for the basic rights of aliens: a crucial source of protection for those who do not fall within the traditional and newer categories of specially protected migrants.

The particular situation of unaccompanied child migrants (a diverse group that may include economic migrants, survival migrants, and victims of exploitation) is the focus of the next article in this section. The central point of Jacqueline Bhabha's piece, "Independent Children, Inconsistent Adults: International Child Migration and the Legal Framework," is that the relevant legal framework does not adequately reflect the circumstances of unaccompanied child migrants or meet their needs. For example, at the national level, laws related to child protection rarely take appropriate account of the special challenges faced by migrant children. National immigration laws are similarly inadequate. International law has generally been much more responsive, long recognizing the multiple vulnerabilities faced by child migrants, particularly those who are separated from their families, and articulating basic principles for their protection and support. Many of these principles, including the prohibition on discrimination and the right to family unity, have been incorporated into different legal instruments. However, the author argues that the international legislative framework is incomplete and ultimately ineffective. The real challenge will be to generate the political will necessary to deliver protection and support to a marginalized and silent population.

The UN Committee on the Elimination of Discrimination Against Women (CEDAW Committee) oversees implementation of the United Nations Convention on the Elimination of All Forms of Discrimination Against Women. This Convention is one of the core international human rights treaties, often referred to as a "bill of rights for women," and is one of the most widely accepted of all the international human rights treaties. It obliges states parties to take steps to eliminate all forms of discrimination against women in public and private life. While the treaty contains no specific provisions about women migrants, it is clear that the Convention's general prohibition applies to this group. In 2008, the CEDAW Committee issued a General Recommendation on women migrant workers that is reproduced in full here. The General Recommendation affirms the importance of migration in creating new opportunities for women, particularly in terms of economic empowerment and participation. However, it notes that migration continues to be highly gendered and can place the rights and security of women—particularly those who are in an irregular situation or are working in certain sectors—at serious risk. It affirms the applicability of all human rights to migrant women and the consequent obligation of states to ensure these rights are protected and respected. The General Recommendation considers the factors influencing female migration and the way in which human rights concerns may arise at each stage of the migration process. For example, women may be compelled to migrate because of family violence or because of discrimination in employment. It concludes with a comprehensive set of recommendations, directed to all involved states (origin, transit, and destination) as well as to the international community.

The final piece in Part 3, "Protecting the Rights of Migrant Workers: A Shared Responsibility," addresses, more broadly, the rights of migrant workers. It is authored by the International Labour Organization (ILO), a United Nations body with primary responsibility for protecting and promoting the rights of workers. The premise of the article is that migration benefits all countries involved—and that responsibility for protection of migrant worker rights must be shared between governments in countries of origin and destination. Countries of origin, for example, have a responsibility to their emigrating citizens. These countries should be actively engaged in supervising and regulating international migration. They should also be cooperating with countries of destination in a shared effort to promote rights and prevent exploitation and abuse, particularly of low-skilled migrants, who are often especially vulnerable. Countries of destination also have specific responsibilities to migrants within their territory. Destination countries should recognize a shared interest in ensuring that migrants are not subject to discrimination and unfair treatment. The article makes a point that is central to the concerns of this anthology: that development gains from migration (for all countries involved) and protection of migrant worker rights are inseparable: each depends on the other. The ILO takes the position that it is in the interests of all involved to prevent irregular migration, which it views as an obstacle to securing the development benefits of migration. The article provides an overview of the international standards (relating to human rights, rights of workers, rights of migrants) that are available to guide countries in formulating and implementing national law and policy on labor migration.

As you read the articles in this part, consider the following questions:
• What are the most important exceptions to the right of states to control who can enter and stay in their territory?
• Should children always be discouraged from migrating for purposes of finding work or other opportunities to better their situation? Also, is it appropriate to put all young people up to age 18 in the same legal category of "children"?
• Many women migrant workers are engaged in domestic work in private households. What are the special challenges in protecting this group

of workers and how could these challenges be effectively addressed? What do you think will be the challenges in securing effective implementation of the 2009 ILO Convention on Domestic Workers?

• What practical steps can be taken by governments in countries of destination to protect the rights of migrant workers? Should these steps be the same irrespective of the legal status of the migrant? To what extent are such steps being taken in your country, and to what effect?

International Legal Protection of Migrants and Refugees: Ghetto or Incremental Protection? Some Preliminary Comments

by Vincent Chetail*

The entitlement by States to admit aliens into their territory and to expel them from it has long been recognized by international law. This power needs however be exercised in conformity with international law standards. This paper deals with two traditional categories of migrants, namely refugees and migrant workers. As is known, the legal status of either category of aliens is regulated by treaties. The steady convergence of the two international legal regimes by the operation of human rights law calls for a contemporary re-assessment of the applicable principles and rules governing migrations.

We live in a time of unprecedented international movement. The contemporary phenomenon of globalization has provoked a growing discrepancy between the social reality of migration and its legal regulation. The social manifestations of globalization are an explosion of cheap and fast means of communication and some convergence of the values and expectations held by people. Goods and capital now circulate with greater ease than ever before, and peoples increasingly move across borders. In contrast, control over migration is generally regarded as one of the last bastions of the truly sovereign State. In this respect, Professor Vera Gowlland-Debbas writes:

> It is indeed ironical at a time when it has become fashionable to speak of the withering away or erosion of State sovereignty that we are witnessing a reinforcement of that last bastion of State sovereignty which is the right to decide who to admit and who to expel.[1]

Admission and expulsion of aliens are indeed traditionally held as an essential element of the sovereignty of States. As a general rule, no country is obliged to allow foreigners onto its territory. The classical writer on international law, Emerich de Vattel, in his book *Le Droit des Gens* (1758) gave due recognition to this principle:

> Every nation has the right to refuse to admit an alien into its territory when to do so would expose it to evident danger or cause it serious trouble. This right is based upon a care for its own security which it owes

as a duty to itself. By reason of its natural liberty it is for each Nation to decide whether it is or is not in a position to receive an alien. Hence, an exile has no absolute right to choose a country at will and settle himself there as he pleases; he must ask permission of the sovereign of the country; and if it is refused, he is bound to submit.[2]

This traditional position has been reiterated in the practice of States. According to the famous *dictum* of the Supreme Court of the United States, delivered in 1892:

> It is an accepted maxim of international law, that every sovereign nation has the power, as inherent in sovereignty, and essential to its self-preservation, to forbid the entrance of foreigners within its dominions, or to admit them only in such cases and upon such conditions as it may see fit to prescribe.[3]

This judicial pronouncement reflects the basic assumption of traditional international law based on Nation-States. By definition, a State possesses primary authority over its territory and population; and, by virtue of its sovereignty, it may therefore decide if and how it will permit non-citizens to enter its territory.

The elusive concept of sovereignty may however be misleading for assessing the role of States in migration control. Asserting that States have sovereign powers to decide upon the admission and expulsion of aliens does not mean that they have absolute discretion to do so. The authority of States and their correlative responsibility in that field may be better understood by reference to the concept of domestic jurisdiction as enshrined in Article 2(7) of the UN Charter.[4] Domestic jurisdiction (or reserved domain) is traditionally understood as the domain of State activities where the jurisdiction of the State is not bound by international law.[5] Domestic jurisdiction is, however, not a monolithic notion. The scope of this domain depends on international law. Already in 1923, the Permanent Court of International Justice explained in the *Nationality Decree Case* that:

> The question whether a certain matter is or is not solely within the [domestic] jurisdiction of a State is an essentially relative question; it depends upon the development of international relations.[6]

From that perspective, the admission and expulsion of aliens—although in principle a domestic issue—have to some extent been internationalized by a set of customary and conventional rules. As a result, States no longer enjoy an absolute and uncontrolled discretion. Although they still enjoy a wide margin of appreciation in determining the grounds for refusing admission or mandating expulsion, the exercise of this competence through the enactment and enforce-ment of domestic law is limited by international law. Typical of this approach is the *Declaration on the Human Rights of Individuals who are not Nationals of the Country in which They Live*, which was adopted by the General Assembly of the United Nations in 1985. Article 2(1) of the Declaration signals the balance between the sovereign prerogatives of States and the legal obligations imposed on States. It provides the following:

> Nothing in this Declaration shall be interpreted as legitimizing the illegal entry into and presence in a State of any alien, nor shall any provision be interpreted as restricting the right of any State to promul- gate laws and regulations concerning the entry of aliens and the terms and conditions of their stay or to establish differences between nationals and aliens. However, such laws and regulations shall not be incompatible with the international legal obligations of that State, including those in the field of human rights.[7]

The main difficulty with this balancing exercise lies in the fact that the ex-act scope of the relevant international obligations is far from being completely clear. At the universal level, a comprehensive international treaty regulating global migration regimes and governing all aspects of international migration does not exist. The law governing the treatment of aliens has been thus equated with 'a giant unassembled juridical jigsaw puzzle', for which 'the number of piec-es is uncertain and the grand design is still emerging'.[8] International obligations of States with regard to migrants are indeed dispersed amongst heterogeneous enactments.

The current international legal framework governing migration consists of a wide variety of principles and rules belonging to numerous branches of interna-tional law (such as refugee law, human rights law, trade law, labour law, air law, consular law, etc.). These principles and rules are supplemented by a large body of bilateral and regional agreements. The *European Union Treaty*,[9] the *North American Free Trade Agreement*[10] or the *Treaty Establishing the West African Eco-nomic Community*[11] exemplify the current search for a more coherent regime for managing migration. While international law does not establish a clear-cut comprehensive migration regime, an increasingly detailed and expanded set of international norms constrains and channels State authority over migration.[12] It is not our intention here to study the multiple and complex facets of these norms, but to briefly highlight some of the most important principles and gen-eral trends governing international migration law.

Traditionally international law has been concerned with two particular and clearly individualized categories of migrants, namely, the refugee and the migrant worker. With regard to the first, probably the most important restriction on the sovereignty of States is the principle of non-refoulement that prohibits States from sending refugees back to their country of origin or to any other country where their life or freedom may be threatened.[13] This principle was first expressed in conventional law in the 1933 *Convention Relating to the Status of Refugees*.[14] Immediately after the Second World War, it emerged as a key principle in regulation of the international protection of refugees.[15] In 1951, it was explicitly codified in Article 33 of the *Geneva Convention Relating to the Status of Refugees* currently ratified by 147 States.[16] This basic protection against removal to a country of persecution is reinforced by Article 31(1) which prohibits the imposition of penalties on account of the illegal entry of refugees.[17] As a consequence, anyone who sets foot on the territory of a Contracting State is protected, regardless of the legal or illegal nature of his or her entry.

Although the prohibition of refoulement does not create an obligation to admit *per se*, it paves the way for *de facto* asylum. As a matter of fact, respect for the principle of non-refoulement entails two possibilities: sending the refugee to a country where there is no threat of persecution (the so-called 'safe third country') or admitting the refugee within its own territory. The 1951 Convention also guarantees certain human rights standards and social benefits to refugees who are admitted into the territory of the State of asylum. The legal status of refugees is defined by reference to three different categories of treatments which are rather complex:

1. Refugees are entitled to *treatment at least as favourable as that accorded to their citizens* with respect to religion (art. 4); protection of intellectual property (art. 14); access to courts and legal assistance (art. 16); rationing measures (art. 20); elementary education (art. 22(1)); public relief and assistance (art. 23); labour legislation and social security (art. 24); as well as fiscal taxes and charges (art. 29).
2. States shall also accord refugees *the most favourable treatment accorded to nationals of a foreign country* with regard to non-political and non-profit-making associations and trade unions (art. 15) and wage-earning employment (art. 17).
3. The 1951 Geneva Convention finally requires that States Parties accord refugees *treatment no less favourable than that accorded to aliens generally* with respect to exemption from legislative reciprocity (art. 7(1)); movable and immovable property (art. 13); self-employment (art. 18); liberal professions (art. 19); housing (art. 21); post-elementary educa-

tion (art. 22(2)); and freedom of movement within the territory of host countries (art. 26).

Migrant workers constitute another important category of aliens that also benefits from the protection afforded by a wide range of universal instruments.[18] The vast majority of these instruments were concluded under the auspices of the International Labour Organisation (ILO), including the *Migration for Employment Convention 1949* (No. 97),[19] the *Migration for Employment Recommendation 1949* (No. 86)[20] and the *Migrant Workers Convention 1975* (No. 143).[21] Certain rights are guaranteed regardless of the legality of the migrant's presence in the territory, e.g., equal remuneration and minimum wage with respect to past employment and maintenance of social security benefits.[22] Other rights are extended only to those lawfully within a territory, e.g., rights to equal opportunities and vocational training.[23] The *1990 International Convention on the Protection of the Rights of All Migrant Workers and Members of Their Families*[24] constitutes another major achievement by specifying and restating the basic rights of this particular vulnerable group of migrants. Although the Convention distinguishes between documented migrant workers and those who are undocumented or in an irregular situation, Part III of the Convention enumerates a comprehensive set of civil, political, economic, social and cultural rights applicable to all migrant workers and members of their families. Among these rights, the principle of equality of treatment between migrant workers and nationals is to be applied before the courts (art. 18) and in respect of remuneration and other working conditions (art. 25). Part IV of the Convention grants additional rights to those migrants who are in a regular situation and Part VI seeks to prevent and eliminate illegal entry and illegal employment of migrant workers.

The adoption and development of specific rules with regard to refugees and migrant workers exemplifies a typical trend in international law to protect selected categories of migrants, rather than to regulate migration in a more comprehensive manner. This traditional driving force of international migration law has been extended during the two last decades to also cover other particularly vulnerable groups such as victims of torture,[25] children migrants,[26] or victims of trafficking.[27] From the perspective of general international law, such a legislative trend begs the inevitable question of whether the development of dispersed and heterogeneous rules constitutes a sort of normative ghetto, or provides for an incremental protection within a broader context.

International human rights law tends, however, to bypass these controversies by providing for a more systemic approach to migration. This expanded branch of international law sets up a sort of *lex generalis* which supplements the specialized treaty regimes applicable to more limited categories of aliens. Beyond the fragmentary nature of international migration law, general human rights law also plays an increasingly important role in the internationalization of migration policy. This significant body of law not only guarantees a general framework for the basic rights of aliens, but more importantly it is crucial for those people who do not fall within traditional categories of protected migrants.[28] Such assessment derives from the very nature of human rights law based on the assumption that human rights apply to everyone, irrespective of nationality or statelessness, because of the inherent dignity of every human being. Like all the other human rights instruments, the *International Covenant on Civil and Political Rights*[29] recalls in Article 2(1) that:

> Each State Party to the present Covenant undertakes to respect and to ensure to all individuals within its territory and subject to its jurisdiction the rights recognized in the present Covenant, without distinction of any kind, such as race, colour, sex, language, religion, political or other opinion, national or social origin, property, birth or other status.

In its General Comment No. 15 on *The Position of Aliens under the Covenant*, the Human Rights Committee explains that:

> The general rule is that each one of the rights of the Covenant must be guaranteed without discrimination between citizens and aliens. Aliens receive the benefit of the general requirement of non-discrimination in respect of the rights guaranteed in the Covenant, as provided for in Article 2 thereof. This guarantee applies to aliens and citizens alike. Exceptionally, some of the rights recognized in the Covenant are expressly applicable only to citizens (art. 25) [relating to the right to vote and to take part in the conduct of public affairs], while Article 13 [on procedural guarantees governing expulsion] applies only to aliens. (§1)

General Comment No. 15 delineates further the basic rights of aliens deriving from the *International Covenant on Civil and Political Rights*:

> Aliens thus have an inherent right to life, protected by law, and may not be arbitrarily deprived of life. They must not be subjected to torture or to cruel, inhuman or degrading treatment or punishment; nor may they be held in slavery or servitude. Aliens have the full right to liberty and security of the person. If lawfully deprived of their liberty, they shall be treated with humanity and with respect for the inherent dignity of their person. Aliens may not be imprisoned for failure to fulfil a contractual obligation. They have the right to liberty of movement and free choice of residence; they shall be free to leave the country. Aliens shall be equal

before the courts and tribunals, and shall be entitled to a fair and public hearing by a competent, independent and impartial tribunal established by law in the determination of any criminal charge or of rights and obligations in a suit at law. Aliens shall not be subjected to retrospective penal legislation, and are entitled to recognition before the law. They may not be subjected to arbitrary or unlawful interference with their privacy, family, home or correspondence. They have the right to freedom of thought, conscience and religion, and the right to hold opinions and to express them. Aliens receive the benefit of the right of peaceful assembly and of freedom of association. They may marry when at marriageable age. Their children are entitled to those measures of protection required by their status as minors. In those cases where aliens constitute a minority within the meaning of Article 27, they shall not be denied the right, in community with other members of their group, to enjoy their own culture, to profess and practise their own religion and to use their own language. Aliens are entitled to equal protection by the law. There shall be no discrimination between aliens and citizens in the application of these rights. These rights of aliens may be qualified only by such limitations as may be lawfully imposed under the Covenant. (§7).

More significantly, human rights law enshrines a qualified freedom of movement through the well-established right to leave any country and to return to one's own country.[30] However, although the right to leave and the right to return are clearly interrelated, their respective content is not similar. Freedom to leave is available to everyone (i.e., to nationals and aliens alike), while the right to return does not ensure a general human right to enter the territory of a State. Article 12(4) of the *International Covenant* does guarantee a right to enter 'his own country'. This broad and somewhat ambiguous expression is commonly argued to cover both nationals and permanent immigrant residents on the territory of States Parties.[31] With regard to admission of aliens in general, the Human Rights Committee acknowledges that:

> In certain circumstances an alien may enjoy the protection of the Covenant even in relation to entry or residence, for example, when considerations of non-discrimination, prohibition of inhuman treatment and respect for family life arise.[32]

Protection against arbitrary detention is one further example, among many others, of this contextualized approach of human rights law in the field of migration. The Committee acknowledged in the well known case of *A v. Australia* that prolonged detention of illegal migrants without a showing of necessity and periodic review is arbitrary and therefore in violation of Article 9 of the Covenant.[33]

The international legal protection of migrants and refugees increasingly tends to be an integral part of human rights law. Its growing and inescapable importance for regulating States' conduct in migration issues is not surprising nor completely new. It derives from the general philosophy of the Charter of the United Nations, one of the main purposes of which, as set out in Article 55, is to promote 'universal respect for, and observance of, human rights and fundamental freedoms for all without distinction as to race, sex, language, or religion'. Rather than signalling a resurgence of the truly sovereign State, developments in the legal protection of migrants reflect the major changes in contemporary international law, which is gradually moving from a State-centred to an individual-oriented paradigm.

ENDNOTES

1. V. Gowlland-Debbas, 'Introduction', in: V. Gowlland-Debbas (ed.), *The Problem of Refugees in the Light of Contemporary International Law Issues*, Martinus Nijhoff, The Hague/Boston/London, Graduate Institute of International Studies, Geneva, 1996, p. xii. See also: I. Brownlie, *Principles of Public International Law*, 6th ed., Oxford University Press, 2003, p. 498; Malcolm N. Shaw, *International Law*, 5th ed., Cambridge University Press, 2003, p. 574.

2. Classics of International Law, Text of 1758, Book 1, Chapter XIX, Sec. 230. See also in the same vein: S. Pufendorf, *Le droit de la nature et des gens*, 1672, traduction de J. Barbeyrac (1759), Bibliotheque de Philosophie politique et juridique, Textes et Documents, Université de Caen, 1987, Liv. Ill, chap. Ill, § IX, p. 336; C. Wolff, *Principes du droit de la nature et des gens*, traduction de S. Formey, (1758), Bibliotheque de Philosophic politique et juridique, Textes et Documents, Université de Caen, 1988, Tome III, Liv. IX, chap. IV, § XV, p. 278.

3. *Nishimura Ekiu v. United States* 142 US 651 (1892), Gray J., 659. See also: Attorney-General for Canada v. Cain [1906] AC 542, 546: 'One of the rights possessed by the supreme power in every State is the right to refuse to permit an alien to enter that State, to annex what conditions it pleases to the permission to enter it, and to expel or deport from the State, at pleasure, even a friendly alien, especially if it considers his presence in the State opposed to its peace order, and good government, or to its social or material interest'. In a judgement delivered in December 2004, the House of Lords recalls that: 'The power to admit, exclude and expel aliens was among the earliest and most widely recognised powers of the sovereign State': *European Roma Rights Centre and others v. Immigration Officer at Prague Airport* [2004] UKHL 55.

4. 'Nothing contained in the present Charter shall authorize the United Nations to intervene in matters which are essentially within the domestic jurisdiction of any state or shall require the Members to submit such matters to settlement under the present Charter'.

5. See notably Articles 1 & 3 of the resolution *The Determination of the 'Reserved Domain' and Its Effects* adopted in Aix en Provence on 29 April 1954 by the Institute of International Law, available at: http://www.idi iil.org/idiF/navig_chronl953.html.

6. PCIJ (1923) Ser. B, N° 4, p. 23.

7. UNGA Res. 40/114 (13 December 1985). The Human Rights Committee recalls in the same perspective that: 'The question whether an alien is 'lawfully' within the territory of a State is a matter governed by domestic law, which may subject the entry of an alien to the territory of a State to restrictions, *provided they are in compliance with the State's international obligations'*: General Comment N° 27 (Freedom of Movement), 1999, § 4, CCPR/C/21/Rev.l/Add.9.

8. R. Lillich, *The Human Rights of Aliens in Contemporary International Law*, Manchester University Press, 1984, p. 122.

9. *Treaty on European Union*, Official Journal C 325, 24 December 2002.

10. *North American Free Trade Agreement Between the Government of Canada, the Government of the United Mexican States and the Government of the United States*, 8–17 December 1992, 32 ILM (1993) p. 289.

11. *Treaty Establishing the West African Economic Community*, 28 May 1975, 1010 UNTS p. 17.

12. For a comprehensive presentation of these International norms, see: R. Plender, *International Migration Law*, 2nd ed., Martinus Nijhoff Publishers, 1988; T.A. Aleinikoff & V. Chetail (eds.), *Migration and International Legal Norms*, T.M.C. Asser Press, The Hague, 2003; V. Chetail (ed.), *Globalization, Migration and Human Rights: International Law under Review*, Bruylant, Brussels, 2007.

13. For an overview of the principle of non-refoulement in International law, see notably: G.S. Goodwin-Gill, *The Refugee in International Law*, 2nd ed., Clarendon Press, Oxford, 1996, pp. 117–171; V. Chetail, 'Le principe de non refoulement et le statut de réfugié en droit international', in: V. Chetail & J.-F. Flauss (eds.), *La Convention de Genève du 28 juillet 1951 relative au statut des réfugiés—50 ans après: bilan et perspectives*, Bruylant, Brussels, 2001, pp. 3–61; E. Lauterpacht & D. Bethlehem, 'The scope and content of the principle of non-refoulement: Opinion', in: E. Feller, V. Turk & F. Nicholson (eds.), *Refugee Protection in International Law*, Cambridge University Press, 2003, pp. 87–164.

14. 159 *LNTS* 3663.

15. See notably: UN Doc. A/Res/8(I) (1946).

16. 28 July 1951, 189 UNTS 150, entered into force April 22, 1954. The first paragraph of this article states that: 'No Contracting State shall expel or return ('refouler') a refugee in any manner whatsoever to the frontiers of territories where his life or freedom would be threatened on account of his race, religion, nationality, membership of a particular social group or political opinion'.

17. 'The Contracting States shall not impose penalties, on account of their illegal entry or presence, on refugees who, coming directly from a territory where their life or freedom was threatened in the sense of article 1, enter or are present in their territory without authorization, provided they present themselves without delay to the authorities and show good cause for their illegal entry or presence.' For an extensive commentary on this provision, see: G.S. Goodwin-Gill, 'Article 31 of the 1951 Convention Relating to the Status of Refugees: non-penalization, detention and protection', in: E. Feller, V. Turk & F. Nicholson (eds.), *Refugee Protection in International Law*, op. cit., pp. 185–252.

18. See on this question: R. Cholewinski, *Migrant Workers in International Human Rights Law*, Clarendon Press, Oxford, 1997.

19. Convention N° 97 *concerning Migration for Employment (Revised)*, 1 July 1949, 120 UNTS 71.

20. *International Labor Conventions and Recommendations*, vol. 1, ILO, 1996.

21. *Convention N° 143 concerning Migration in Abusive Conditions and the Promotion of Equality of Opportunity and Treatment of Migrant Workers*, 24 June 1975, 1120 UNTS 324.

22. *Convention N° 97 concerning Migration for Employment (Revised)*, art. 6.

23. *ILO Migrant Workers Recommendation*, 1975 (No. 51), para. 8).

24. G.A. Res. 45/158 (Annex), 18 December 1990.

25. See Article 3 of the Convention against Torture, 10 December 1984, 1465 UNTS 85.

26. See for example: Articles 9 to 11 of the *Convention on the Rights of the Child*, 20 November 1989, 1577 UNTS 44.

27. *Protocol to Prevent, Suppress and Punish Trafficking in Persons, especially Women and Children, supplementing the United Nations Convention against Transnational Organized Crime*, 15 November 2000, G.A. Res. 55/25.

28. See on this question: R. Lillich, *The Human Rights of Aliens in Contemporary International Law, op. cit.*; C. Tiburcio, *The Human Rights of Aliens under International and Comparative Law*, Martinus Nijhoff Publishers, The Hague, 2001; J. Fitzpatrick, The Human Rights of Migrants', in: T.A. Aleinikoff & V. Chetail (eds.), *Migration and International Legal Norms, op. cit.*, pp. 169-184; V. Chetail (ed.), *Globalization, Migration and Human Rights: International Law under Review*, Bruylant, Brussels, 2007.

29. 999 UNTS 171.

30. *See* notably on this question: R. Higgins, 'The Right in International Law of an Individual to Enter, Stay In and Leave a Country', *International Affairs*, 1973, pp. 341–357; H. Hannum, *The Right to Leave and Return in International Law and Practice*, Martinus Nijhoff, Dordrecht/Boston, 1987; V. Chetail, 'Freedom of Movement and Transnational Migrations: A Human Rights Perspective', in: T.A. Aleinikoff & V. Chetail (eds.), *Migration and International Legal Norms, op. cit.*, pp. 47–60.

31. General Comment N° 27 (Freedom of Movement), *op. cit.*, § 20.

32. General Comment N° 15 (The Position of Aliens under the Covenant), *op. cit.*, § 5.

33. *A v. Australia*, CCPR/C/59/D/560/1993 (30 April 1997), §§ 9.4–9.5.

*Vincent Chetail is the director of the Programme for the Study of Global Migration and professor of public international law at the Graduate Institute of International and Development Studies, Geneva.

Chetail, Vincent. "International Legal Protection of Migrants and Refugees: Ghetto or Incremental Protection? Some Preliminary Comments." *Law of Refugees: Global Perspectives* (2005), 33–45 (essay first presented at the European Society of International Law Research Forum on International Law: Contemporary Issues at the Graduate Institute of International Studies, Geneva, May 26–28, 2005).

Used by permission.

Independent Children, Inconsistent Adults: International Child Migration and the Legal Framework

*by Jacqueline Bhabha**

". . . decision-making politicians appear sometimes to be confused about how to treat migrant children. On the one hand, they state their full support of the idea that children do have rights and also recognize that our aging continent will need migration, not least young migrants. On the other hand a number of them appear not to be able to draw the necessary conclusions [about the rights of migrant children]."[1]

[. . .]

THE LEGAL FRAMEWORK

International, regional and domestic law impinging on international child migration includes three broad approaches, each of which covers only part of the relevant phenomena. One approach is punitive and criminalizing, the oldest strain in migration legislation, dating back to prohibition of the so-called 'white slave trade' in the nineteenth century. In its contemporary form, it includes conventions criminalizing trafficking in persons, including children, though not trafficked persons. It is based on a dichotomy between criminal traffickers and victim trafficked persons. This approach focuses on penalizing and preventing exploitative child migration. It is, by definition, inhibitory rather than facilitatory. In this body of legislation, crystallized by the Trafficking Protocol to the 2000 Transnational Organized Crime Convention, victimhood is constitutive of the child migrant. As a matter of legal definition and unlike their adult counterparts, child migrants can never consent to exploitative migration facilitated by intermediaries.[2] Where mediation and an intention to exploit exist, such migration therefore always constitutes the crime of trafficking. An adolescent looking for employment and a way out of a Kosovar refugee camp who agrees to accompany an agent to a west European capital to work in the sex trade counts as a trafficking victim just as an Indian child sold into domestic service by her parents. Insofar as this categorization results in the mobilization of protections and human rights entitlements for trafficked children, the results may be positive. In the United States, for example, a 'T Visa' which provides lawful immigration status for 4 years and can lead to permanent residence, is available (though only vary rarely granted) to child victims of trafficking. But often classification as a trafficking victim leads to additional migration obstacles for the child at the border or forced return of the migrant child to his or her place of origin. This may hamper the long term realization of human rights and opportunities for child migrants, and frustrate plans actively chosen which they consider their best available options. The process of criminalization of traffickers can also confront children with dangerous options: in some countries, access to protection is conditional on the agreement of the child to testify against the trafficker in court, a strategy which can backfire on relatives and be detrimental and/or dangerous for the child.

A second legal approach to child migration is regulatory, the primary thrust of most domestic and regional migration related law. It establishes the parameters for legal migration, including the migration of children. It is based on the notion that children are family dependents who lack autonomous agency. As has been pointed out in the context of the United States, but the point applies more generally, "for purposes of immigration law, a 'child' only exists in relation to a parent".[3] Family reunion depends on proof of the parent-child relationship, and of the child's dependence. It takes place around parents, not children. The European Union Council Directive on the Right to Family Reunification, for example, only requires member states to admit children for family reunion without additional qualifications if they are below the age of 12. Beyond that age, states can impose additional requirements, such as proof that the child meets "a condition for integration".[4] As a result, much contemporary independent child migration fits imperfectly into the template, leading to a status of illegality or irregularity for the migrant child. In the United Kingdom, for example, single parents who cannot demonstrate that they have had 'sole responsibility' for children over 12 who are seeking to join them, will be disqualified from bringing them in.

A third approach is protective, the most recent human rights-related strain. It includes international law directed at the protection of specific groups; e.g., refugees, migrant workers and their families, children, victims of the worst forms of child labour. Over the past fifteen years or so, there has been a growing acknowledgement that child migration is a significant and increasingly important phenomenon that requires the development of a more effective, protective approach. As a result, despite the absence of comprehensive legislation, there is now a body of international standards including both the Convention on the Rights of the Child (CRC)[5] but also some 'soft law' measures which directly address child migration. For example, several migration destination countries such as Canada, the United States and the United Kingdom, have developed guidelines for child asylum-seekers,[6] regional bodies and institutions including the EU have produced recommendations targeting child migrants,[7] and the UN Committee on the Rights of the Child has issued a detailed and comprehensive General Comment on the topic.[8] Regional groupings of NGOs, such as ECPAT in Asia, and the Separated Children in Europe Project, have developed specific recommendations on particular categories of child migrants, such as sexually exploited and asylum-seeking children.[9] Human rights groups have directed research and advocacy towards targeted issues such as child labourers in Italy (MSF) and child workers and street children in Morocco and Spain (HRW).[10] International organizations such as the United Nations High Commissioner for Refugees (UNHCR) now regularly track child migration statistics for refugee and internally displaced persons, and have issued a series of Executive Committee (or EXCOM) recommendations and guidelines about refugee children.[11]

The emphasis of this body of work has been on child migrants' distinctive vulnerability, their triple burden of alienage, minority and family separation, and on the need for protective policies to ensure their safety and welfare. In this focus, the work has followed one of the general principles of the UN Convention on the Rights of the Child (CRC), the best interests' principle:

'In all actions concerning children, whether undertaken by public or private social welfare institutions, court of law, administrative authorities or legislative bodies, the best interests of the child shall be a primary consideration.'[12]

The other, complementary, general principle, equally central to the international child rights framework but newer in its conception, has not featured as prominently. This is the principle of child agency or voice:

'State parties shall assure to the child who is capable of forming his or her own views the right to express those views freely in all matters affecting the child, the views of the child being given due weight in accordance with the age and maturity of the child.'

"For this purpose, the child shall in particular be provided the opportunity to be heard in any judicial and administrative proceedings affecting the child, either directly or through a representative or an appropriate body, in a manner consistent with the procedural rules of national law".[13]

When this principle is applied to the analysis of child migration, a different perspective emerges, with child migrants as agents, decision makers, initiators and social actors in their own right. From this vantage point, vulnerability and the need for protection are only one element of the social policy agenda; the other role is facilitation, non-discrimination, inclusion, the promotion of opportunity and the acknowledgement of capacity for autonomous responsible action, and for child participation in policy formation. This perspective has been virtually non-existent in the evolution of the legal framework governing child migration, where denial of the child migrant's capacity for autonomous agency has been the guiding principle. Independent child migrants, as a matter of law, have generally been regarded as suspect, either passive victims of exploitation (trafficked), or undeserving illegals (petty thieves, beggars, domestic workers pretending to need asylum) or adults masquerading as children.[14] In the words of an American juvenile immigration officer, they are "either runaways or throwaways".

DEFINITIONS

What are some of the current legal provisions that govern the situation of child migrants and how might they be improved? One can define independent child migrants as children who migrate across national borders separately (though not necessarily divorced) from their families, and include within this definition four broad categories defined by the primary purpose of travel:

a) Children who travel in search of opportunities, whether educational or employment related

b) Children who travel to survive—to escape persecution or war, family abuse, dire poverty

c) Children who travel for family reunion—to join documented or undocumented family members who have already migrated[15]

d) Children who travel in the context of exploitation (including trafficking).

These groups are not mutually exclusive. Like adults, children travel independently for reasons which may overlap. The refugee may also be seeking family reunion and hoping for enhanced educational opportunities; the trafficked child may find him or herself in this situation because of dire poverty and may have no better alternatives than employment abroad. Much of the applicable general legal framework applies to all four categories of independent child migrant. The most important and fundamental human rights protections are comprehensive in their scope. As stated above, there are some additional measures which apply more specifically to trafficked and persecuted children, and there are immigration regulations governing access for families. Children who travel independently, in search of education and/or work opportunities are least catered to by specific child migration measures. A fortiori, legislative provisions that apply to them apply to the other groups of child migrants too.

MIGRATING TO ADVANCE OPPORTUNITIES

There is no clear understanding of how many children migrate alone in search of better opportunities, for education and or employment, but the number is undoubtedly significant and probably growing. Generic factors such as global inequalities, increasingly available travel opportunities, social imaginaries which include the possibility of life elsewhere combine with situation specific circumstances to produce a very large and diverse population of children migrating to advance their opportunities. Here are two vignettes encompassing four continents.

The first describes the large migration of Moroccan children to Spain. As the Moroccan director of an NGO providing services to the children in Ceuta, the Spanish enclave on the northern coast of Morocco, commented.

"They are not street children, but youth from poor neighbourhoods who are the only support for their families. They have no job skills and leave school early because they have no hope that schools will improve their situation. . . . [The children] plan for a long time; sometimes they travel with the agreement of their families, who pay clandestine travel fees to the "smugglers". . . They know not to bring papers, but for the last two years they also know that with documents they can get status and they know who to ask for in Cordoba or Marseille to get help with status. We have never met a youth who comes back who says he failed."

Children describe their journeys as motivated by poverty and lack of opportunities, but also by a more general desire to seek out a better life.

A sixteen year old boy explained: "I want to go to Spain to work and to help my family. My family is very poor". A thirteen year old girl, who sold sundry food items on the streets, begged and collected leftover food from cafes said: "We come to eat. . . I had to leave school about a year ago". According to a fifteen year-old who left his job in Tangier to travel to mainland Spain hidden under a large truck but was detected at the border and returned: "My heart told me to go to Spain so I went. My parents let me do what I want. . . I see my future in Spain. The next time I will go over and become a butcher. I will go to school there and learn."[16]

Not all journeys undertaken are between adjacent countries. Some children embark on transcontinental travel to pursue their dreams or those of their families. A well-worn route transports thousands of children on their own from the Fujian province of South-Eastern China to northern metropoli, including New York. The journeys are invariably dangerous and unpredictable, mediated by intermediaries who stand to gain financially from the transport. Children's re-actions on arrival are complex and varied. Some indicate an elaborate plan, involving what one might call "mutually advantageous exploitation"; others evidence regret, fear, the obligation of filial obedience, disorientation. Here are two different responses to similar journeys, given by Chinese children inter-viewed in New York in December 2000.

An eighteen year old girl told us: "My family used to live in a village by the ocean in Fuzhou province. My father owned a big business, a sock factory, but his business went bankrupt and then we moved back to my grandmother's house on an island in Fuzhou . . . I had a happy childhood there . . . My Dad started a new transport business. Now my Dad only comes back home once a month. My Mom has a home business. She wakes up early to get fresh fish and sell it in the market. . . . Most of my friends have left my village. Almost all the young people leave, about 90 per cent . . . They are foolish people. They want to send their kids away to save face. They are proud. Families think that at least one of their children should go to live somewhere else. Some of them are too proud to really care about their children's future. I have two younger brothers. My oldest brother wants to come to the United States, but I don't think he should. . . . Today the passage costs about US$60,000 and it is very dangerous. I don't think I should have come. I miss China. I wish I had not come. I don't think life in Fuzhou is that difficult really. . . . The latest trend is for people in the village to borrow money from their neighbours or relatives at a very high interest rate in order to send their kids away. . . . When my Mom talked to me about coming to the United States, I disagreed with her very strongly, but then she started to cry. She begged me. I didn't want to disappoint her, so eventually I agreed to go . . . They are my parents so I have to obey them."

By contrast, this was the perspective of an eighteen year-old boy from the same area: "My father used to work in the Communist government, but he was fired when I was born (one child policy). . . . He became a corn farmer. My family became much poorer . . . Then five or six years ago my father died. My family's financial situation became much more difficult . . . I was 16 years old when I left China. My mom didn't want me to go at first. I was the only son left . . . But I knew I had to go to help my family."[17]

A range of legal instruments are relevant to independent child migrants in these situations; as previously stated, no single consolidated statute or convention specifically addresses them. Though there is an authoritative international definition of a child—"every human being below the age of 18 . . . unless under the law applicable to the child, majority is attained earlier",[18] there is no comparable definition of a migrant. Applicable law can be divided into two broad categories, international human rights law and labour law. Other areas of law, such as refugee law and criminal law may be relevant in some cases too; they most directly cover the situation of children migrating for survival and for exploitation.

1. INTERNATIONAL HUMAN RIGHTS LAW

The minimum floor of rights pertaining to migrants, including child migrants, derives from two clusters of human rights law, namely the international bill of rights which sets out general human rights protections for all, and specific conventions which address the rights of particular groups. Though all the principal human rights which are relevant to child migrants are codified in the 1989 Convention on the Rights of the Child, which consolidates previous international legal commitments, it is useful to review the more generic human rights instruments since child migrants' rights should be understood and defended within the context of general and universal human rights obligations as well as by reference to more specific and limited legal undertakings.

(a) The International Bill of Rights

The Universal Declaration of Human Rights (UDHR), the International Covenant on Civil and Political Rights (ICCPR) and the International Covenant on Economic, Social and Cultural Rights (ICESCR) set out a broad range of basic human rights which apply to all, including therefore child migrants, irrespective of nationality, legal status or age. By virtue of these provisions, child migrants, whatever their immigration status, have an unqualified right to the basic human rights. The most fundamental principle is the non-discrimination principle, which prohibits all distinctions between people which are arbitrary, disproportionate or unjustifiable.[19] Cultural, moral and religious arguments are often advanced to justify migration decisions imposed on children (e.g. it is in the child's best interests to be sent home to their family); and political and economic factors are also used to rebut criticisms of arbitrary exclusion of migrant children from services (e.g. from education grants, from free health care). Given the moral and legal imperative of treating all humans as of equal worth,[20] the onus of justifying these measures is on those who seek to bring themselves within an exception to the equality principle. In practice, discussions about what exclusionary policies are arbitrary, unjustifiable or disproportionate, are ongoing and central to the evolution of any society, especially one experiencing rapid demographic changes. And access to legal services required to enforce rights is as unevenly distributed as the rights themselves, rendering the letter of the law illusory in most practical situations.

More specific rights include 'life, liberty and security', freedom from torture, cruel or degrading treatment or punishment, full access to the court system, equality before the law, protection from 'arbitrary arrest, detention or exile', full procedural protections in the event of arrest and detention associated with a criminal process, payment of a fair wage for work performed, police protection from physical or sexual abuse, publicly funded emergency health care when available within the state, and shelter and other forms of social assistance necessary to preserve life. Individuals also have a right to some less commonly cited protections including 'recognition as a person before the law' and the right to a nationality. In addition they have a right to leave any country including their own, unless restrictions to this right are required as a matter of "national security, public order (order public), public health or morals or the rights and freedoms of others".[21]

These human rights provisions impinge directly on some common aspects of the situation of independent child migrants. Generic human rights obligations to protect life (strengthened by maritime law and specific regulations about rescue at sea) implicate state responsibility for children stranded trying to cross a border through the desert, or injured as a result of dangerous transport arrangements (undercarriages of planes, boots of trucks, containers in lorries) or in distress at sea. Procedures which create insuperable hurdles for children seeking to leave their own countries and do not fall within the exceptions listed above, or which subject them to summary removal and return at borders without individualized proceedings, also fall foul of these provisions, as do arbitrary or abusive detention practices or other deprivations of liberty to which migrant children are frequently subjected. Even where the detention of child migrants is lawful and envisaged as a measure of last resort and for the shortest period of time, it must conform with a range of procedural protections, including the right to be informed of the reasons for detention, the right to be brought before a court promptly, the right to challenge the legality of the detention and to seek compensation in the event of wrongful detention. Where child migrants are denied access to guardianship or to free legal representation, the effectiveness of their right to challenge detention can be called into question. According to UNHCR, the detention of child asylum-seekers is always against their best interests. It follows from their view that justifications, such as the need to 'protect' them from traffickers or snakeheads have the same validity as incarceration of child abuse victims would.

The right to equality before the law combined with the right to fair working conditions and to work that is not hazardous, does not interfere with the child's education and is not harmful to the child's health or development (CRC art. 32) should enable child migrants to claim redress for abusive employment situations. And the right to liberty and security and to the enjoyment of just working conditions imposes a duty on states to protect migrant children from working conditions that are inhuman or degrading, and from third party threats to their safety, including from smugglers and employers. Conversely, however, human rights law also includes very general provisions regarding the right to work: the ICESCR notes that states "shall recognize the right to work, which includes the right of everyone to the opportunity to gain his living by work which he freely chooses or accepts".[22] States can limit this right to promote full employment and adequate rates of pay, provided adequate social assistance is afforded to those excluded from the labour market. And states can also limit the types and conditions of employment permissible for children, including providing for a minimum age for admission to employment.[23] EU directives, for example, prohibit the employment of children under 15. Subject to these provisions, however, general non-discrimination provisions apply and migrant children should not be arbitrarily excluded from employment available to domestic children.

Other social and economic rights relevant to child migrants, including housing, health care and education, are also protected by international human rights law. The ICESCR recognizes the "right of everyone to an adequate standard of living including adequate . . . housing, and to the continuous improvement of living conditions", a generic right which in the case of children is strengthened by more explicit CRC obligations on states to "assist parents and others responsible for the child to implement the right to a standard of living adequate for the child's physical, mental, spiritual, moral and social development and to provide where necessary material assistance and support programs, particularly with regard to nutrition, clothing and housing".[24] There is a serious question about whether the bed and breakfast accommodation provided by some states to adolescent child migrants without an additional support complies with this requirement.

Regarding health care, the ICESCR notes that "every person has the right to enjoy the highest attainable standard of physical and mental health".[25] This encompasses the right to access health care, and not to face discrimination on the basis of nationality or other status. Whereas the scope of the obligation for undocumented adult migrants may be limited to provision of emergency health care, with other broader health care obligations residing with the country of origin,[26] in the case of child migrants the obligation is undoubtedly broader, encompassing "the provision of necessary medical assistance and health care to all children with emphasis on the development of primary health care".[27] Many migration destination states have embraced these inclusive provisions providing emergency, necessary and in some cases comprehensive health care to child migrants irrespective of status. Within Europe, for example, there appears to be a broad spectrum of approaches. Spain and Italy provide free health care for all within the same comprehensive health care system; France, Belgium and the Netherlands administer separate systems for migrants, but envisage free access for some types of health care needs; the United Kingdom and Portugal have more restrictive systems, and Hungary and Germany allow free health care only in limited cases, but require providers to inform on users with an irregular migration status. Poland only provides access to medical care to children who are asylum seekers, who are obliged to go through medical screening. In practice however, even in countries where access to health care is permitted, child migrants encounter obstacles to medical treatment arising out of discrimination because they lack health insurance. In the Netherlands, restrictive interpretations of what constitutes 'necessary care' have prevented access for some child migrants. In France, child migrants need a regular address to access emergency medical care if they do not have documents. Some NGOs, including the Association Jeunes Errants, provide their own address to overcome this hurdle; children not in touch with helpful NGOs however would find themselves excluded. In the United States, by contrast, undocumented child migrants must be provided with emergency care but they are not otherwise eligible for publicly-funded health services. In the state of California alone, there are an estimated 136,000 undocumented children without health insurance. State policies which subject migrant children to prolonged and harsh incarceration, whether as a result of age determination procedures or delays in immigration processing, are inconsistent with the international health obligations just outlined, as well as with relevant international juvenile justice standards.

The right to education is recognized as fundamental for children. The ICE-SCR requires states parties to "recognize the right of everyone to education" and in particular to ensure that primary education is free and available to all, that secondary education, including technical and vocational education, is "made generally available and accessible to all by every appropriate means", and that "higher education is equally accessible to all, on the basis of capacity".[28] These obligations are reinforced in identical terms by the CRC; the Convention for the Protection of the Rights of Migrant Workers (CPRMW) prohibits refusal of access to schools on the basis of a child's irregular status. In practice states have again broadly embraced these provisions. In the United States, all children irrespective of immigration status have the right to primary and secondary education, while access to higher education varies by state. Some states have passed legislation permitting undocumented children who have graduated from US schools to enrol in state colleges at the same tuition rates as legal residents. The DREAM Act, which has been introduced in the last 3 Congresses but is still only a proposal, would provide legal status to a subset of undocumented children who complete their secondary education in the United States.

European countries vary in their approaches to the education of undocumented child migrants. In Italy, for example, school is compulsory for all children under 18 and undocumented children have the right to attend; human rights groups however report non-attendance by significant numbers of migrant children working in agriculture.[29] In Poland, by contrast, though the same compulsory education provisions apply, undocumented children have to pay to attend. In practice, there is considerable evidence that undocumented children encounter obstacles to attending school in Europe. In some cases school authorities require identification documents as a precondition of enrolment (because the schools only get reimbursed from the ministry if they include these details in their financial reporting). In other cases, undocumented families withhold their children from school for fear that this will lead to detection by immigration authorities.

(b) Conventions Addressing Specific Interest Groups

In addition to the protections derived from the bill of rights, child migrants enjoy the protection of several other instruments. They include the Convention on the Rights of the Child and the Convention against Torture, the Convention on the Elimination of all forms of Racial Discrimination, the Convention on the Elimination of all forms of Discrimination against Women, the Convention on the Rights of the Child and the Convention on the Protection of the Rights of All Migrant Workers and Members of their Families. Many of the protections afforded restate or reinforce rights set out in the 2 Covenants, amplifying particular aspects of rights protection for the relevant constituency. In what follows, the two most relevant conventions, the CRC and the CPRMW are considered.

The focus of analysis switches from the protective to the enabling perspective to inquire whether and to what extent these two targeted international human rights conventions address the needs and promote the interests of independent child migrants.

(i) The Convention on the Rights of the Child (CRC)

The CRC, as is well known, is a very widely ratified, consolidating convention that draws together the disparate human rights provisions relevant to children, synthesizing and deepening their impact by creating an implementation structure that includes reporting obligations to and scrutiny by the Committee on the Rights of the Child, the treaty body established to oversee the Convention's workings. It represents a watershed in thinking about the rights of children for several reasons. First, it signals the centrality of children to the general preoccupations of the human rights movement, something that had been lacking at the legal level and is still in its infancy at the policy and political level. The Convention establishes without ambiguity the imperative obligation on states parties to consider children's human rights in general, and their best interests in particular, more vigorously than they had. Second, the CRC enlarges the scope of children's rights by emphasizing the importance of child agency and participation in addition to the traditional concern with child protection and best interest. In other words, the CRC establishes a framework for thinking about children as rights-bearing subjects and agents, as well as objects of adult protective attention. Moreover, the Committee on the Rights of the Child has issued a General Comment, no. 6, which specifically and holistically addresses the obligations of states parties towards unaccompanied and separated children outside their country of origin.[30] By drawing attention to the particularly vulnerable position of this population, the General Comment sets out the "multifaceted challenges faced by States and other actors in ensuring that such children are able to access and enjoy their rights",[31] "irrespective of the nationality, immigration status or statelessness".[32] For example, the General Comment urges States Parties to engage in a "clear and comprehensive" assessment of a child's identity when undertaking the best interest process.[33] This policy has potentially far-reaching consequences. For example it requires government officials to put to one side simplistic and general assumptions that :home is the best place for a child" or essentialist simplifications about what is in the interests of "African" or "Chinese" children in favour of much more nuanced appraisals of the components of a child's sense of self worth, of identification, of expressed desires and ambitions.

Apart from the measures already discussed including the protection of rights to education, to health, to shelter, the prohibition on discrimination, arbitrary detention, inhuman treatment—one additional set of provisions is worth reviewing. It concerns family unity, and the very strong protection afforded to its aspects, the right not to be separated and the right to reunification, by the Convention. The CRC notes that states parties have a mandatory obligation not to separate a child from his or her parents against their will unless this is necessary for the child's best interests.[34] It goes on to require of states that they deal with family reunion applications by a child or his or her parents "in a positive, humane and expeditious manner".[35] These broad stipulations do not specify which parties provide the base, and which reunify. They thus cover not only the common situation in which children join parents who migrated before them, usually a right qualified by the ability to support and accommodate the child at a certain level and earned by parents following law-abiding residence in the destination state. The CRC right also includes the opposite possibility—reunion of parents travelling to join a child who migrated first. This is important. Most domestic laws exclude this possibility, and indeed there is considerable suspicion of so-called "anchor children" sent off as front runners to secure a foothold before the rest of the family follows. Traditionally, family reunion in immigration law is a unidirectional principle that assumes the movement of child to parent, not parent to child. As a general rule, despite the mandatory phrasing of CRC Art. 9 and Art. 3 and 12, legislation has not been put in place to ensure that children with citizenship or legal immigration status have the right to bring their parents or other relatives to join them. In the United States, for example, even children who are granted the 'Special Immigrant Juvenile Status', a visa created to provide a permanent legal status for children found to have been 'abused, abandoned or neglected' can never exercise family reunion rights. The idea that a child could provide the base around which his or her family later gathers is considered as illegitimate, as was once the situation of men to follow their wives or fiancées (see the case of ACB v. United Kingdom).[36] Yet the CRC clearly envisages the possibility of such situations, and ratifying states have an obligation to allow them as they arise. At present, however, such possibilities are not reflected in law and policy. Children can only bring their parents to join them once they become adults themselves and establish the parents' dependency on them. Independent child migrants are thus deprived of the nuclear family reunification entitlements that other migrant workers enjoy.

(ii) The Convention for the Protection of the Rights of Migrant Workers and Their Families (CPRMW)

This Convention, much less comprehensively ratified and therefore in practice much less significant as a policy instrument than the CRC, provides a comprehensive protective framework for migrant workers. It is a remarkably inclusive document, which encompasses undocumented and irregular workers as much as regular legal ones in most of its provisions. Migrant workers irrespective of their status have a right to fair and public court hearings, to protection from collective expulsion, and to equal treatment regarding employment terms and conditions. In particular: "States Parties shall take all appropriate measures to ensure that migrant workers are not deprived of any rights derived from [the principle of equality] by reason of any irregularity in their stay or employment."[37] The Convention reinforces the inclusive rights to emergency health care (but not education) set out in other instruments.

Two aspects of the CPRMW are relevant for the present discussion. First, the Convention adopts an age-neutral definition of migrant worker and establishes a comprehensive principle of equality regarding the group as a whole. Unlike the CRC which focuses on child labour and child work with the goal of preventing abuse, exploitation and the curtailment of other rights (e.g. to education and health), the CPRMW covers the rights of all child migrant workers on a par with adults (though the rights of trainees and students are excluded). It is left to states to determine the minimum age of employment and other matters regarding conditions of work, within the rights respecting parameters defined by the Convention.

Second, and by contrast, the Convention's definition of family members reflects the traditional view of migrants as adults. As a result the enumerated relationships are the spouse and the children; not parents or siblings. The definition does include 'other dependent persons who are recognized as members of the family' by domestic legislation, but this breaks no new ground in advancing the family unity rights of independent child migrants or in facilitating their ability to migrate autonomously and eventually bring relatives to join them. The only explicit mention of child migrants' rights in the Convention covers the situation where criminal charges are brought against juveniles.[38] In the light of international standards, the Convention requires states parties to separate juvenile from adult offenders,[39] to treat them appropriately taking into account their age and promote rehabilitation where possible.[40]

2. LABOUR LAW

Labour law provides a different legal framework for child migrants, based on their activity rather than their status. It takes as its starting point the reality of child labour. The International Labour Organization (ILO), which has been at the forefront of labour rights legislation and standard setting since the early twentieth century, operates quite differently in relation to its mandate from the

Committee on the Rights of the Child. Its role is regulatory and its conventions do not have the force of law, though they may and frequently do provide the framework for subsequent legislation. The institutional and legislative separation between human rights and labour rights has not served migrant child workers particularly well; the implementation strategies for the labour provisions are underdeveloped and as a result many of the most relevant provisions lack effective practical impact.

Most of the general provisions promulgated by the organization apply incidentally to child migrant workers as they do to the workforce as a whole. Like international human rights law discussed earlier, international labour law establishes the right of all migrant workers, including those in an irregular immigration status, to fair working conditions and pay. For example, the ILO 1975 Migrant Workers Convention requires states parties to ensure "equality of treatment" for irregular migrant workers who face expulsion "in respect of rights arising out of past employment as regards remuneration, social security and other benefits".[41] If the migrant worker has been employed in an ostensibly regular context and has made contributions to the social security system, both the CPRMW and the ILO Migrant Workers Convention (as well as the ICESCR and the CRC in the case of the child[42]) protect his or her right to receive social security payments without discrimination.

Of particular relevance to the situation of independent child migrants are ILO conventions on forced labour and on child labour. The former include the Convention on Forced Labour[43] and the Abolition of Forced Labour Convention.[44] They call on all states to suppress forced or compulsory labour, which is defined as "all work or service which is exacted from any person under the menace of any penalty, and for which the said person has not offered himself voluntarily". Many independent child migrants may fit this definition. For example, children such as the Chinese children (quoted earlier) who have to work to repay a smuggling debt are frequently threatened with severe sanctions against themselves or their families if they fall behind in their payments.[45] Establishing the voluntariness of their agreement to work may also be complicated: in the absence of good employment options or other means of livelihood, many child migrants 'voluntarily' agree to highly exploitative working conditions.[46] The regulation and prohibition of these employment situations may work against the medium and long term interests of independent child migrants unless prohibiting states set in place alternatives for them other than expulsion or repatriation. Child rights, migrants' rights and labour rights organizations need to establish common guidelines and standards as a basis for government policies.

The ILO has taken the lead internationally in formulating policy on child labour. The Minimum Age Convention[47] and the Convention on the Worst Forms of Child Labour[48] address the situation of all children, including migrant children. The Minimum Age Convention requires member states to "ensure the effective abolition of child labour" and to progressively raise the age for admission to employment.[49] The Convention establishes 15 as the minimum age for employment, except for potentially hazardous work where the minimum age is set at 18,[50] or for 'light' work not likely to be harmful to health or prejudicial to school attendance.[51] Much of the work performed by independent child migrants falls within the categories envisaged. But implementation is weak and children's alternatives are often non-existent. As a result the impact of labour law regulation on the working lives of child migrants is generally minimal.

MIGRATING FOR SURVIVAL

UNHCR data suggests that between 4 per cent and 5 per cent of all asylum applications received by industrialized countries come from unaccompanied minors. Conversely, given the paucity of immigration statuses available to independent child migrants, many are encouraged to apply for asylum. The refugee protection system, however, is anything but a panacea for independent child migrants. Many child asylum applicants receive some form of protection during their minority—humanitarian leave, temporary permission to remain, discretionary status. Long term permanent legal status, however, is far less common. Moreover, procedural problems undermine the efficacy of the rules in place. In general, securing a valid legal status is dependent on the child having access to effective mentorship and legal representation, which is frequently not the case. In the absence of this support, children frequently give up rights to challenge the refusal of status (e.g. many child migrants in the United States agree to sign 'voluntary departure' forms presented with the alternative of long-term detention).

Children are also beset with other problems which make the available remedies less accessible or effective than claimed. A pervasive climate of disbelief, reflected in the proliferation of age disputed cases, detention of children and rejection of children's testimony affects child migrants in many sectors of the migration system. Ignorance by child welfare or social work officials of the intricacies of immigration law contributes to the absence of competent representation. As a result a substantial number of unaccompanied child migrants end up undocumented, in temporary and unsatisfactory statuses where their future rights cannot be assured.

Within the options available, asylum is perhaps the most familiar protection outcome for unaccompanied minors, not because it is easily secured, but because it corresponds to the protection required of all states parties to the 1951 Refugee Convention (as modified by the 1967 Protocol). However, many difficulties are faced by children attempting to secure asylum over and above the access, guardianship and legal representation issues already raised. A central concern is the persistent failure of immigration officials and decision makers to effectively apply the refugee definition to children. This is the case both where children face similar harms to those faced by adults—such as political persecution or religious persecution—and where children face 'child-specific' forms of persecution. Whereas the United States has promulgated specific guidelines concerning children's asylum applications, it has not fostered the development of a consistent body of decision-making which incorporates some of the recommendations in the guidelines. A comprehensive doctrine of child-specific persecution which complements the broader, more generic concept is necessary to correct the prevailing blindness towards the special problems facing children. At the same time, it is important to note that in the United States there have been some significant improvements in the application of refugee law to children in some specific cases. For example, sexual violence inflicted on a girl by her father has counted as the basis for an asylum claim, as has female circumcision, persecution as a street child and child abuse. In this respect the United States provides some laudable examples of good practice, which other countries could do well to emulate. Australia, by contrast, has not produced any child-specific asylum guidelines and case law expanding the refugee concept to child-specific situations is still in its infancy, despite the large number of Afghani child asylum seekers fleeing the Taliban that have been processed through the Australian system.

MIGRATING FOR EXPLOITATION

States have developed other statuses for according protection to migrant children. Many states have instituted special anti-trafficking statutes for victims of trafficking including children. The main purpose of these measures is to criminalize the commercial networks involved in trafficking, but an important secondary goal is to provide protections for those who are trafficked and to establish that they are not prosecuted or penalized for their irregular entry. The United States law has created a special 'T Visa' which is available to victims of severe forms of trafficking in persons; children under 18 can benefit from this status and in theory they do not need to cooperate with law enforcement investigations by giving evidence against their traffickers. In practice, however, certification of a child as a victim of trafficking has come to depend on confirmation from law enforcement agencies of the child's involvement, a practice which has deterred some children from applying for the visa for fear of retaliation. Moreover the burden of proof on the child is very high. As a result only a tiny number of children have received 'T visas' (32 unaccompanied children between October 2001 and January 2005!).[52]

In Australia, a special visa subclass for trafficked persons—Class UM and Class DH visas—has been created to provide protection for victims; initially limited to a temporary stay of two years, the visa can be extended to a permanent stay if the need for protection is ongoing. Children are eligible for this visa but they must cooperate in the prosecution of their trafficker, as a matter of law. This is an unfortunate requirement which places law enforcement above protection and acts as a deterrent for child victims. Numbers of child victim beneficiaries of these visas are negligible.

CONCLUSION

As presently constituted, the legislative framework applicable to the situation of independent child migrants suffers from two significant defects. It is radically incomplete, because it fails to cover the circumstances of most independent child migrants; and it is dramatically ineffective, because even where binding obligations or legal requirements exist, their implementation is erratic, left to the vagaries of under-funded and ill-equipped legal services. The real challenge is to generate political will to address a series of acute challenges facing a population that has no vote, no effective voice, and scanty political or economic clout. Employment pressures and demographic considerations, which rely on children's energy and agency, may be the best allies for this constituency in the future.

ENDNOTES

1. Thomas Hammarberg, Commissioner for Human Rights, Council of Europe, presentation, March 2007

2. Trafficking Protocol, Art. 3.

3. David Thronson, 'Choiceless Choices: Deportation and the Parent-Child Relationship', 6(3) Nevada Law Journal 2006, 1181.

4. Council Directive 2003/86/EC of 22 September 2003 on the right to family reunification, OJ L251, Art. 1(d).

5. Art. 2 non-discrimination on any ground including social or national original or any other status; 3, 12, and 1 and 2 Art 9, 10, 22 and 37.

6. UK Refugee Council Panel of Advisers for Unaccompanied Refugee Children established in 1994; Canadian Immigration and Refugee Board: 'Child Refugee Claimants: Procedural and Evidentiary Issues' 1996; US Guidelines for Children's Asylum Claims, 1998.

7. See for example European Network of Experts on Fundamental Rights, Thematic Comment on Children in the EU, section on child migrants.

8. UN Committee on the Rights of the Child, General Comment No. 6.

9. See for example Code of Conduct for the Protection of Children from Sexual Exploitation and Tourism, www. thecode.org/; Statement of Good Practice, Separated Children in Europe Programme, www. separated-children-europe-programme.org/ separated_children/good_practice.

10. For example, Human Rights Watch, United States—Detained and Deprived of Rights: Children in the Custody of the U.S. Immigration and Naturalization Service, December 1998 vol. 10 No. 4 (G); Amnesty International, Most Vulnerable of All: The Treatment of Unaccompanied Children in the UK, 1999.

11. UNHCR, Policy on Refugee Children, 1993, E/SCP/82; UNHCR, Refugee Children: Guidelines on Protection and Care (1994); UNHCR, Guidelines on Policies and Procedures in Dealing with Unaccompanied Children Seeking Asylum (February 1997).

12. Convention on the Rights of the Child (CRC), Art. 3(1).

13. CRC, art 12(1) and (2).

14. According to a recent UK study, 45 per cent of all those who claim asylum as children in the UK are age disputed by the Home Office and treated as adults. Heaven Crawley, When is a Child not a Child?, ILPA 2007.

15. This category should also logically include the 30,000 trans-national adoptee who migrate across borders each year for family reunion purposes. However they are not included in this analysis.

16. *Human Rights Watch*, Nowhere to Turn: State Abuses of Unaccompanied Migrant Children by Spain and Morocco, *Vol. 14, No. 4(D), May 2002.*

17. Interviews conducted by Celeste Froehlich in New York, December 2000, unpublished on file with the author.

18. CRC Art. 1.

19. ICCPR Art. 13.

20. UDHR Art. 1.

21. ICCPR Art. 12(2) and (3).

22. ICESCR Art. 4.

23. CRC Art. 32.

24. CRC Art. 27.

25. ICESCR Art. 12.

26. CPRMW Art. 28.

27. CRC Art. 24.

28. ICESCR Art. 13.

29. MSF Personal Communication, April 2007.

30. Committee on the Rights of the Child, General Comment No. 6, Treatment of Unaccompanied and Separated Children Outside their Country of Origin, CRC/GC/2005/6(2005).

31. GC 6, para 1.

32. GC 6, para 12.

33. GC No. 6, para 20.

34. CRC Art. 9.

35. CRC Art. 10(1).

36. 'Abdulaziz, Cabales, and Balkandali v. United Kingdom', European Court of Human Rights, Application no. 9214/80; 9473/81, 9474/81, 28 May 1985.

37. CPRMW Art. 25 (3).

38. CPRMW Art. 17, 18.

39. Art. 17(4).

40. Art. 18(4).

41. Art. 9(1).

42. See CRC Art. 26.

43. C 29, 1930.

44. C 105, 1957.

45. Jacqueline Bhabha, Frying Pan to the Fire, Gao Yun, Chinese Migrants and Forced Labour in Europe, ILO Research paper, July 2004.

46. Jacqueline Bhabha, *Boston Review* article.

47. C 138, 1973.

48. C 182, 1999.

49. C 138, Art. 1.

50. C 138, Art. 3.

51. C 138, Art. 7.

52. Seeking Asylum Alone, Comparative Report, 185.

*Jacqueline **Bhabha** is Jeremiah Smith, Jr., Lecturer on Law at Harvard Law School, director of research at Harvard's Francois-Xavier Bagnoud Center for Health and Human Rights, and adjunct lecturer on public policy at the Harvard Kennedy School.

Bhabha, Jacqueline. "Independent Children, Inconsistent Adults: International Child Migration and the Legal Framework." *Innocenti Discussion Paper No. IDP 2008-02*. Florence: UNICEF Innocenti Research Centre, 2008.

Used by permission.

General Recommendation No. 26 on Women Migrant Workers[1]

by *The United Nations Committee on the Elimination of Discrimination Against Women**

INTRODUCTION

1. The Committee on the Elimination of Discrimination against Women (the Committee), affirming that migrant women, like all women, should not be discriminated against in any sphere of their life, decided at its thirty-second session (January 2005), pursuant to article 21 of the Convention on the Elimination of All Forms of Discrimination against Women (the Convention), to issue a general recommendation on some categories of women migrant workers who may be at risk of abuse and discrimination.[2]

2. This general recommendation intends to contribute to the fulfilment of the obligations of States parties to respect, protect and fulfil the human rights of women migrant workers, alongside the legal obligations contained in other treaties, the commitments made under the plans of action of world conferences and the important work of migration-focused treaty bodies, especially the Committee on the Protection of the Rights of All Migrant Workers and Members of their Families.[3] While the Committee notes that the International Convention on the Protection of the Rights of All Migrant Workers and Members of Their Families protects individuals, including migrant women, on the basis of their migration status, the Convention on the Elimination of All Forms of Discrimination against Women protects all women, including migrant women, against sex- and gender-based discrimination. While migration presents new opportunities for women and may be a means for their economic empowerment through wider participation, it may also place their human rights and security at risk. Hence, this general recommendation aims to elaborate the circumstances that contribute to the specific vulnerability of many women migrant workers and their experiences of sex- and gender-based discrimination as a cause and consequence of the violations of their human rights.

3. While States are entitled to control their borders and regulate

migration, they must do so in full compliance with their obligations as parties to the human rights treaties they have ratified or acceded to. That includes the promotion of safe migration procedures and the obligation to respect, protect and fulfil the human rights of women throughout the migration cycle. Those obligations must be undertaken in recognition of the social and economic contributions of women migrant workers to their own countries and countries of destination, including through caregiving and domestic work.

4. The Committee recognizes that migrant women may be classified into various categories relating to the factors compelling migration, the purposes of migration and accompanying tenure of stay, the vulnerability to risk and abuse, and their status in the country to which they have migrated, and their eligibility for citizenship. The Committee also recognizes that these categories remain fluid and overlapping, and that therefore it is sometimes difficult to draw clear distinctions between the various categories. Thus, the scope of this general recommendation is limited to addressing the situations of the following categories of migrant women who, as workers, are in low-paid jobs, may be at high risk of abuse and discrimination and who may never acquire eligibility for permanent stay or citizenship, unlike professional migrant workers in the country of employment. As such, in many cases, they may not enjoy the protection of the law of the countries concerned, at either de jure or de facto levels. These categories of migrant women are:[4] (a) Women migrant workers who migrate independently; (b) Women migrant workers who join their spouses or other members of their families who are also workers; (c) Undocumented[5] women migrant workers who may fall into any of the above categories.

The Committee, however, emphasizes that all categories of women migrants fall within the scope of the obligations of States parties to the Convention and must be protected against all forms of discrimination by the Convention.

5. Although both men and women migrate, migration is not a gender-neutral phenomenon. The position of female migrants is different from that of male migrants in terms of legal migration channels, the sectors into which they migrate, the forms of abuse they suffer and the consequences thereof. To understand the specific ways in which women are impacted, female migration should be studied from the perspective of gender inequality, traditional female roles, a gendered

labour market, the universal prevalence of gender-based violence and the worldwide feminization of poverty and labour migration. The integration of a gender perspective is, therefore, essential to the analysis of the position of female migrants and the development of policies to counter discrimination exploitation and abuse.

APPLYING PRINCIPLES OF HUMAN RIGHTS AND GENDER EQUALITY

6. All women migrant workers are entitled to the protection of their human rights, which include the right to life, the right to personal liberty and security, the right not to be tortured, the right to be free of degrading and inhumane treatment, the right to be free from discrimination on the basis of sex, race, ethnicity, cultural particularities, nationality, language, religion or other status, the right to be free from poverty, the right to an adequate standard of living, the right to equality before the law and the right to benefit from the due processes of the law. These rights are provided for in the Universal Declaration of Human Rights and the many human rights treaties ratified or acceded to by States Members of the United Nations.

7. Women migrant workers are also entitled to protection from discrimination on the basis of the Convention, which requires States parties to take all appropriate measures without delay to eliminate all forms of discrimination against women and to ensure that they will be able to exercise and enjoy de jure and de facto rights on an equal basis with men in all fields.

FACTORS INFLUENCING WOMEN'S MIGRATION

8. Women currently make up about one half of the world's migrant population. Various factors, such as globalization, the wish to seek new opportunities, poverty, gendered cultural practices and gender-based violence in countries of origin, natural disasters or wars and internal military conflicts determine women's migration. These factors also include the exacerbation of sex-specific divisions of labour in the formal and informal manufacturing and service sectors in countries of destination, as well as a male-centred culture of entertainment, the latter creating a demand for women as entertainers. A significant increase in the number of women migrating alone as wage earners has been widely noted as part of this trend.

Sex- and Gender-Based Human Rights Concerns Related to Migrant Women

9. Because violations of the human rights of women migrant workers occur in countries of origin, countries of transit and countries of destination, this general recommendation will address all three situations in order to facilitate the use of the Convention, further the rights of women migrant workers and advance substantive equality of women and men in all spheres of their lives. It is also recalled that migration is an inherently global phenomenon, requiring cooperation among States in multilateral, bilateral and regional levels.

In Countries of Origin Before Departure[6]

10. Even before they leave home, women migrant workers face myriad human rights concerns, including complete bans or restrictions on women's out-migration based on sex or sex combined with age, marital status, pregnancy or maternity status, occupation-specific restrictions or requirements that women must have written permission from male relatives to obtain a passport to travel or migrate. Women are sometimes detained by recruiting agents for training in preparation for departure, during which time they may be subject to financial, physical, sexual or psychological abuse. Women may also suffer the consequences of restricted access to education, training and reliable information on migration, which may lead to increased vulnerability in relation to employers. Exploitative fees may be charged by employment agents, which sometimes cause women, who generally have fewer assets than men, to suffer greater financial hardships and make them more dependent, for example, if they need to borrow from family, friends, or moneylenders at usurious rates.

In Countries of Origin upon Return

11. Women migrant workers may face sex- and gender-based discrimination, including compulsory HIV and AIDS testing for women returnees, moral "rehabilitation" for young women returnees and increased personal and social costs compared to men, without adequate gender-responsive services. For example, men may return to a stable family situation, whereas women may find disintegration of the family upon their return, with their absence from home regarded as the cause of such disintegration. There may also be a lack of protection against reprisals from exploitative recruiting agents.

In Countries of Transit

12. Women migrant workers may face a variety of human rights concerns when transiting through foreign countries. When travelling with an agent or escort, women migrants may be abandoned if the agent encounters problems in transit or upon arrival in the country of destination. Women are also vulnerable to sexual and physical abuse by agents and escorts when travelling in countries of transit.

In Countries of Destination

13. Once they reach their destinations, women migrant workers may encounter multiple forms of de jure and de facto discrimination. There are countries whose Governments sometimes impose restrictions or bans on women's employment in particular sectors. Whatever the situation, women migrant workers face additional hazards compared to men because of gender-insensitive environments that do not allow mobility for women, and that give them little access to relevant information about their rights and entitlements. Gendered notions of appropriate work for women result in job opportunities that reflect familial and service functions ascribed to women or that are in the informal sector. Under such circumstances, occupations in which women dominate are, in particular, domestic work or certain forms of entertainment.

14. In addition, in countries of destination, such occupations may be excluded from legal definitions of work, thereby depriving women of a variety of legal protections. In such occupations, women migrant workers have trouble obtaining binding contracts concerning terms and conditions of work, causing them sometimes to work for long hours without overtime payment. Moreover, women migrant workers often experience intersecting forms of discrimination, suffering not only sex- and gender-based discrimination, but also xenophobia and racism. Discrimination based on race, ethnicity, cultural particularities, nationality, language, religion or other status may be expressed in sex- and gender-specific ways.

15. Because of discrimination on the basis of sex and gender, women migrant workers may receive lower wages than do men, or experience non-payment of wages, payments that are delayed until departure, or transfer of wages into accounts that are inaccessible to them. For example, employers of domestic workers often deposit the worker's wages into an account in the employer's name. If a woman and her spouse both have worker status, her wages may be paid into an account in the name of her spouse. Workers in female-dominated sectors may not be paid for weekly

days of rest or national holidays. Or, if they are heavily burdened by debt from recruitment fees, women migrant workers may not be able to leave abusive situations since they have no other way to repay those debts. Such violations may of course be faced by non-migrant local women in similar female-dominated jobs. However, non-migrant local women have better job mobility. They have the choice, however limited, of leaving an oppressive job situation and obtaining another job, whereas, in some countries, a woman migrant worker may become undocumented the minute she leaves her job. Non-migrant local women workers may, more-over, have some economic protection by way of family support if they are unemployed, but women migrant workers may not have such protection. Women migrant workers thus face hazards on the basis of sex and gender, as well as on the basis of their migrant status.

16. Women migrant workers may be unable to save or transmit savings safely through regular channels due to isolation (for domestic workers), cumbersome procedures, language barriers, or high transaction costs. This is a great problem since in general they earn less than men. Women may further face familial obligations to remit all their earnings to their families to a degree that may not be expected of men. For example, single women may be expected to support even extended family members at home.

17. Women migrant workers often suffer from inequalities that threaten their health. They may be unable to access health services, including re-productive health services, because insurance or national health schemes are not available to them, or they may have to pay unaffordable fees. As women have health needs different from those of men, this aspect requires special attention. They may also suffer from a lack of arrange-ments for their safety at work, or provisions for safe travel between the worksite and their place of accommodation. Where accommodation is provided, especially in female-dominated occupations such as factory, farm or domestic work, living conditions may be poor and overcrowded, without running water or adequate sanitary facilities, or they may lack privacy and hygiene. Women migrant workers are sometimes subjected to sex-discriminatory mandatory HIV/AIDS testing or testing for other infections without their consent, followed by provision of test results to agents and employers rather than to the worker herself. This may result in loss of job or deportation if test results are positive.

18. Discrimination may be especially acute in relation to pregnancy. Women migrant workers may face mandatory pregnancy tests followed

by deportation if the test is positive; coercive abortion or lack of access to safe reproductive health and abortion services, when the health of the mother is at risk, or even following sexual assault; absence of, or inadequate, maternity leave and benefits and absence of affordable obstetric care, resulting in serious health risks. Women migrant workers may also face dismissal from employment upon detection of pregnancy, sometimes resulting in irregular immigration status and deportation.

19. Women migrant workers may be subjected to particularly disadvantageous terms regarding their stay in a country. They are sometimes unable to benefit from family reunification schemes, which may not extend to workers in female-dominated sectors, such as domestic workers or those in entertainment. Permission to stay in the country of employment may be severely restricted, especially for women migrant workers in domestic work when their time-fixed contracts end or are terminated at the whim of the employer. If they lose their immigration status, they may be more vulnerable to violence by the employer or others who want to abuse the situation. If they are detained, they may be subject to violence perpetrated by officials in detention centres.

20. Women migrant workers are more vulnerable to sexual abuse, sexual harassment and physical violence, especially in sectors where women predominate. Domestic workers are particularly vulnerable to physical and sexual assault, food and sleep deprivation and cruelty by their employers. Sexual harassment of women migrant workers in other work environments, such as on farms or in the industrial sector, is a problem worldwide (see E/CN.4/1998/74/Add.1). Women migrant workers who migrate as spouses of male migrant workers or along with family members face an added risk of domestic violence from their spouses or relatives if they come from a culture that values the submissive role of the women in the family.

21. Access to justice may be limited for women migrant workers. In some countries, restrictions are imposed on the use of the legal system by women migrant workers to obtain remedies for discriminatory labour standards, employment discrimination or sex- and gender-based violence. Further, women migrant workers may not be eligible for free government legal aid, and there may be other impediments, such as unresponsive and hostile officials and, at times, collusion between officials and the perpetrator. In some cases, diplomats have perpetrated sexual abuse, violence and other forms of discrimination against women migrant domestic workers while enjoying diplomatic immunity. In some countries, there

are gaps in the laws protecting migrant women workers. For example, they may lose their work permits once they make a report of abuse or discrimination and then they cannot afford to remain in the country for the duration of the trial, if any. In addition to these formal barriers, practical barriers may prevent access to remedies. Many do not know the language of the country and do not know their rights. Women migrant workers may lack mobility because they may be confined by employers to their work or living sites, prohibited from using telephones or banned from joining groups or cultural associations. They often lack knowledge of their embassies or of services available, due to their dependence on employers or spouses for such information. For example, it is very difficult for women migrant domestic workers who are scarcely ever out of sight of their employers to even register with their embassies or file complaints. As such, women may have no outside contacts and no means of making a complaint, and they may suffer violence and abuse for long periods of time before the situation is exposed. In addition, the withholding of passports by employers or the fear of reprisal if the women migrant worker is engaged in sectors that are linked to criminal networks prevent them from making a report.

22. Undocumented women migrant workers are particularly vulnerable to exploitation and abuse because of their irregular immigration status, which exacerbates their exclusion and the risk of exploitation. They may be exploited as forced labour, and their access to minimum labour rights may be limited by fear of denouncement. They may also face harassment by the police. If they are apprehended, they are usually prosecuted for violations of immigration laws and placed in detention centres, where they are vulnerable to sexual abuse, and then deported.

RECOMMENDATIONS TO STATES PARTIES[7]

Common Responsibilities of Countries of Origin and Destination

23. Common responsibilities of countries of origin and destination include:
(a) Formulating a comprehensive gender-sensitive and rights-based policy: States parties should use the Convention and the general recommendations to formulate a gender-sensitive, rights-based policy on the basis of equality and non-discrimination to regulate and administer all aspects and stages of migration, to facilitate access of women migrant workers to work opportunities abroad, promoting safe migration and ensuring the protection of the rights of women migrant workers (articles 2 (a) and 3);

(b) Active involvement of women migrant workers and relevant non-governmental organizations: States parties should seek the active involvement of women migrant workers and relevant non-governmental organizations in policy formulation, implementation, monitoring and evaluation (article 7 (b));

(c) Research, data collection and analysis: States parties should conduct and support quantitative and qualitative research, data collection and analysis to identify the problems and needs faced by women migrant workers in every phase of the migration process in order to promote the rights of women migrant workers and formulate relevant policies (article 3).

Responsibilities Specific to Countries of Origin

24. Countries of origin must respect and protect the human rights of their female nationals who migrate for purposes of work. Measures that may be required include, but are not limited to, the following:

(a) Lifting of discriminatory bans or restrictions on migration: States parties should repeal sex-specific bans and discriminatory restrictions on women's migration on the basis of age, marital status, pregnancy or maternity status. They should lift restrictions that require women to get permission from their spouse or male guardian to obtain a passport or to travel (article 2 (f));

(b) Education, awareness-raising and training with standardized content: States parties should develop an appropriate education and awareness-raising programme in close consultation with concerned non-governmental organizations, gender and migration specialists, women workers with migration experience and reliable recruiting agencies. In that regard, States parties should (articles 3, 5, 10 and 14):

(i) Deliver or facilitate free or affordable gender- and rights-based pre-departure information and training programmes that raise prospective women migrant workers' awareness of potential exploitation, including: recommended contents of labour contracts, legal rights and entitlements in countries of employment, procedures for invoking formal and informal redress mechanisms, processes by which to obtain information about employers, cultural conditions in countries of destination, stress management, first aid and emergency measures, including emergency telephone numbers of home embassy, and services; information about safety in transit, including airport and airline orientations and information on general and reproductive health, including HIV/AIDS prevention. Such training programmes should be targeted to women who are prospective migrant workers through an effective outreach programme and held in decentralized training venues so that they are accessible to women;

(ii) Provide a list of authentic, reliable recruitment agencies and create a unified information system on available jobs abroad;

(iii) Provide information on methods and procedures for migrating to work for women workers who wish to migrate independently of recruitment agencies;

(iv) Require recruitment agencies to participate in awareness-raising and training programmes and sensitize them on the rights of women migrant workers, the forms of sex- and gender-based discrimination, the exploitation women could experience and responsibilities of agencies towards the women;

(v) Promote community awareness-raising concerning the costs and benefits of all forms of migration for women and conduct cross-cultural awareness- raising activities addressed to the general public, which should highlight the risks, dangers and opportunities of migration, the entitlement of women to their earnings in the interest of ensuring their financial security and the need to maintain a balance between women's familial responsibility and their responsibility to themselves. Such an awareness-raising programme could be carried out through formal and informal educational programmes;

(vi) Encourage the media, information and communication sectors to contribute to awareness-raising on migration issues, including on the contributions women migrant workers make to the economy, women's vulnerability to exploitation and discrimination and the various sites at which such exploitation occurs;

(c) Regulations and monitoring systems, as follows:

(i) States parties should adopt regulations and design monitoring systems to ensure that recruiting agents and employment agencies respect the rights of all women migrant workers. States parties should include in their legislation a comprehensive definition of irregular recruitment along with a provision on legal sanctions for breaches of the law by recruitment agencies (article 2 (e));

(ii) States parties should also implement accreditation programmes to ensure good practices among recruitment agencies (article 2 (e));

(d) Health services: States parties should ensure the provision of standardized and authentic health certificates if required by countries of destination and require prospective employers to purchase medical insurance for women migrant workers. All required pre-departure HIV/AIDS testing or pre-departure health examinations must be respectful of the human rights of women migrants. Special attention should be paid to voluntariness, the provision of free or affordable services and to the problems of stigmatization (articles 2 (f) and 12);

(e) Travel documents: States parties should ensure that women have equal and independent access to travel documents (article 2 (d));

(f) Legal and administrative assistance: States parties should ensure the availability of legal assistance in connection with migration for work. For example, legal reviews should be available to ensure that work contracts are valid and protect women's rights on a basis of equality with men (articles 3 and 11);

(g) Safeguarding remittances of income: States parties should establish measures to safeguard the remittances of women migrant workers and provide information and assistance to women to access formal financial institutions to send money home and to encourage them to participate in savings schemes (articles 3 and 11);

(h) Facilitating the right to return: States parties should ensure that women who wish to return to their countries of origin are able to do so free of coercion and abuse (article 3);

(i) Services to women upon return: States parties should design or oversee comprehensive socio-economic, psychological and legal services aimed at facilitating the reintegration of women who have returned. They should monitor service providers to ensure that they do not take advantage of the vulnerable position of women returning from work abroad, and should have complaint mechanisms to protect the women against reprisals by recruiters, employers or former spouses (articles 2 (c) and 3);

(j) Diplomatic and consular protection: States parties must properly train and supervise their diplomatic and consular staff to ensure that they fulfil their role in protecting the rights of women migrant workers abroad. Such protection should include quality support services available to women migrants, including timely provision of interpreters, medical care, counselling, legal aid and shelter when needed. Where States parties have specific obligations under customary international law or treaties such as the Vienna Convention on Consular Relations, those obligations must be carried out in full in relation to women migrant workers (article 3).

Responsibilities Specific to Countries of Transit

25. States parties through which migrant women travel should take all appropriate steps to ensure that their territories are not used to facilitate the violation of the rights of women migrant workers. Measures that may be required include, but are not limited to, the following:

(a) Training, monitoring and supervision of Government agents: States parties should ensure that their border police and immigration officials are adequately trained, supervised and monitored for gender-sensitivity and non-discriminatory practices when dealing with women migrants (article 2 (d));

(b) Protection against violations of migrant women workers' rights that take place under their jurisdiction: States parties should take active measures to prevent, prosecute and punish all migration-related human rights violations that occur under their jurisdiction, whether perpetrated by public authorities or private actors. States parties should provide or facilitate services and assistance in situations where women travelling with an agent or escort have been abandoned, make all attempts to trace perpetrators and take legal action against them (articles 2 (c) and (e));

Responsibilities Specific to Countries of Destination

26. States parties in countries where migrant women work should take all appropriate measures to ensure non-discrimination and the equal rights of women migrant workers, including in their own communities. Measures that may be required include, but are not limited to, the following:

(a) Lifting of discriminatory bans or restrictions on immigration: States parties should repeal outright bans and discriminatory restrictions on women's immigration. They should ensure that their visa schemes do not indirectly discriminate against women by restricting permission to women migrant workers to be employed in certain job categories where men predominate, or by excluding certain female-dominated occupations from visa schemes. Further, they should lift bans that prohibit women migrant workers from getting married to nationals or permanent residents, becoming pregnant or securing independent housing (article 2 (f));

(b) Legal protection for the rights of women migrant workers: States parties should ensure that constitutional and civil law and labour codes provide to women migrant workers the same rights and protection that are extended to all workers in the country, including the right to organize and freely associate. They should ensure that contracts for women migrant workers are legally valid. In particular, they should ensure that occupations dominated by women migrant workers, such as domestic work and some forms of entertainment, are protected by labour laws, including wage and hour regulations, health and safety codes and holiday and vacation leave regulations. The laws should include mechanisms for monitoring workplace conditions of migrant women, especially in the kinds of jobs where they dominate (articles 2 (a), (f) and 11);

(c) Access to remedies: States parties should ensure that women migrant workers have the ability to access remedies when their rights are violated. Specific measures include, but are not limited to, the following (articles 2 (c), (f) and 3):

(i) Promulgate and enforce laws and regulations that include adequate legal remedies and complaints mechanisms, and put in place easily accessible dispute resolution mechanisms, protecting both documented and undocumented women migrant workers from discrimination or sex-based exploitation and abuse;

(ii) Repeal or amend laws that prevent women migrant workers from using the courts and other systems of redress. These include laws on loss of work permit, which results in loss of earnings and possible deportation by immigration authorities when a worker files a complaint of exploitation or abuse and while pending investigation. States parties should introduce flexibility into the process of changing employers or sponsors without deportation in cases where workers complain of abuse;

(iii) Ensure that women migrant workers have access to legal assistance and to the courts and regulatory systems charged with enforcing labour and employment laws, including through free legal aid;

(iv) Provide temporary shelters for women migrant workers who wish to leave abusive employers, husbands or other relatives and provide facilities for safe accommodation during trial;

(d) Legal protection for the freedom of movement: States parties should ensure that employers and recruiters do not confiscate or destroy travel or identity documents belonging to women migrants. States parties should also take steps to end the forced seclusion or locking in the homes of women migrant workers, especially those working in domestic service. Police officers should be trained to protect the rights of women migrant workers from such abuses (article 2 (e));

(e) Non-discriminatory family reunification schemes: States parties should ensure that family reunification schemes for migrant workers are not directly or indirectly discriminatory on the basis of sex (article 2 (f));

(f) Non-discriminatory residency regulations: when residency permits of women migrant workers are premised on the sponsorship of an employer or spouse, States parties should enact provisions relating to independent residency status. Regulations should be made to allow for the legal stay of a woman who flees her abusive employer or spouse or is fired for complaining about abuse (article 2 (f));

(g) Training and awareness-raising: States parties should provide mandatory awareness-raising programmes concerning the rights of migrant women workers and gender sensitivity training for relevant public and private recruitment agencies and employers and relevant State employees, such as criminal justice officers, border police, immigration authorities, border police and social service and health-care providers (article 3);

(h) Monitoring systems: States parties should adopt regulations and design monitoring systems to ensure that recruiting agents and employers respect the rights of all women migrant workers. States parties should closely monitor recruiting agencies and prosecute them for acts of violence, coercion, deception or exploitation (article 2 (e));

(i) Access to services: States parties should ensure that linguistically and culturally appropriate gender-sensitive services for women migrant workers are available, including language and skills training programmes, emergency shelters, health-care services, police services, recreational programmes and programmes designed especially for isolated women migrant workers, such as domestic workers and others secluded in the home, in addition to victims of domestic violence. Victims of abuse must be provided with relevant emergency and social services, regardless of their immigration status (articles 3, 5 and 12);

(j) The rights of women migrant workers in detention, whether they are documented or undocumented: States parties should ensure that women migrant workers who are in detention do not suffer discrimination or gender-based violence, and that pregnant and breastfeeding mothers as well as women in ill health have access to appropriate services. They should review, eliminate or reform laws, regulations, or policies that result in a disproportionate number of women migrant workers being detained for migration-related reasons (articles 2 (d) and 5);

(k) Social inclusion of women migrant workers: States parties should adopt policies and programmes with the aim of enabling women migrant

workers to integrate into the new society. Such efforts should be respectful of the cultural identity of women migrant workers and protective of
their human rights, in compliance with the Convention (article 5);

(l) Protection of undocumented women migrant workers: the situation
of undocumented women needs specific attention. Regardless of the lack
of immigration status of undocumented women migrant workers, States
parties have an obligation to protect their basic human rights. Undocumented women migrant workers must have access to legal remedies and
justice in cases of risk to life and of cruel and degrading treatment, or if
they are coerced into forced labour, face deprivation of fulfilment of basic
needs, including in times of health emergencies or pregnancy and maternity, or if they are abused physically or sexually by employers or others. If they are arrested or detained, the States parties must ensure that
undocumented women migrant workers receive humane treatment and
have access to due process of the law, including through free legal aid. In
that regard, States parties should repeal or amend laws and practices that
prevent undocumented women migrant workers from using the courts
and other systems of redress. If deportation cannot be avoided, States
parties need to treat each case individually, with due consideration to the
gender-related circumstances and risks of human rights violations in the
country of origin (articles 2 (c), (e) and (f));

Bilateral and Regional Cooperation

27. Measures that are required include but are not limited to the following:

(a) Bilateral and regional agreements: States parties who are sending or
receiving and transit countries should enter into bilateral or regional
agreements or memorandums of understanding protecting the rights of
women migrant workers as elaborated in this general recommendation
(article 3);

(b) Best practices and sharing of information, as follows:

(i) States parties are also encouraged to share their experience of best
practices and relevant information to promote the full protection of the
rights of women migrant workers (article 3);

(ii) States parties should cooperate on providing information on perpetrators of violations of the rights of women migrant workers. When
provided with information regarding perpetrators within their territory, States parties should take measures to investigate, prosecute
and punish them (article 2 (c)).

Recommendations Concerning Monitoring and Reporting

28. States parties should include in their reports information about the legal framework, policies and programmes they have implemented to protect the rights of women migrant workers, taking into consideration the sex- and gender-based human rights concerns listed in paragraphs 10 to 22 and guided by the recommendations given in paragraphs 23 to 27 of this general recommendation. Adequate data should be collected on the enforcement and effectiveness of laws, policies and programmes and the de facto situation of women migrant workers, so that the information in the reports is meaningful. This information should be provided under the most appropriate articles of the Convention, guided by the suggestions given against all the recommendations.

Ratification or Accession to Relevant Human Rights Treaties

29. States parties are encouraged to ratify all international instruments relevant to the protection of the human rights of migrant women workers, in particular, the International Convention on the Protection of the Rights of All Migrant Workers and Members of Their Families.

ENDNOTES

1. The Committee acknowledges the contribution of the Committee on the Protection of the Rights of All Migrant workers and Members of their Families during the preparation of this general recommendation.

2. The Committee on the Elimination of Discrimination against Women acknowledges and seeks to build on the important work on the rights of migrants completed by the other human right treaty bodies, the Special Rapporteur on the Human Rights of Migrants, the United Nations Development Fund for Women, the Division for the Advancement of Women, the Commission on the Status of Women, the General Assembly, and the Sub-Commission on the Promotion and Protection of Human Rights. The Committee also refers to its earlier general recommendations, such as general recommendation No. 9 on the gathering of statistical data on the situation of women, especially general recommendation No. 12 on violence against women, general recommendation No. 13 on equal remuneration for work of equal value, general recommendation No. 15 on the avoidance of discrimination against women in national strategies for the prevention and control of acquired immunodeficiency syndrome (AIDS), general recommendation No. 19 on violence against women and general recommendation No. 24 on women's access to health care, as well as the concluding comments made by the Committee when examining the reports of States parties.

3. Besides treaties and conventions, the following programmes and plans of action are applicable. The United Nations Vienna Declaration and Programme of Action approved at the 1993 World Conference on Human Rights (part II, paras. 33 and 35). Programme of Action of the Cairo International Conference on Population and Development (chapter X). Programme

of Action of the World Summit for Social Development (chap. 3). Beijing Declaration and Platform for Action, Fourth World Conference on Women, World Conference against Racism, Racial Discrimination, Xenophobia and Related Intolerance August-September 2001. International Labour Organization Plan of Action for Migrant Workers, 2004.

4. This general recommendation deals only with the work-related situation of women migrants. While it is a reality that in some instances women migrant workers may become victims of trafficking due to various degrees of vulnerability they face, this general recommendation will not address the circumstances relating to trafficking. The phenomenon of trafficking is complex and needs more focused attention. The Committee is of the opinion that this phenomenon can be more comprehensively addressed through article 6 of the Convention which places an obligation on States parties "to take all appropriate measures, including legislation, to suppress all forms of traffic in women and exploitation of prostitution of women". The Committee emphasizes however, that many elements of the present general recommendation are also relevant in situations where women migrants have been victims of trafficking.

5. Undocumented workers are those migrant workers who are without a valid residence or work permit. There are many circumstances under which this could have happened. For example, they may have been given false papers by unscrupulous agents or they may have entered the country with a valid work permit, but may have subsequently lost it because the employer may have arbitrarily terminated their services, or become undocumented because employers may have confiscated their passports. Sometimes workers may have extended their stay after the expiry of the work permit or entered the country without valid papers.

6. Paragraphs 10 and 11 describe some of the sex- and gender-related human rights concerns that women experience in their countries of origin, both before departure and upon return. Concerns related to transit and life abroad are discussed in paragraphs 12 to 22. These sections are illustrative and are not meant to be exhaustive. It should be noted that certain human rights concerns described here may render a woman's decision to migrate involuntarily under relevant international law; in such cases, reference should be made to those norms.

7. The articles listed for each recommendation refer to the articles of the Convention on the Elimination of All Forms of Discrimination against Women.

United Nations Committee on the Elimination of Discrimination Against Women is an expert body established in 1982, composed of 23 independent experts on women's issues from around the world. It is responsible for overseeing implementation of the United Nations Convention on the Elimination of All Forms of Discrimination Against Women.

UN Committee on the Elimination of Discrimination Against Women (CEDAW). *General Recommendation No. 26 on Women Migrant Workers*, 5 December 2008, CEDAW/C/2009/ WP.1/R, available at: http://www.unhcr.org/refworld/docid/4a54bc33d.html.

Used by permission.

Protecting the Rights of Migrant Workers: A Shared Responsibility

*by The International Labour Organization**

1. INTRODUCTION AND CONTEXT

This paper specifically focuses on countries' shared responsibility to protect migrant workers' rights. Virtually all countries are countries of origin, transit, *and* destination. Labour migration takes place between developed and developing countries and among developing countries as well, with different challenges. The term "development" as used here is much broader than economic development. It encompasses economic, social, cultural, political, and human development. In regard to migration, it refers to development in both countries of origin and destination, as well as the welfare and full development of the capabilities of migrant workers and their families.

Migration is today, as it has always been, a function of the search for greater opportunity. "Throughout human history, migration has been a courageous expression of the individual's will to overcome adversity and to live a better life."[1] As always, and in many forms, migration involves work to support oneself and one's family. It is has been estimated that in 2005, some 94 million of the world's approximately 191 million migrants were economically active. These migrant workers, with their families, accounted for almost 90 per cent of total international migrants.[2] More recent estimates suggest that the number of international migrants has reached 200 million. Almost half of those migrants are women, who are increasingly migrating on their own for purposes of work.[3]

The countries from which these workers come and those in which they work have a shared responsibility to lessen the burdens on them by protecting and promoting their rights. This can be done by increasing the supervision and regulation of international labour migration and engaging in international cooperation in the interest of promoting their rights and preventing abusive conditions.

2. THE LINKAGE BETWEEN THE RIGHTS OF MIGRANT WORKERS AND DEVELOPMENT

Development gains from migration for the countries involved and the protection of the rights of migrant workers are inseparable. Such development gains are significant not only to origin countries, but also to destination countries where migrant workers provide their labour. Migrant workers contribute to development in origin countries by, among other things, alleviating pressures on labour markets, sending remittances home, acquiring increased skills, and making investments, all of which help to alleviate poverty. In destination countries, they contribute to development by meeting the demand for workers, increasing the demand for goods and services, particularly where they receive decent wages, and contributing their entrepreneurial skills. In some of the most critical service areas for development and growth in origin and destination countries, women migrant workers predominate, for example, in nursing, domestic work, and care-giving. Protecting the rights of migrant workers has a positive effect on productivity, in that it results in fewer lost hours of work, reduces health care costs, and increases output.[4]

Protecting the rights of migrant workers additionally benefits destination countries by preventing the development of an unprotected working underclass of migrants which harms national workers by undercutting their pay and working conditions. It is in the best interests of destination countries to prevent the emergence of migrant dependent economic sectors. It is in the interests of all involved to prevent irregular migration, which is an obstacle to the development benefits of migration, as those migrant workers in irregular status are most often excluded from labour and social rights. Of course, for the migrant workers themselves, protection of human and labour rights furthers their earning capacity and personal development and that of their families in many ways.

Migrants of all skill levels are crossing international borders to work, from the professional and highly skilled to those with lesser skills and even those with little or no previous work experience or formal training. The migration of highly skilled workers can increase returns to education and contribute to the knowledge base of origin countries. For those of lesser skills, migration can provide jobs they might not be able to find in their own countries and thereby increase income for the poor and their families. Migration can be an empowering experience for the less skilled and for women from traditional societies, enabling them to contribute more to development in both countries in which they have contacts. Even though both the highly skilled and lesser skilled can benefit greatly from labour migration, the lesser skilled are not as likely to be in a position to assert their rights, including the rights to fair pay and living and working conditions. Protecting the human and labour rights of the less skilled is significant, because it has a higher potential for poverty reduction in countries of development. In parallel, migration of low-skilled workers also has a larger impact on the social and economic development of host countries. Not only low-skilled migrant workers contribute directly to the national production, but also are found in the dirty, dangerous and difficult jobs often left aside by Nationals for higher skilled occupations. For these reasons, this following discussion on the rights of migrant workers will focus more heavily on the needs of the less skilled and the shared responsibility of those countries involved in their migration to protect their rights.

3. THE SHARED RESPONSIBILITY

The three basic stages in the labour migration process are before workers leave their home countries, after they leave and while they work in destination countries, and after they return to their home countries. Migrant workers benefit when international cooperation takes place during all of these stages. Countries can cooperate by, among other things, exchanging information with each other, engaging in regular dialogue and cooperation on labour migration policy for the protection of workers' rights, and entering into bilateral, multilateral, and regional agreements. They can cooperate in locating and sanctioning those who violate the rights of migrant workers. Where possible, countries should include a role for civil society and employee and employer organizations in their cooperative efforts to manage labour migration and protect workers' rights. International cooperation in furthering development and increasing opportunities for decent work is also of great benefit to migrant workers.[5]

While origin and destination countries share the responsibility to protect the rights of migrant workers, their respective responsibilities differ for two reasons. First, different events take place during workers' migration experiences in their own countries before they leave, than take place after their departure and during their work in destination countries. Second, origin and destination countries have the ability to exercise more supervision in their own countries and much less ability to control what takes place in another. Therefore, during the first stage before migrants leave home, greater responsibility to protect their rights rests on their countries of origin. During the second stage, that is, after their arrival and while they work, greater responsibility rests on countries of destination. During the third stage when they return home, greater responsibility shifts back again to their countries of origin. Although different events are taking place in origin and destination countries that require different approaches to protection during these times, they can and should cooperate with each other in the search for the best approaches to protect migrant workers and further their rights.

Another way of considering the issue of respective responsibilities is as follows:

• The role of origin countries in protecting individuals involved in the labour migration process during the pre-departure and return stages when they are physically present, and during the post-departure and work stage when they are not physically present;

• The role of destination countries in protecting individuals involved in the labour migration process during the post-departure and work stage when they are physically present, and during the pre-departure and return stages when they are not physically present.

4. Responsibilities of Origin Countries

Pre-Departure

The time period before individuals decide to migrate for work—when they are potential migrant workers—is crucial. There are many possible pitfalls if their decision is based on insufficient or false information. Thus, the best line of defense and protection before the decision is made is to provide realistic and accurate information. It should be provided when it is most helpful, including before substantial action toward implementing the decision has been taken, such as paying recruitment fees.

Potential migrant workers should be given organized assistance in finding employment, if possible, and information about things such as costs they must pay to obtain jobs, the migration process, and actual terms and conditions of work in the destination country. There are many good practices that provide concrete examples of action being taken in these and other areas of labour migration.[6] A good example provided by the Egyptian Ministry of Manpower and Emigration is its operation of a website with a job match-making system, databases of job opportunities abroad and potential candidates, and practical information about destination countries.[7] Tunisia has a specialized government agency that assists skilled citizens in finding work in other countries.[8] In Tajikistan, an Information Resource Centre for Labour Migrants provides information to migrants on travel, documentation, admission, and employment in other countries, including the risks involved.[9]

Citizens should be thoroughly educated about unscrupulous private recruiters, traffickers and trafficking in human beings, and the dangers and risks of migrating under irregular conditions. Attention must be paid to educating and warning women about the special problems and conditions they could face because they are women, such as trafficking, and the conditions of certain forms of work held predominantly by women migrant workers, such as domestic work.

A good practice in this area is information provided to women in the Philippines by a non-government organization on how to avoid illegal recruitment and what to do if victimized.[10] Citizens should be educated as well on how to migrate under regular conditions and under conditions which protect their human rights. Both government and civil society can perform this function. They should provide information wherever private recruiters, traffickers, and smugglers search for persons to transport across borders for work, be it in cities, small towns, or the countryside. In Thailand, Cambodia, and Lao People's Democratic Republic, radio programs warning about trafficking and other migration dangers have been broadcast.[11] In Nigeria, public-awareness campaigns regarding trafficking are conducted, and anti-trafficking clubs in secondary schools warn students about precautions to take before accepting job offers in other countries.[12] The Bali Ministerial Conference on People Smuggling, Trafficking in Persons and Related Transnational Crime is a regional consultative process involving the governments of about 40 countries, which share information on trafficking and smuggling and address root causes, including the need for development in origin countries.[13]

Those who have decided to migrate must next be protected during the recruitment process itself. Victimization by unscrupulous private recruitment agents frequently leads to further abuse after individuals migrate and during their work experience. Abuses include giving them little, no, or false information about the terms and conditions of their jobs, failing to provide information about other conditions of work and life in the destination country, charging high recruitment fees to migrant workers, sending them to unsafe or dangerous jobs, jobs where they are not paid or not given their full pay, and even taking large fees from them without providing any job at all. Other abusive practices include giving migrant workers contracts which are not valid, are in a language they do not understand, or are substituted for different, less favourable contracts after they have departed. Beyond educating migrant workers about these unethical and exploitive practices, origin countries should enact legislation and regulations and enforce them to prevent such abuses from taking place and sanction those who have engaged in them. Where the rights of migrant workers have been violated, all persons involved in the chain of their recruitment and employment should be legally accountable, to prevent workers from being left without any remedy. When such persons cross national borders themselves in committing violations against migrant workers, origin countries must cooperate with transit and destination countries to put a stop to their conduct. Thus, for example, a migrant worker may be cheated by a local recruiter who represents another recruiter higher on the chain. All those working together in the chain should be held accountable, whether they operate within national borders or across them.

Origin countries should license and supervise private recruiters and sanction those who do not comply with minimum standards that protect the rights of migrant workers, including by prohibiting them from conducting business. They should require written employment contracts containing minimum standards of terms and conditions of employment for their citizens in the areas of wages, working hours and time off, safety and health, medical care, the right to retain their identity documents, and other important terms and conditions. Where employers provide housing and food, the written contracts should cover that as well and should contain minimum standards. If employers charge their workers for housing and food, the rates charged should be fair. A good example of licensing and regulation of private recruiters is provided by the Philippines Overseas Employment Administration, a specialized agency which performs this and other functions. The agency has a website with information on licensed recruiters, consulates in other countries, and warnings about unethical practices.[14]

Other ways in which countries can assist migrant workers before they depart is to simplify and reduce the costs of administrative processes. This not only lessens the burden on migrants, but can also keep them from turning to irregular channels because of an inability to pay the fees. It is of great help to migrant workers to receive information about the culture and conditions of life that exist in the destination country before they leave. Other forms of helpful information, such as financial literacy training and low-cost ways to transmit remittances, in order to maximize their value, can also be given. Contact information for assistance in the destination country, including sources of emergency assistance there, is helpful. Origin countries should even be ready to provide assistance in halting the process at any time there is an indication that their citizens could be departing into a situation which would violate their human and labour rights.

Post-Departure and Work

By continuing to monitor the treatment of their citizens when they are no longer within their borders, transit and destination countries will have a greater incentive to protect their rights as well. Thus, origin countries should work with transit and destination countries to assist their citizens who have been victimized by traffickers and smugglers and to locate and sanction those who commit such acts. Unfortunately, prosecution of traffickers by countries in which they operate is probably the weakest part of the anti-trafficking system at this time.[15]

Bilateral agreements with destination countries spelling out how responsibilities are to be shared can be a significant means of providing minimum standards and rights for a country's citizens. Origin countries can negotiate for greater rights, particularly for less-skilled workers, which conform to international standards, with compliance guaranteed by the agreements. Exploitation can also be reduced by providing access to regular migration and the formal labour market. Agreements can contain provisions on such things as how origin and destination countries will cooperatively manage pre-departure and return processes, transfer social security earnings or allow portability of pensions. They can also contain dispute settlement procedures and remedies for violation of rights. These agreements are most effective when they contain specific mechanisms and procedures for resolving problems and grievances, such as monitoring missions or joint committees with representatives from the countries involved. A good example of a bilateral agreement is that between Spain and Ecuador, which includes procedures and requirements on educational campaigns for potential migrants, offers of employment, evaluation of qualifications, travel, selection of workers, employment contracts, visas, information to be given to migrant workers before they depart, residence and work permits, equality of pay and working conditions with nationals, social security, and return, including development assistance.[16]

Another effective means of intervention and protection by origin countries is to establish consular services with labour attaches and both male and female staff to whom migrant workers may come for assistance. This is particularly important in countries where a large number of their citizens work. Consular services can also perform outreach to certain groups of migrant workers who are particularly vulnerable to abuse, such as women, or those who are isolated, especially domestic workers, who are mostly women and thereby doubly vulnerable. They may be called upon to provide emergency assistance, especially when their citizens have nowhere else to turn. They can facilitate the systematic transmission of information regarding abusive employers and industries to officials at home to take measures to prevent their citizens from migrating to work for them. Sri Lanka and the Philippines are examples of two countries which have labour attaches in their consulates in countries where large numbers of their citizens work to assist migrant workers. The Sri Lankan consulate services pay particular attention to the assistance of women migrant workers.[17]

Origin countries can further assist and protect their citizens by helping to establish welfare funds for migrants and their families, which can be either publicly or privately operated. Sri Lanka, Pakistan and the Philippines have welfare fund programs to assist migrant workers, which provide death and disability insurance, and other services for them and their families, such as loans for housing and small businesses upon return.[18]

Return

Origin countries should try to assist those migrant workers who need it with reintegration back into society upon their return. One way in which they can do this and further development at the same time is to assist workers in investing their remittances in a productive way, including by setting up enterprises or micro-enterprises. Sustainable socio-economic reintegration should be encouraged in order to further long-term benefits for development. A good practice is shown by Senegal, which has an office within the Ministry of Foreign Affairs to facilitate migrant workers' return and reintegration.[19] Mexico has a fund-matching remittance investment program in which approved proposals by migrant workers to use their remittances for infrastructure development, public services, or job creation receive matching funds from the government.[20]

For origin countries which have large numbers of citizens leaving for work in other countries, the underlying issue is a development issue. That is, it is developing countries' fundamental responsibility to increase employment opportunities at home so that their citizens have the option of not having to migrate to other countries to find work—so that they migrate out of choice and not necessity or despair. Essential roots of extensive outmigration lie in deficits in decent work in countries of origin, reflected by unemployment, underemployment, and poverty. The creation of more productive, freely chosen employment and decent work will allow citizens the right to remain in their own countries for work if they wish.

5. RESPONSIBILITIES OF DESTINATION COUNTRIES

Pre-Departure

While destination countries have a much lesser capacity to protect migrants before they are within their borders, they can nevertheless engage in bilateral dialogue and cooperation to help protect them during that stage. For example, they can provide information to origin countries about known, unethical recruiters and abusive employers, so that immediate preventive action can be taken. They can work with origin countries to establish computerized recruitment services that are easier to supervise, can more rapidly adapt to changing labour needs, and can protect against use by unethical recruiters and lessen their role in labour migration. Destination countries can also provide training and orientation in migrant's home countries before they leave. A good practice in this regard is a pre-departure training program for persons migrating to Italy for work, which consists of 40 hours of orientation and 80 hours of language training. Legal, labour market, cultural and social, and psycho-social orientation is covered in the orientation portion of the training.[21]

Destination countries can engage in bilateral and multilateral dialogue and cooperation to combat irregular migration, trafficking, and smuggling, including by coordinating their police efforts to ensure that those who engage in this unlawful conduct do not evade detection due to a lack of international coordination. When in need of foreign workers, they can further their protection by entering into bilateral agreements with origin countries which conform to international human rights and labour standards, as described earlier. Provisions on social security portability can be included within bilateral and multilateral agreements, such as those contained in the European Union legal framework, which grants portability to nationals of both the EU and third countries.[22] Ten countries have entered into the ASEAN Declaration on the Protection and Promotion of the Rights of Migrant Workers, which sets forth obligations of destination and origin countries.[23]

Destination countries should guarantee labour and social rights for migrants entering and working under temporary or circular migration schemes as well. These schemes, which are being used for workers of all skill levels, vary greatly and may or may not be the subject of bilateral agreements. They can be based on a country's system of granting temporary work permits or upon an arrangement providing for workers return home after a specified period of employment. The principle of equal treatment between migrant and national workers should be respected to guard against the development of substandard conditions. A good practice in this area is a memoranda of understanding which Canada has with Mexico and Caribbean countries for temporary migrant agricultural workers to assist them with entry and which requires minimum employment and welfare standards.[24]

Post-Departure and Work

After migrant workers enter their borders is when destination countries' primary responsibility for protecting their rights begins. Written information in a language migrant workers can understand on labour and employment rights, social and welfare rights, and where to seek assistance should be provided to them. If migrants have been transported to the country and abandoned without work, they should be assisted with accommodation and help in returning home. Trafficking victims should similarly receive the help they need to escape their traffickers. For example, the Italian government has set up a toll-free telephone hotline to enable immediate reporting of cases of trafficking.[25]

Destination countries should ensure that migrant workers are covered by their labour and employment laws. In most countries, employment and labour laws cover all workers, including migrant workers, on the same basis, and in some countries discrimination against them in employment is prohibited.[26] However, there may be other, inconsistent laws within the same country, resulting in migrant workers having fewer rights than nationals, even when they perform the same work. If not currently covered, those migrant workers especially vulnerable and with little protection, such as domestic workers, should be included. Laws and regulations should provide equal treatment of regularly admitted migrant workers with national workers in the workplace. Whenever possible, restrictions on migrant workers being tied to a single employer should be removed, as increased dependency and exploitation can result when workers have to choose between working under abusive conditions or not working at all and leaving the country. Thus, for example, in the United Kingdom, migrant domestic workers are permitted to change their employers. Those who have left their original employer because of abuse or exploitation and are in an irregular situation, may apply for regularization.[27]

Migrant workers are entitled to fundamental workers' rights, such as the right to freedom of association and the right to be free from discrimination, to which national workers are entitled. They are also entitled to safe and healthy working conditions and reasonable working hours. Destination countries should ensure that migrant workers are not paid lower wages than national workers for the same work, that their wages are paid directly to them, and that they are paid all wages due, particularly before they leave the country, when it becomes almost impossible to collect them. If necessary to stay in the country to collect unpaid wages, they should be permitted to do so. Establishing remittance services where migrant workers can transfer their earnings home safely and at low cost, helps protect the wages of migrant workers as well. Such services exist in various countries.[28] The retention of migrant workers' identity documents by others should be prohibited, as is the case in Taiwan, Republic of China.[29]

Attention should be paid to those migrant workers who are especially vulnerable, such as those in irregular status and women. While migrant workers in irregular status may not have the right to remain in the country on the same basis as migrants in regular status, they nevertheless have human rights and workplace rights as workers. Regardless of their legal status, employers, and indirectly the destination country as well, profit from the labour they have performed and have a duty to respect their rights as human beings and as workers. Destination countries should prevent employers from treating them as a lower class of workers, undercutting their own citizens, and creating undesirable jobs that their citizens will not accept. Women migrant workers often face "double" discrimination, as women and as migrants.[30] In recognition of this, Canada applies a gender based analysis to new migration policies to ensure that gender considerations are taken into account during policy-making.[31] Women may be especially isolated or vulnerable to abuse due to their gender and should be protected from violence and sexual abuse. Conditions for domestic workers should be improved, as they often have very long work days and may not even have days off.

Destination countries should ensure that laws and regulations protecting migrant workers are actually enforced and are effective deterrents. For example, there should be regular inspections of working and living conditions and supervision of compliance with employment contracts and with bilateral agreements. In Mauritius, the Ministry of Labour has a Special Migrant Workers Unit, which inspects the working, housing, and food conditions of migrant workers, who have the same rights as nationals.[32] Jordan has recently strengthened its labour inspection program in the garment sector, which is largely staffed by migrant workers, to increase compliance with labour laws. In a few instances, factories where serious violations of workers' rights were committed were shut down.[33] Mistreatment of workers should lead to effective sanctions. Where the rights of migrant workers have been violated, all persons involved should be legally accountable to prevent workers' from being left without any remedy. A good practice in this area is a Portuguese law holding both the direct employer and the general contractor responsible for the payment of wages to migrant workers. If the employer fails to pay wages due, the general contractor must pay.[34] Ensuring accountability for mistreatment of migrant workers may require cooperation with origin and transit countries.

Complaint procedures and remedies for violations should be freely available to migrant workers, and destination countries should ensure that they are aware of their right to complain and seek remedies if their rights are violated. They should have the right to voice grievances without fear of intimidation or retaliation. Destination countries should refrain from engaging in mass detentions and deportations of migrant workers. Instead, they should engage in dialogue with origin countries in the interest of finding mutually satisfactory solutions to problems involving large groups of migrant workers. Legal services should be available to migrant workers, if necessary. Trade unions and civil society should be permitted to promote the welfare of migrant workers and assist them in asserting their rights.

With regard to social welfare, health insurance and medical care should be available to migrant workers. Measures to prevent social exclusion, discrimination and xenophobia in the larger society and encourage the recognition of migrant workers as needed and productive members of society will increase social cohesion. This is of undeniable benefit to destination countries. At all times, destination countries should be cooperative and responsive to concerns and reports of abuse, whether made by origin countries, through their consular services or otherwise, by private parties concerned with migrant workers, or by migrant workers themselves.

Migrant resource centers in destination countries can be of great assistance to workers. In Portugal, the Information and Resource Centre for Migrants, among other things, provides information to migrant workers on their rights and assists them with processing requests for family reunification.[35] Trade unions operate information centers in Finland and Estonia to provide information and resources to migrant workers and to prevent a two-track labour market from developing with lower standards for migrant workers than nationals. Spanish trade unions operate centers throughout the country to provide information and assistance.[36]

Other rights and protections for the families of migrant workers should be respected when migrants are accompanied by them. For example, their children must have the right to education, and their families the right to medical care and decent housing. When migrants become permanent settlers in their new countries, those countries should give them the same rights as nationals as much as possible, so that they can fully integrate into the society. They should have the opportunity to advance in their careers, just as citizens do. Non-discrimination and integration enable destination countries to take full advantage of migrant workers' capabilities.

Return

Even when migrant workers are finished with their work and return home, the destination country is involved in facilitating the termination of work and in making sure that the travel to the origin country is as secure as possible. In cases where migrant workers have been contributing to pension schemes, countries of destination and origin have to explore channels for portability of social security benefits. There are also ways in which those countries can assist the migrant workers to reintegrate into their own countries and further develop there. For example, they can participate in resettlement support programs and co-development schemes. France, for example, links migration and development policies and provides development assistance to francophone Africa. Germany, Italy, and Spain have similar programs with other countries from which their migrant workers come.[37] Destination countries can also assist migrant workers in transferring their skills and investments to small businesses in their countries.

6. INTERNATIONAL STANDARDS PROTECTING THE RIGHTS OF MIGRANT WORKERS

International standards providing rights and protection during all stages of the labour migration process are available to guide countries in formulating and implementing national law and policy. They are contained in international and ILO Conventions and other international instruments, such as human rights instruments. Countries may wish to ratify and implement the terms of these international instruments for the benefit of migrant workers. When all parties follow the same rules, there is a more equal playing field. The use of reporting mechanisms under the human rights instruments and international conventions on behalf of migrant workers advances their rights. Even when countries have not ratified international instruments beneficial to migrant workers, they can adhere to their terms. International human rights law contains the most basic rights, which apply to all human beings, such as the 1948 Universal Declaration of Human Rights[38] setting forth rights held by all persons "without distinction of any kind," the 1966 International Covenant on Economic, Social and Cultural Rights,[39] and the 1966 International Covenant on Civil and Political Rights.[40]

There are three international Conventions specifically addressing the rights of migrant workers. Two are ILO Conventions, the Migration for Employment Convention (Revised), 1949 (No. 97)[41] and the Migrant Workers (Supplementary Provisions) Convention (No. 143),[42] each of which have accompanying Recommendations.[43] Convention No. 97 applies to migrant workers in regular status and covers issues involving their departure, journey, and reception, and transfer of earnings. Two Annexes address recruitment, placement, and conditions of labour. This Convention requires that migrants in regular status receive treatment no less favourable than those of nationals in certain matters pertaining to employment. Convention 143, on the other hand, focuses on labour migration under abusive conditions and equality of opportunity and treatment. It addresses the need to suppress clandestine movements of migrants and their employment in irregular status by taking action against their organizers and employers (not the workers themselves). It also provides some rights to migrant workers in irregular status arising out of their employment.

The third international Convention specifically pertaining to migrant workers is the 1990 International Convention on the Protection of the Rights of All Migrant Workers and Members of Their Families.[44] This Convention covers the entire migration process and provides many areas of protection for migrant workers and their families. In addition to issues related to employment, it includes provisions on human rights, slavery and forced labour, liberty and security of person, protection against violence, confiscation of identity documents, expulsion, medical care, the education of migrant workers' children, family reunification, transfer of earnings, recruitment, the right to the protection and assistance of their countries' consular services, and other issues. Another Convention related to the situation of migrant workers is the 2000 Convention against Transnational Organized Crime, and its two protocols, the Protocol to Prevent, Suppress and Punish Trafficking in Persons, Especially Women and Children and the Protocol against the Smuggling of Migrants by Land, Sea and Air.[45]

While these Conventions are directed toward workers' *migrant* status, all ILO Conventions generally apply to them as well, because of their status as *workers*. There are eight fundamental ILO Conventions which are considered human rights at work. They cover freedom of association and the right to collective bargaining, the abolition of forced labour, equality and non-discrimination in employment and occupation, and the elimination of child labour.[46] The Private Employment Agencies Convention, 1997, No. 181,[47] is of particular relevance to the protection of migrant workers, as it provides for a system of licensing or certification of private recruiters, rights for employees who use their services, and protection against abuses.

The 2006 ILO Multilateral Framework on Labour Migration, Nonbinding principles and guidelines for a rights-based approach to labour migration,[48] provides, as evident by its title, *rights-based* practical guidance to governments and to employers' and workers' organizations with regard to the development, strengthening and implementation of national and international labour migration policies. It has been drawn from principles contained in relevant international instruments, promotes the rights of migrant workers, and provides guidance in the prevention of and protection against abusive migration practices. It additionally addresses decent work, means for international cooperation on labour migration, global knowledge base, effective management of labour migration, the migration process, social integration and inclusion, and migration and development.

7. Summary and Conclusion

The development benefits of labour migration depend upon the degree to which migrants are protected and empowered by the origin countries from which they come and the destination countries in which they live and work. Development gains accrue to both origin and destination countries. There are three basic stages in the labour migration process during which migrants' rights must be protected. These are the pre-departure stage, the post-departure and work stage, and the return stage. While origin and destination countries have a shared responsibility to protect the rights of migrant workers through all of these stages, their responsibilities differ. That is because different events are taking place before and after departure, and because countries have the ability to exercise more supervision in their own countries and much less ability to control what takes place in another. The need to protect migrant workers during the various stages of their migration experience and the ways in which they can be protected should be seen from the standpoint of origin and destination countries, keeping in mind international cooperation to further these ends.

Specific issues and challenges include the formulation and implementation of labour migration policies that respond to the needs of the labour market, coherence between migration laws and labour laws, and respect of rights of all migrant workers and their families. Steps towards the effective protection of migrant workers can take into consideration the ratification and effective implementation of ILO fundamental Conventions and Conventions on migrant workers (C.97 and C.143), the use of guidelines and principles provided by the ILO Multilateral Framework on Labour Migration, the promotion of labour and social security bilateral agreements between sending and receiving countries, the monitoring through labour inspection systems, the reduction of cost of remittances and recognition and efficient use of skills.

Examples of good practices exist, which have been implemented in different regions of the world and can be replicated by other countries. These examples show that development gains from migration for both countries of origin and destination, as well as migrant workers themselves, are inseparable from the protection of their rights. ILO and UN Conventions and the ILO Multilateral Framework on Labour Migration provide guidance in formulating and implementing national law and policy for the protection of migrant workers.

ENDNOTES

1. United Nations (2006). International migration and development: Report of the Secretary-General. New York, A/60/871, United Nations, June 2006. http://www.un.org/esa/ population/migration/hld/Text/Report%20of%20the%20SG% 28June%2006%29_English.pdf.

2. United Nations Population Division (2006), Trends in Total Migrant Stock: The 2005 Revision, New York, 2006; International Labour Migration and Development: The ILO Perspective, International Migration Brief, 2007.

3. OSCE, IOM, ILO Handbook on Establishing Effective Labour Migration Policies in Countries of Origin and Destination, 2006, p. 19.

4. Migration and Development, a Human Rights Approach, Office of the UN High Commissioner for Human Rights, pp. 3–5, 8–10, www.ohchr.org/english/bodies/cmw/docs/.

5. The ILO Multilateral Framework on Labour Migration, Non-binding principles and guidelines for a rights-based approach to labour migration, 2005, provides guidance in the area of international cooperation, http://www.ilo.org/public/english/protection/migrant/download/multilat_fwk_en.pdf.

6. Collections of good practices from all regions of the world to protect and promote the rights of migrant workers and further development in origin and destination countries can be found in various sources. For example, the ILO Multilateral Framework on Labour Migration contains an annex with a selection of 132 such practices. Good practices can also be found in OSCE, IOM, ILO Handbook on Establishing Effective Labour Migration Policies in Countries of Origin and Destination, 2006; OSCE, IOM, ILO Handbook on Establishing Effective Labour Migration Policies, Mediterranean Edition, 2007; Guide to Private Employment Agencies, ILO, 2007, http://www.ilo.org/wcmsp5/groups/public/---ed_norm/--declaration/documents/ instructionalmaterial/wcms_083275.pdf.; An Information Guide, Preventing Discrimination, Exploitation and Abuse of Women Migrant Workers, ILO, 2003, http://www.ilo.org/ public/english/ employment/gems/ advocacy/protect.htm.

7. OSCE, IOM, ILO Handbook on Establishing Effective Labour Migration Policies, Mediterranean Edition, 2007, p. 72.

8. Idem, p. 70.

9. OSCE, IOM, ILO Handbook on Establishing Effective Labour Migration Policies in Countries of Origin and Destination, 2006, p. 54.

10. An Information Guide, Preventing Discrimination, Exploitation and Abuse of Women Migrant Workers, ILO, 2003, Booklet 3, p. 49.

11. ILO Multilateral Framework on Labour Migration, best practice No. 81.

12. Idem, best practice No. 78.

13. Idem, best practice No. 84.

14. Idem, best practice Nos. 37 and 95.

15. An Information Guide, Preventing Discrimination, Exploitation and Abuse of Women Migrant Workers, ILO, 2003, Booklet 6, p. 83; Migration and Development, a Human Rights Approach, Office of the UN High Commissioner for Human Rights, pp. 18–19. http://www2.ohchr.org/english/bodies/cmw/docs/HLMigration/MigrationDevelopment HC'spaper.pdf.

The section below on International Standards Protecting the Rights of Migrant Workers discusses international standards which can guide legislation in this area.

16. OSCE, IOM, ILO Handbook on Establishing Effective Labour Migration Policies in Countries of Origin and Destination, 2006, pp. 225–230.

17. ILO Multilateral Framework on Labour Migration, best practice Nos. 95, 96.

18. OSCE, IOM, ILO Handbook on Establishing Effective Labour Migration Policies in Countries of Origin and Destination, 2006, pp. 56–58.

19. ILO Multilateral Framework on Labour Migration, best practice No. 125.

20. Idem, best practice No. 121.

21. OSCE, IOM, ILO Handbook on Establishing Effective Labour Migration Policies in Countries of Origin and Destination, 2006, p. 224.

22. ILO Multilateral Framework on Labour Migration, best practice No. 71.

23. http://www.aseansec.org/19264.htm.

24. ILO Multilateral Framework on Labour Migration, best practice No. 41; OSCE, IOM, ILO Handbook on Establishing Effective Labour Migration Policies in Countries of Origin and Destination, 2006, p. 118.

25. An Information Guide, Preventing Discrimination, Exploitation and Abuse of Women Migrant Workers, ILO, 2003, Booklet 6, p. 83.

26. ILO Multilateral Framework on Labour Migration, best practice No. 69.

27. ILO Multilateral Framework on Labour Migration, best practice No. 82.

28. OSCE, IOM, ILO Handbook on Establishing Effective Labour Migration Policies in Countries of Origin and Destination, 2006, p. 75; ILO Multilateral Framework on Labour Migration, best practice Nos. 117, 119, 122, 123, 124, 132.

29. Idem, best practice No. 80.

30. OSCE, IOM, ILO Handbook on Establishing Effective Labour Migration Policies in Countries of Origin and Destination, 2006, p. 20.

31. GFMD Background Paper, Roundtable 1, Session 1.2, Brussels, 2007, p. 9; www.gfmd-fmmd.org/en/system/files/Background+Paper+Session+1.2+EN.pdf; http://www.swc-cfc.gc.ca/pubs/gbaperformance/index_e.html.

32. ILO Multilateral Framework on Labour Migration, best practice No. 74; OSCE, IOM, ILO Handbook on Establishing Effective Labour Migration Policies, Mediterranean Edition, 2007, p. 144.

33. Labor Compliance in Jordan's Apparel Sector, Actions to Date and Next Steps, Ministry of Labor, Amman, Hashemite Kingdom of Jordan, March 2007, http://www.mol.jo/report/ActionPlan-FINALMarch30.pdf.

34. Portuguese Ministry of Internal Administration, Law Decree No. 34/2003, 25 February 2003, Art. 144.4.

35. OSCE, IOM, ILO Handbook on Establishing Effective Labour Migration Policies in Countries of Origin and Destination, 2006, p. 148.

36. ILO Multilateral Framework on Labour Migration, best practice Nos. 90, 112.

37. Idem, best practice No. 1.

38. http://www.unhchr.ch/udhr/lang/eng.htm.

39. www.ohchr.org/english/law/cesr.htm.

40. www.ohchr.org/english/law/ccpr.htm. These and the other four international human rights treaties are monitored by the human rights treaty bodies, which can advance the protection of the rights of migrant workers, http://www.ohchr.org/EN/HRBodies/Pages/ HumanRightsBodies.aspx. Those others are the 1965 International Convention on the Elimination of All Forms of Racial Discrimination, http://www.ohchr.org/english/law/cerd. htm, the 1979 Convention on the Elimination of All Forms of Discrimination Against Women, http://www.ohchr.org/english/law/ cedaw.htm; the 1984 Convention Against Torture and Other Cruel, Inhuman or Degrading Treatment or Punishment, http:// www.ohchr.org/ english/law/cat.htm; and the 1989 Convention on the Rights of the Child, http://www.ohchr. org/english/law/crc.htm.

41. http://www.ilo.org/ilolex/cgi-lex/convde.pl?C097.

42. http://www.ilo.org/ilolex/cgi-lex/convde.pl?C143.

43. http://www.ilo.org/ilolex/cgi-lex/convde.pl?R086 and http://www.ilo.org/ilolex/cgi- lex/ convde.pl?R151.

44. http://www.ohchr.org/english/law/cmw.htm.

45. http://www.unodc.org/pdf/crime/a_res_55/res5525e.pdf.

46. Freedom of Association and Protection of the Right to Organise Convention, 1948 (No. 87), http://www.ilo.org/ilolex/cgi-lex/convde.pl?C087; Right to Organise and Collective Bargaining Convention, 1949 (No. 98), http://www.ilo.org/ilolex/cgi-lex/convde.pl?C098; Forced Labour Convention, 1930 (No. 29), http://www.ilo.org/ilolex/cgi-lex/convde. pl?C029; Abolition of Forced Labour Convention, 1957 (No. 105), http://www.ilo. org/ilolex/cgi-lex/ convde.pl?C105; Equal Remuneration Convention, 1951 (No. 100), http://www.ilo.org/ ilolex/cgi-lex/convde.pl?C100; Discrimination (Employment and Occupation) Convention, 1958 (No. 111), http://www.ilo.org/ilolex/cgi-lex/convde. pl?C111; Minimum Age Convention, 1973 (No. 138), http://www.ilo.org/ilolex/cgi-lex/ convde.pl?C138; Worst Forms of Child Labour Convention, 1999 (No. 182), http://www. ilo.org/ilolex/cgi-lex/convde.pl?C182.

47. http://www.ilo.org/ilolex/cgi-lex/convde.pl?C181.

48. http://www.ilo.org/public/english/protection/migrant/download/multilat_fwk_en.pdf; available in Arabic, Chinese, English, French, Russian, and Spanish.

*The **International Labour Organization** (ILO) is a United Nations specialized agency that seeks the promotion of social justice and internationally recognized human and labor rights. The ILO is responsible for drawing up and overseeing international labor standards.

International Labour Organization. *Protecting the Rights of Migrant Workers: A Shared Responsibility.* Geneva, International Labour Office (2009): 1–24. Copyright © International Labour Organization 2009.

Used by permission.

Part 4: Toward the Future

The purpose of this final section is to encourage a broader and more thoughtful reflection on migration, human rights, and development with a selection of pieces that challenge traditional thinking and present innovative pathways for change.

Restrictions on migration are universally accepted as part of the sovereign right of states to control their own borders and as an inevitable element of a properly functioning society. While people will often argue that a particular restriction is unfair or unjustly applied, they will rarely challenge the right of states to create such restrictions and the logic behind their imposition. The first article in this section, "Why Should We Restrict Immigration?" by Bryan Caplan, seeks to challenge this orthodoxy in the specific context of United States migration policy. Caplan asserts a moral presumption in favor of open borders and asks why we should restrict migration in the first place: Is this the only remedy to the "problem" that immigration restrictions are supposed to be solving? If cheaper or more humane alternative solutions exist, then why are these not being tried? The author examines the alleged negative effects of immigration on the host country (loss of jobs; economic costs; threats to culture, liberty, and property rights). He concludes that immigration is not a significant threat on any of these fronts and that even if it was, immigration restrictions cannot be shown to be the best way of addressing them.

The second piece in this final section, by Cristina Rodríguez, continues the theme of new visions. In "Building Capacity for the Transnational Regulation of Migration," the author examines the dynamics and future of the U.S. – Mexico immigration relationship. She challenges several myths in the public debate about labor migration and illegal migration. The first of these is the assumption that irregular migration is "fixable" by the United States through the perfection of domestic enforcement mechanisms. This assumption ignores the reality that migration is a shared concern; that its management requires engagement with other governments; and that certain aspects will always be beyond U.S. control. The second, related assumption is that migration is a problem to be solved, rather than a complex structural and historical phenomenon that will evolve over time but never disappear. The author notes the growing importance of bilateral and transnational frameworks (involving both public and civil society institutions and networks) in the process and management of migration. In the context of the U.S.–Mexico relationship, she considers how the very different mechanisms that are active in this area can help to manage migration in a manner that ensures both sides of the bilateral relationship reap benefits and bear costs. In the longer term such involvement should help to promote greater accountability in immigration policy.

In her wide-ranging article "Migration and Development: The Flavour of the 2000s," Birgitte Brønden reflects on the decade that has elapsed since migration and development were formally linked, surging to the top of the international development agenda and gaining the attention of academics as well as policymakers in countries of origin and destination. This support is based on a widespread belief that, through remittances and other benefits such as skill transfers, migration can help to lift countries out of poverty as well as transform individual lives. Brønden notes, however, that there has been ongoing debate about the nature and value of the migration–development nexus. For example, the assumption that all parties (origin countries, destination countries, and migrants) are winners has been challenged by those who point out that policies and practices are often skewed toward the interests of wealthy countries of destination. The author acknowledges these criticisms while arguing that migration remains one of the most potent weapons against poverty. The challenge for the future will be to confront the complexity of the issues and also to ensure that discussions about migration and development are not isolated from wider debates around global power, wealth, and inequality, as well as consideration of the rights of migrants.

The anthology concludes with the text of a message delivered by the United Nations Secretary-General, Ban Ki-moon, on International Migrants Day, 18 December 2011. This brief but powerful statement directly confronts the false assumptions that have shaped irrelevant and even dangerous migration policy: that migrants are a burden; that women migrants are inevitably victims; that irregular migrants are criminals who must be stopped at all costs. The Secretary-General affirms the sovereign prerogative of states to manage their borders. But, like other contributors to this anthology, he warns that they also have a responsibility to abide by their international legal obligations, most particularly the obligation to protect and respect fundamental human rights. As he explains: "Human rights are not a matter of charity, nor are they a reward for obeying immigration rules. Human rights are the inalienable entitlement of every person, including the world's 214 million international migrants as well as their family members."[1]

As you read the articles in this part, consider the following questions:

• Should there be a moral presumption in favor of open borders, with the burden shifting to proponents of immigration restrictions to justify their position? To what extent may one's personal family history influence one's views on these matters?

• Are economic arguments for open borders, such as the following view put forward by economist Philippe Legrain, persuasive?

[The] case for free migration follows logically from that for free trade. Just as it's beneficial for goods and services to flow freely across borders, so, too, the people who produce them. Freer trade has made Americans much richer over the past 50 years; unfreezing labor flows could deliver vast gains over the next 50. According to some estimates, removing immigration controls could more than double the size of the world economy.[2]

• Do you agree with Stephen Castles that "migration alone cannot remove structural constraints to economic growth, social change and greater democracy."[3] What implications does this statement have for policies that aim to promote development through migration? Is a human rights perspective part of what is missing?

NOTES

1. The United Nations Secretary-General, Ban Ki-moon, "Message on International Migrants Day," 18 December 2011.

2. Philippe Legrain, "Let Them In," Forbes.com, http://www.forbes.com/forbes/2010/0628/special-report-immigration-opening-borders-mexico-let-them-in_print.html.

3. Stephen Castles, "Bringing Human Rights into the Migration and Development Debate," Global Policy 2, no. 3 (2011): 250.

Why Should We Restrict Immigration?

*by Bryan Caplan**

Consider the following thought experiment: Moved by the plight of desperate earthquake victims, you volunteer to work as a relief worker in Haiti. After two weeks, you're ready to go home. Unfortunately, when you arrive at the airport, customs officials tell you that you're forbidden to enter the United States. You go to the American consulate to demand an explanation. But the official response is simply, "The United States does not have to explain itself to you."

You don't have to be a libertarian to admit that this seems like a monstrous injustice. The entire ideological menagerie—liberals, conservatives, moderates, socialists, and libertarians—would defend your right to move from Haiti to the United States. What's so bad about restricting your migration? Most obviously, because life in Haiti is *terrible*. If the American government denies you permission to return, you'll live in dire poverty, die sooner, live under a brutal, corrupt regime, and be cut off from most of the people you want to associate with. Hunger, danger, oppression, isolation: condemning you to even one seems wrong. Which raises a serious question: if you had been born in Haiti, would denying you permission to enter the United States be any less wrong?[1]

This thought experiment hardly proves that people have an absolute right of free migration. After all, many things that seem wrong on the surface turn out to be morally justified. Suppose you knock me unconscious, then slice me open with a knife. This is normally wrong. But if you're performing surgery required to save my life, and I gave my informed consent, then your action is not just morally permissible, but praiseworthy. Nevertheless, my thought experiment does establish one weak conclusion: immigration restrictions seem wrong on the surface. To justifiably restrict migration, you need to overcome the moral *presumption* in favor of open borders (Huemer 2010).

How would one go about overcoming this presumption? For starters, you must show that the evils of free immigration are fairly severe. Immigration restrictions trap many millions in Third World misery. Economists' consensus estimate is that open borders would roughly double world GDP, enough to virtually eliminate global poverty (Clemens 2011). The injustice and harm that immigration restrictions prevent has to be at least comparable to the injustice and harm that immigration restrictions impose.

But hard evidence that immigration has major drawbacks is not enough. The proponent of immigration restrictions also has to show that there is no cheaper or more humane way to mitigate the evils of immigration. Surgery wouldn't be morally justified if a $1 pill were an equally effective treatment. Why not? Because even if surgery will save the patient's life, there is a cheaper, more humane way to do so.

The rest of this paper examines the alleged evils of immigration through this moral lens. In each case, I begin with a balanced survey of the relevant social science. The point is not to determine whether immigration has good overall effects. The point, rather, is to determine whether any of the effects of immigration are bad enough to credibly overcome the moral presumption in favor of open borders. After reviewing the social science, each section then turns to a deeper question: assuming the worst about immigration, are immigration restrictions the only viable remedy? If cheaper, more humane alternatives exist, then immigration restrictions remain unjustified even if my summary of the social science is hopelessly biased.

PROTECTING AMERICAN WORKERS?

The most popular argument for immigration restrictions is that we need them to protect American workers from poverty. The mechanism is simple: Without these laws, the supply of labor would drastically increase—and American wages would plummet to Third World levels.

Many of the assumptions behind this argument are true. After the highest-growth decade in the history of the world (Chandy and Gertz 2011, Maddison 2009), billions remain desperately poor. About a billion people live on the equivalent of a dollar a day or less (Collier 2007). About a quarter of the world's population would like to permanently move to another country (Torres and Pelham 2008). Contrary to populist complaints, current immigration restrictions clearly achieve their intended purpose: excluding almost all of the people who want to move here. Without immigration restrictions, the supply of labor in the United States would rapidly increase.

Yet these assumptions do not imply that American workers owe their standard of living to immigration restrictions. Under open borders, low-skilled wages are indeed likely to fall, but *most Americans are not low-skilled*. Over 87 percent of Americans over the age of 25 are high-school graduates (U.S. Census Bureau 2011). Most of the world's would-be immigrants are, at best, substitutes for American high-school drop-outs.

Mainstream estimates confirm this point: immigration has little or no effect on *overall* wages. Educated Americans are primarily customers, not competitors, of new arrivals. As Kerr and Kerr (2011: 12) explain in their state-of-the-art literature survey:

> The documented wage elasticities are small and clustered near zero. Dustmann et al. (2008) likewise found very little evidence for wage effects in their review of the UK experience. This parallels an earlier conclusion by Friedberg and Hunt (1995) that immigration had little impact on native wages; overall, their survey of the earlier literature found that a 10 percent increase in the immigrant share of the labor force reduced native wages by about 1 percent. Recent meta-surveys by Longhi et al. (2005, 2008) and Okkerse (2008) found comparable, small effects across many studies.

George Borjas, the most academically reputable critic of immigration, lands comfortably inside this consensus. Together with Lawrence Katz (Borjas and Katz 2005: 49), Borjas finds that between 1980 and 2000, Mexican immigration reduced overall native wages by 3.4 percent in the short run, and 0 percent in the long run. These are *not* annual effects; they are the *total* effect of two decades of immigration. Drop-outs suffered more, but the effect is surprisingly mild: –8.2 percent in the short run, –4.8 percent in the long run. Borjas and Katz also report that moderately educated natives—high-school graduates without college degrees—enjoyed long-run gains.

Standard estimates admittedly have a serious flaw: They assume that native and foreign workers with the same educational credentials have exactly the same skills. In reality, the two groups' skills differ; for starters, natives speak much better English than "identically educated" foreigners. In a series of papers, Giovanni Peri and his co-authors show that this oversight makes mainstream estimates overly pessimistic (Ottaviano and Peri forthcoming, D'Amuri and Peri 2011, Peri and Sparber 2009, Ottaviano and Peri 2008). When immigration increases, physical skills become more plentiful relative to demand, but language skills become more scarce. Since most jobs are a mix of physical and language skills, and people can change jobs, immigration might actually *increase* native wages.

This distinction between physical and language skills turns out to be empirically important. When immigration increases, native workers really do respond by switching to more language-based occupations—escaping lower pay for their physical skills, and capturing higher pay for their language skills. Peri and Sparber (2009: 162) find that this mechanism cuts the estimated effect of immigration on low-skilled natives' wages by 75 percent. On standard assumptions, immigration from 1990–2000 reduced low-skilled wages by 1.2 percent; on Peri-Sparber's more realistic assumptions, the hit was only 0.3 percent. Using a similar approach, Ottaviano and Peri (2008: 59) conclude that immigration from 1990–2006 raised average native wages by 0.6 percent.

Immigration can benefit American workers even if it reduces their wages. How? By increasing the value of workers' non-labor assets, like pensions and real estate. The admittedly small literature finds surprisingly large effects. In the United States, housing prices and rents rise by roughly 1 percent when immigration raises a city's population by 1 percent (Saiz 2007, 2003). Gonzalez and Ortega (2009) find an even larger effect for Spain. Since Americans own almost all American residential real estate, immigration is a quiet but massive transfer from immigrants to native homeowners. In an era of massive bailouts for underwater mortgages, taxpayers benefit too.

Contrary to popular opinion, then, "protecting American workers" is a weak rationale for immigration restrictions. Immigration makes low-skilled natives worse off, especially if they rent. But most Americans gain. Even if you reject these conclusions, though, immigration restrictions remain unjustified. You do not have to restrict migration to protect native workers from the consequences of immigration. There is a cheaper and more humane alternative: Charge immigrants surtaxes and/or admission fees, then use the extra revenue to compensate low-skilled Americans. For example, you could issue green cards to Haitians who agree to perpetually pay a 50 percent surtax on top of their ordinary U.S. tax liability. Haitians used to earning a dollar a day would jump at the opportunity, and the extra revenue could fund, say, tax cuts for low-income natives. Critics can tailor the details to fit the magnitude of the harm they believe immigrants inflict on native workers. Whatever the magnitude of this harm might be, extracting compensation is cheaper and more humane than forcing foreigners to languish in the Third World.

PROTECTING AMERICAN TAXPAYERS?

The American welfare state pays more for idleness than many countries pay for work. Should we not fear that, under open borders, many would immigrate merely to take advantage of the system? Milton Friedman himself famously remarked, "You cannot simultaneously have free immigration and a welfare state."[2] Immigration restrictions seem like the natural way for American taxpayers to protect themselves from billions of potential parasites.

Despite Friedman's endorsement, this argument is much weaker than it looks. Kerr and Kerr (2011) again provide a state-of-the-art summary of existing research on the net fiscal effects of immigration. Some studies find that immigrants receive more in benefits than they pay in taxes; others find the opposite. The United States does better than northern Europe. By all accounts, though, effects are small:

> The estimated net fiscal impact of migrants also varies substantially across studies, but the overall magnitudes relative to the GDP remain modest. This variance is partly due to different settings and policies, but also due to differences in methodology and assumptions. The more credible analyses typically find small fiscal effects [Kerr and Kerr 2011: 21].

How small is small? Consider Borjas and Trejo's (1991) relatively pessimistic calculations. They estimate that the average native family uses $7,900 in welfare over a lifetime, versus $13,600 for the average immigrant family that arrived between 1975 and 1980. That's a difference of just $5,700 (in 1989 dollars) for an entire family for an entire lifetime—no more than a few dollars a month per person.

Numbers like this may seem too good to be true. But before you dismiss the best available evidence, consider two key facts.

First, contrary to popular stereotypes, welfare states focus on the *old*, not the poor. Social Security and Medicare dwarf means-tested programs (Office of Management and Budget 2010: 153–55). Since immigrants tend to be young, they often end up supporting elderly natives rather than "milking the system." Illegal immigrants who pay taxes on fake Social Security numbers are pure profit for the Treasury. In 2005, Social Security's chief actuary estimated that without all the taxes paid on invalid Social Security numbers, "the system's long-term funding hole over 75 years would be 10 percent deeper" (Porter 2005).

Second, a high share of government spending is "nonrival"— government can serve a larger population for little or no extra cost. National defense is the most obvious example. If the population of the U.S. doubled, the current military could still ably defend it. You certainly wouldn't need to double the total defense budget. An even clearer case: if the population of the U.S. doubled overnight, the national debt (not deficit) would remain the same, and the per capita debt would halve. The lesson: Immigrants can pull their own fiscal weight even if their tax bills are well below average.

Suppose, however, that you remain convinced that immigrants impose a large fiscal burden on native taxpayers. Before you embrace immigration restrictions, you should still look for cheaper, more humane solutions. They're not hard to find. The simplest is to freely admit immigrants, but make them permanently ineligible for benefits. "Net fiscal burden" is not a physical constant. It is a function of policy. If immigrants paid normal taxes and received zero benefits, their "net fiscal effect" would almost automatically be positive. If permanent ineligibility seems unfair, surely it is less unfair than refusing to admit immigrants in the first place. And there are many intermediate approaches. You could impose a waiting period: No benefits for 10 years.[3] You could reduce or limit benefits: Half benefits for life, or double Medicare co-payments. You could set thresholds: Immigrants become eligible for benefits after their cumulative taxes exceed $100,000. Whether you love or loathe these proposals, they are certainly cheaper and more humane responses to the fiscal effects of immigration than the status quo.

PROTECTING AMERICAN CULTURE?

Another common complaint about immigrants is that they harm our culture. Many fail to learn English, and cling to the backward ways of their homelands. Do we really want America to become Mexico? If not, immigration restrictions seem like a commonsense response.

Claims about English fluency are easy to evaluate. The Pew Hispanic Center ran six high-quality surveys between 2002 and 2006 (Hakimzadeh and Cohn 2007). If you consider only first-generation Hispanic immigrants, popular complaints check out: a mere 23 percent speak English very well. But lack of English fluency is not hereditary: 88 percent of second-generation and 94 percent of third-generation Hispanics speak fluent English. Samuel Huntington, a leading proponent of the cultural complaint about immigration, admits these facts (Huntington 2004: 231). Hispanics are learning English about as well as earlier waves of non-English-speaking immigrants.

Vaguer cultural complaints are harder to evaluate. However, if we equate "culture" with "high culture" or "popular culture," we see a curious pattern. America's top two cultural centers, California and New York, have the largest foreign-born populations in the country—26 percent and 20 percent, respectively (U.S. Census Bureau 2003). While states with few immigrants—like Alabama (2 percent foreign-born), Arkansas (3 percent), Montana (2 percent), North Dakota (2 percent), South Dakota (2 percent), and West Virginia (1 percent)—enjoy great natural beauty, even their tourism bureaus would not paint them as cultural meccas. You could dismiss these patterns as mere correlation. But immigrants causally improve at least one form of culture prized by snobs and philistines alike: cuisine. And if we're being honest, don't most Americans care more about food than literature and museums?

Finally, if you equate "culture" with "trust" or "social capital," real estate markets are a helpful measuring stick. If social capital is important and immigration has large negative effects on an area's social capital, then immigration would cause housing prices and rents to *fall*. Immigrants would directly increase housing demand by renting and buying homes, but indirectly decrease housing demand by making their destinations unpleasant places to live. In fact, as discussed earlier, immigration has a strong positive effect on cities' real estate prices (Gonzalez and Ortega 2009; Saiz 2003, 2007). If immigration hurts trust or social capital, the effect must be small.

Regardless of your cultural views, there are certainly cheaper and more humane ways to address them than immigration restrictions. If you're worried about the decline of English, we could admit any immigrant who passes a test of English fluency. If you're worried about culture in some vaguer sense, we could admit any immigrant who passes a test of cultural literacy. In the interest of fairness, though, you should make sure that the typical native can pass your test. If most Americans cannot name the decade of the American Civil War, why should we expect more from immigrants?

PROTECTING AMERICAN LIBERTY?

Most immigrants come from countries that are less free than the United States. Since even dictatorships are somewhat responsive to public opinion (Caplan 2008), we should expect immigrants to lean statist. Immigrants fleeing domestic repression might hold atypically libertarian views. But *economic* migrants presumably share the policy outlook of the typical voter from their country of origin. If enough statists come, won't our democracy switch to the kinds of policies that immigrants struggle to escape? Economists—or at least economists with strong free-market sympathies—would call this a "political externality." The only way to protect American liberty, you might conclude, is to strictly limit the liberty of foreigners to enter the country.

This is probably libertarians' favorite argument against open borders. My own research confirms many of its underlying assumptions. In *The Myth of the Rational Voter* (Caplan 2007), I conclude that democracies choose bad policies because bad policies are popular, and bad policies are popular because voters have systematically biased beliefs about their effects. Almost all of my evidence admittedly comes from the United States, where high-quality public opinion data are most abundant. Still, if some countries have worse policies than others, the most plausible explanation is that some electorates are more biased than others. Libertarians seem to face a tragic choice between compromising their principles and retaining the liberty they already have.

Since the political externality story primarily concerns libertarians (and, to a lesser extent, conservatives), we cannot turn to a mature academic literature to estimate the severity of the problem. Nevertheless, there are good reasons to think that the political externality of immigration is less negative than it appears.

First, immigrants and their descendents have lower voter turnout than natives (Xu 2005; Cassel 2002). Looking at 2000 data, Citrin and Highton (2002: 16) found that Hispanics were 26 percent of California's adult population, 18 percent of its citizen population, and only 14 percent of its voting population. For the United States as a whole, Hispanics were 5 percent of the adult population, 3 percent of its citizen population, and just 2 percent of its voting population. Roughly the same pattern holds for Asians. Citrin and Highton (2002: 67–74) project that in 2040, whites will be just over a third of California's population but remain 53 percent of its voters. Non-libertarians often treat immigrants' low turnout as yet another strike against them. But if you fear political externalities, immigrants' political apathy is a blessing in disguise.

Second, voters have what psychologists call "status quo bias" (Sachs 1994, Samuelson and Zeckhauser 1988). They have a strong tendency to favor whatever already exists *because* it already exists. In 2010, most Americans favored Medicare but opposed "Obamacare." Why? In large part, because we already *had* Medicare. Status quo bias is the psychological underpinning for political aphorisms like "Never waste a good crisis" (Harrison 2009). In normal times, the public prefers to stay the course; you have to wait for a crisis to persuade the public to try something new.

What does status quo bias have to do with immigration? Simple. If people have a generic tendency to prefer what already exists, admitting them to a more libertarian society effectively makes them more libertarian: "Liberty is what you already have here. Fine, let's stick with that." Immigrants from Bismarckian Germany and Czarist Russia came from extremely authoritarian societies, but when they arrived in the United States, they made little effort to recreate their homelands. Instead, they accepted their new society as it was.[4] Migration may not change people's fundamental philosophy, but it doesn't have to. If human beings accept the status quo and the status quo happens to be liberty, liberty wins by default.

The opposite holds, naturally, when people move to more statist societies. If people have status quo bias, statist societies effectively make people more statist. But if libertarians are right about the connection between freedom and prosperity, status quo bias is our friend. Migrants will flow from statist countries to freer countries and become less statist in the process—subtly moving global public opinion in a libertarian direction.

My point is not that status quo bias completely negates the effect of country of origin on political opinions. My point, rather, is that status quo bias makes the political externality of immigration less negative than it appears. Immigrants from statist countries may lean statist, but few yearn to remake their new homeland's policies in the image of their mother country's. "People who come here will see the wonders of liberty with their own eyes" may well be wishful thinking. But "People who come here will largely accept our status quo as long as it more or less works" is realism.

Immigration also has political benefits that libertarians neglect. The empirical literature on the political economy of the welfare state reaches two seemingly contradictory conclusions (Alesina, Glaeser, and Sacerdote 2001, henceforth AGS; Gilens 1999). First, as believers in the political externality story would expect, non-whites are more supportive of the welfare state than whites. Second, as racial diversity increases, the welfare state *shrinks*. The standard resolution of the paradox: diversity undermines solidarity. People happily support welfare for members of "their" group, but resent paying taxes to help "the other." Racially homogeneous societies have large welfare states because almost everyone, rich and poor alike, agrees that the recipients are deserving. Racially mixed societies like the United States have less consensus and smaller welfare states. As AGS (2001: 229) explain:

> Americans think of the poor as members of some different group than themselves, whereas Europeans think of the poor as members of their own group. Racial differences between the poor and the nonpoor in the United States will tend to create the perception of the poor as "other," but geographic or social isolation might do this as well.

The estimated effect of AGS's mechanism is large and robust. Internationally, they find a −.66 correlation between redistribution and racial fragmentation, a correlation which persists controlling for per capita GDP, region, and age composition. Moving from minimum to maximum racial fragmentation reduces redistribution as a share of GDP by an estimated 7.5 percentage points (AGS 2001: 231). Domestically, AGS find a −.49 correlation between U.S. states' AFDC benefits and their black population shares, a correlation that persists controlling for median state income.[5] A 10-percentage-point increase in the black population share reduces AFDC benefits for a family of three by an estimated $69 per month in 1990 dollars (AGS 2001: 236).

If AGS's story is correct, immigration could actually make the welfare state shrink. As individuals, immigrants probably do favor a larger welfare state than natives. But collectively, immigrants' very presence undermines the welfare state by *reducing* native support.[6] Social democrats may find this tension between diversity and solidarity disturbing. But libertarians should rejoice: increasing foreigners' freedom of movement may indirectly increase natives' freedom to decide who deserves their charity.

To the best of my knowledge, no researcher has specifically tested whether AGS's results extend to immigration.[7] But we should expect them to. Immigrants are the ultimate out-group. Even today, Americans publicly complain about "immigrants" in language they would never use for blacks or gays. If the knowledge that foreigners attend "our" public schools and seek treatment in "our" hospitals does not undermine support for government spending on education and health care, nothing will.

Finally, there is at least one issue where immigrants are sharply *more* libertarian than natives: immigration itself. Materially, recent immigrants have the most to lose from additional immigration. Ottaviano and Peri (2008: 59) estimate that immigration from 1990–2006 depressed foreign-born workers' wages by over 7 percent. But immigrants, like human beings generally, do not derive their political philosophies from material self-interest (Mansbridge 1990). The General Social Survey asks respondents to put their views on immigration on a 1–5 scale, with 5 being most hostile.[8] People with two native-born parents have an average response of 3.9, with a median of 4; people with at least one foreign-born parent have an average response of 3.1, with a median of 3. By way of comparison, people who call themselves "extremely liberal" have an average response of 3.3—versus 4.0 for the "extremely conservative." People with foreign-born parents rarely favor open borders, but economists and libertarians aside, no one is less opposed to immigration.

Suppose, however, that you remain convinced that immigration has serious political externalities. You have to ask yourself: are immigration restrictions really the cheapest, most humane way to address the problem? The answer, again, is No. Consider a simple alternative: admit immigrants to live and work, but not to vote. If necessary, we could make their non-voting status hereditary. Or suppose you worry about immigrants' political ignorance. If so, we could restrict the vote to immigrants who successfully pass a civics test. Are you afraid of class warfare? We could give immigrants the right to vote once their lifetime tax payments surpass $100,000. Whatever your complaint, there exists a remedy far less objectionable than exclusion and deportation.

PROTECTING PROPERTY RIGHTS?

The most fundamental objection to my argument is to deny the moral presumption in favor of free migration. Maybe forcibly preventing a person from working, renting, and shopping for no good reason is morally permissible as long as he was born in another country. To make this case, defenders of immigration restrictions often appeal to the distinction between killing and letting die (Rachels 2001). Donating a few hundred dollars to charity could easily save a life, but we do not call a man a "murderer" if he chooses to buy a plasma TV instead. Why then should we condemn countries that take care of their own instead of admitting millions of penniless strangers?

Unfortunately for this argument, immigration restrictions are not merely a passive refusal to help. Immigration restrictions forbid people to help themselves by trading with willing partners. As philosopher Michael Huemer (2009: 4–5) explains:

> Suppose that, through no fault of mine, Marvin is in danger of starvation. He asks me for food. If I refuse to give him food, I thereby *fail to confer a benefit* on Marvin and, at the same time, *allow* Marvin to go hungry. If Marvin then starves to death, those who accept the doing/allowing distinction would say that I have not *killed* Marvin, but merely *allowed* him to die. And some believe that this is much less wrong than killing, possibly not even wrong at all. But now consider a different case. Suppose that Marvin, again in danger of starvation, plans to walk to the local market to buy some food. In the absence of any outside interference, this plan would succeed—the market is open, and there are people willing to trade food for something that Marvin has. Now suppose that, knowing all this, I actively and forcibly restrain Marvin from reaching the market. As a result, he starves to death. In this situation, I would surely be said to have killed Marvin, or at least done something morally comparable to killing him.

Millions of Haitians want to move here. Millions of American landlords, employers, and stores would be happy to house, hire, and feed them. For the U.S. government to criminalize these transactions for no good reason is not merely uncharitable. It is unjust.

Critics of immigrants also often compare them to trespassers. If an individual has a spare bedroom, we don't expect him to justify his refusal to allow a total stranger to live there. Why should we hold countries to a higher standard?

The problem with this argument is that standard property law *already* protects owners against trespassers, both foreign and domestic. The point of immigration restrictions is not to protect property rights, but to restrict them.[9] Some landlords want to rent to immigrants. Some employers want to hire them. Some stores want to sell to them. Under open borders, landlords, employers, and stores can do so if they see fit. Immigration restrictions force them to deal solely with people pre-approved by the state.[10]

More empirically minded critics may object that the social science of immigration focuses too much on the United States. The labor market and fiscal effects of immigration seem worse in other parts of the world—especially Europe. My reply is twofold. First, the estimated effects of immigration are only moderately worse for Europe than they are for the United States (Kerr and Kerr 2011, D'Amuri and Peri 2011). Second, and more importantly, European nations have cheaper and more humane ways to cope. They could deregulate labor markets and scale back their welfare states across the board. They could move to a two-tier system: heavy regulation and high benefits for native workers, light regulation and low benefits for immigrant workers. Scapegoating immigrants for the pathologies of the welfare state is politically popular but morally perverse.

Critics might also object that my proposed "cheaper and more humane" alternatives to immigration restrictions are politically impossible. But you could say the same about any radical policy change. If you're convinced that a Grand Bargain—open borders plus conditions—would make the world a better place, how is "political impossibility" a reason not to advocate it? A variant on the "politically impossible" critique objects that the Grand Bargain would not be politically credible; once the immigrants arrive, the terms would not be enforced. This is overly pessimistic. Before the Grand Bargain would stand a chance, public opinion would have to *drastically* change. If you can imagine public opinion accepting the Grand Bargain in the first place, why is it so hard to believe that the public would insist on strict adherence to its terms?

The strongest empirical objection to my thesis is that open borders is far "out of sample." The last time a major country approximated open borders was roughly a century ago. Social scientists show that moderate liberalization of immigration has good effects. Full liberalization could still be disastrous. We don't know enough to rule out worst-case scenarios.

If you embrace something like the Precautionary Principle (Sunstein 2005), this is a powerful objection to immediate open borders. The society we have works extremely well by world and historic standards. If you live in the First World, you're doing fine. Why take chances?

From an amoral, risk-averse point of view, there is no good response to this objection. But if you take the moral presumption in favor of free migration seriously, this is a weak argument indeed. Immigration restrictions are not a minor inconvenience we impose on the rest of the world for our peace of mind. Immigration restrictions literally ruin many millions of lives—forcibly denying people the opportunity to do business with their best customers. "We're trapping millions in Third World misery because we *know* that free migration has very bad consequences" arguably overcomes the presumption in favor of open borders. "We're trapping millions in Third World misery because there's a *small chance* that free migration has very bad consequences" does not. Think of the moral progress that the Precautionary Principle would have precluded: until a society tried freedom of religion or the abolition of slavery, no one could be sure the experiment wouldn't end in disaster.

In any case, the Precautionary Principle lends no support to the status quo. Existing research confirms that moderate liberalization of immigration has excellent overall consequences. If the "out of sample" problem bothers you, the obvious solution is to expand the sample gradually. Step one: liberalize slightly more than any other country. Step two: see what happens. Step three: in the absence of very bad consequences, liberalize a little more and return to step two.

Conclusion: The Presumption in Favor of Immigration

Between 2000 and 2010, the United States government officially deported almost three million people and intimidated another 11 million into "voluntarily" leaving the country (Office of Immigration Statistics 2011: 94). At least 10 million residents of the United States endure the humiliation and fear of "being illegal" (Hoefer, Rytina, and Baker 2011: 4). In the broad scheme of things, these immigrants are the lucky ones. Mexicans and Central Americans can cross the U.S. border if they are in good health and willing to pay smugglers a few years' wages (Roberts et al. 2010). For most would-be immigrants from South America, Asia, and Africa, however, the cost of illegal entry is prohibitive. With legal permission, even the poorest could eventually scrape together money for a boat ticket. But for low-skilled workers from the Third World, legal permission to enter the United States is almost impossible to obtain (Anderson 2010: 93–4).

Many libertarians would condemn these facts as "inexcusable." I rest my argument on a weaker premise: whether or not the facts are "inexcusable," they do *require an excuse*. On the surface, it seems wrong to prohibit voluntary exchange between natives and foreigners. Proponents of immigration restrictions have to show why, moral appearances notwithstanding, immigration restrictions are morally justified.

They fail to do so. Immigration restrictions are not necessary to protect American workers. Most Americans benefit from immigration, and the losers don't lose much. Immigration restrictions are not necessary to protect American taxpayers. Researchers disagree about whether the fiscal effects of immigration are positive or negative, but they agree that the fiscal effects are small. Immigration restrictions are not necessary to protect American culture. Immigrants make our culture better—and their children learn fluent English. Immigration restrictions are not necessary to protect American liberty. Immigrants have low voter turnout and accept our political status quo by default. By increasing diversity, they undermine native support for the welfare state. And on one important issue—immigration itself—immigrants are much more pro-liberty than natives.

Even if all these empirical claims are wrong, though, immigration restrictions would remain morally impermissible. Why? Because there are cheaper and more humane solutions for each and every complaint. If immigrants hurt American workers, we can charge immigrants higher taxes or admission fees, and use the revenue to compensate the losers. If immigrants burden American taxpayers, we can make immigrants ineligible for benefits. If immigrants hurt American culture, we can impose tests of English fluency and cultural literacy. If immigrants hurt American liberty, we can refuse to give them the right to vote. Whatever your complaint happens to be, immigration restrictions are a needlessly draconian remedy.

ENDNOTES

1. You might claim that life in Haiti isn't nearly as bad for Haitians, because at least they have their families with them. But suppose your relief mission included your relatives. Would you feel better if the U.S. government denied *your whole family* permission to return, rather than you alone?

2. From Milton Friedman's session at the 18th Annual Institute for Liberty and Policy Analysis (August 20–22, 1999).

3. Many such limitations are already on the books. For example, immigrants have to work (not merely reside) in the United States for at least 10 years before they can collect Social Security benefits (Social Security Online 2011). I owe this point to Michael Clemens.

4. I owe this point to Michael Clemens.

5. AGS report only the results for maximum AFDC benefits, not total social spending. But their result is still noteworthy. Since blacks support higher welfare spending than whites, you would expect larger black population shares to predict *higher* AFDC benefits. The opposite is true.

6. But what if immigration were high enough to make natives a minority? Careful readers will note that blacks remain a minority in every U.S. states; if blacks actually formed a majority, the negative relationship between welfare and black population share would presumably reverse. On reflection, though, there is a crucial disanalogy: Immigrants, unlike African Americans, have never seen themselves as a single group. Immigrants identify with other immigrants from their homeland, not immigrants in general. Indeed, in-group divisions between "early" and "late" immigrants quickly emerge: see for example the divisions between Jewish immigrants in the 19th and early 20th centuries (Sowell 1981).

7. The most sophisticated analyses to date are probably two blog posts by Tino Sanandaji (2011a, 2011b). For a critique of Sanandaji, see Caplan (2011).

8. The question, LETIN1, reads, "Do you think the number of immigrants to America nowadays should be . . ." The response options are: increased a lot (=1), increased a little (=2), remain the same as it is (=3), reduced a little (=4), and reduced a lot (=5).

9. Socialists could of course insist that Americans collectively own America. No one "really" owns real estate or a business; so-called "owners" are merely stewards for society. But are conservatives—much less libertarians—really willing to accept this premise?

10. Some libertarians object that, due to discrimination laws, individuals and firms are not free to refuse to deal with immigrants. As a practical matter, though, these laws—unlike immigration restrictions—are rarely binding and mildly enforced (Caplan 2010). For libertarians to use discrimination laws to justify immigration restrictions is truly a case of straining out a gnat and swallowing a camel.

References

Alesina, A.; Glaeser, E.; and Sacerdote, B. (2001) "Why Doesn't the U.S. Have a European-Style Welfare State?" *Brookings Papers on Economic Activity* 2: 187–254.

Anderson, S. (2010) Immigration. Santa Barbara, Calif.: Greenwood.

Borjas, G., and Katz, L. (2005) "The Evolution of the Mexican-Born Workforce in the United States." In G. Borjas (ed.) *Mexican Immigration to the United States*, 13–55. Chicago: University of Chicago Press.

Borjas, G., and Trejo, S. (1991) "Immigrant Participation in the Welfare System." *Industrial and Labor Relations Review* 44 (2): 195–211.

Caplan, B. (2007) *The Myth of the Rational Voter: Why Democracies Choose Bad Policies*. Princeton, N.J.: Princeton University Press.

———. (2008) "Mises's Democracy-Dictatorship Equivalence Theorem." *Review of Austrian Economics* 21 (1): 45–59.

———. (2010) "Association, Exclusion, Liberty, and the Status Quo." *EconLog*. Available at http://econlog.econlib.org/ archives/2010/06/association_exc.html.

———. (2011) "Ethnic Diversity and the Size of Government: A Belated Reply to Sanandaji." *EconLog*. Available at http:// econlog.econlib.org/archives/2011/09/ethnic_diversit.html.

Cassel, C. (2002) "Hispanic Turnout: Estimates from Validated Voting Data." *Political Research Quarterly* 55 (2): 391–408.

Chandy, L., and Gertz, G. (2011) *Poverty in Numbers: The Changing State of Global Poverty from 2005 to 2015*. Washington: Brookings Institution.

Citrin, J., and Highton, B. (2002) *How Race, Ethnicity, and Immigration Shape the California Electorate*. San Francisco: Public Policy Institute of California.

Clemens, M. (2011) "Economics and Emigration: Trillion-Dollar Bills on the Sidewalk?" *Journal of Economic Perspectives* 25 (3): 83–106.

Collier, P. (2007) *The Bottom Billion: Why the Poorest Countries Are Failing and What Can Be Done about It*. New York: Oxford University Press.

D'Amuri, F., and Peri, G. (2011) "Immigration, Jobs, and Employment Protection: Evidence from Europe." NBER Working Paper No. 17139.

Gilens, M. (1999) *Why Americans Hate Welfare: Race, Media, and the Politics of Anti-Poverty Policy*. Chicago: University of Chicago Press.

Gonzalez, L., and Ortega, F. (2009) "Immigration and Housing Booms: Evidence from Spain." IZA Discussion Paper No. 4333. Bonn, Germany: Institute for the Study of Labor.

Hakimzadeh, S., and Cohn, D. (2007) "English Usage among Hispanics in the United States." Washington: Pew Hispanic Center.

Harrison, P. (2009) "Never Waste a Good Crisis, Hillary Clinton Says on Climate." Reuters (7 March).

Hoefer, M.; Rytina, N.; and Baker, B. (2011) "Estimates of the Unauthorized Immigrant Population Residing in the United States: January 2010." Washington: Office of Immigration Statistics.

Huemer, M. (2010) "Is There a Right to Immigrate?" *Social Theory and Practice* 36 (3): 249–61.

Huntington, S. (2004) *Who Are We? The Challenges to America's National Identity*. New York: Simon & Schuster.

Kerr, S., and Kerr, W. (2011) "Economic Impacts of Immigration: A Survey." NBER Working Paper No. 16736.

Maddison, A. (2009) "World Population, GDP and per Capita GDP, 1–2003 AD." Groningen, Netherlands: University of Groningen. Available at www.ggdc.net/maddison/Historical_Statistics/ horizontal-file_03-2007.xls

Mansbridge, J. (1990) *Beyond Self-Interest*. Chicago: University of Chicago Press.

Office of Immigration Statistics (2011) *2010 Yearbook of Immigration Statistics*. Washington: U.S. Department of Homeland Security.

Office of Management and Budget (2010) *Budget of the U.S. Government: Fiscal Year 2011*. Washington: U.S. Government Printing Office.

Ottaviano, G., and Peri, G. (2008) "Immigration and National Wages: Clarifying the Theory and the Empirics." NBER Working Paper No. 14188.

———. (forthcoming) "Rethinking the Effects of Immigration on Wages." *Journal of the European Economic Association*.

Peri, G., and Sparber, C. (2009) "Task Specialization, Immigration, and Wages." *American Economic Journal: Applied Economics* 1 (3): 135–69.

Porter, E. (2005) "Illegal Immigrants Are Bolstering Social Security with Billions." *New York Times* (5 April).

Rachels, J. (2001) "Killing and Letting Die." In L. Becker and C. Becker (eds.) *Encyclopedia of Ethics*, 947–50. New York: Routledge.

Roberts, B.; Hanson, G.; Cornwall, D.; and Borger, S. (2010) "An Analysis of Migrant Smuggling Costs across the Southwest Border." Washington: Office of Immigration Statistics.

Sachs, J. (1994) "Life in the Economic Emergency Room." In J. Williamson (ed.) *The Political Economy of Policy Reform*, 503–23. Washington: Institute for International Economics.

Saiz, A. (2003) "Room in the Kitchen for the Melting Pot: Immigration and Rental Prices." *Review of Economics and Statistics* 85 (3): 502–21.

———. (2007) "Immigration and Housing Rents in American Cities." *Journal of Urban Economics* 61 (2): 345–71.

Samuelson, W., and Zeckhauser, R. (1988) "Status Quo Bias in Decision Making." *Journal of Risk and Uncertainty* 1 (1): 7–59.

Sanandaji, T. (2011a) "Ethnic Diversity and the Size of Government." *Super-Economy.* Available at http://super-economy.blogspot.com/2011/05/ethnic-diversity-and-size-of-government.html.

———. (2011b) "Bryan Caplan Is Wrong about Open Borders and the Size of Government." *Super-Economy.* Available at http://super-economy.blogspot.com/2011/09/bryan-caplan-is-wrong-about-open.html.

Social Security Online (2011) "How You Earn Credits." Washington: Social Security Administration. Available at www.ssa.gov/pubs/10072.html

Sowell, T. (1981) *Ethnic America: A History.* New York: Basic Books

Sunstein, C. (2005) *The Laws of Fear: Beyond the Precautionary Principle.* Cambridge: Cambridge University Press.

Torres, G., and Pelham, B. (2008) "One-Quarter of World's Population May Wish to Migrate." *Gallup.* Available at www.gallup.com/poll/108325/onequarter-worlds-population-may-wish-migrate.aspx

U.S. Census Bureau (2003) "The Foreign-Born Population: 2000." *Census 2000 Brief.*

———. (2011) "Educational Attainment: Table 2." Available at www.census.gov/hhes/socdemo/education/data/cps/2010/Table2-Both.xls

Xu, J. (2005) "Why Do Minorities Participate Less? The Effects of Immigration, Education, and Electoral Process on Asian American Voter Registration and Turnout." *Social Science Research* 34 (4): 682–702.

*Bryan Caplan is professor of economics at George Mason University and research fellow at the Mercatus Center.

Caplan, Bryan. "Why Should We Restrict Immigration?" *Cato Journal* 32, no. 1 (Winter 2012): 5–24.

CATO JOURNAL Copyright 2012.

Used by permission.

Building Capacity for the Transnational Regulation of Migration

by Cristina M. Rodríguez*

Two significant conceptual errors frame the public debate concerning labor migration and the related phenomenon of illegal immigration. Each error stems from lawmakers' failure or refusal to recognize the ongoing and transnational nature of migration. First, the immigration debate occurs largely within a domestic political framework, and the assumption that the United States can address immigration issues, particularly illegal immigration, through the perfection of domestic enforcement mechanisms pervades the discourse. But migration is inherently international, and its management requires engagement with other governments and with social facts beyond U.S. control. Second, the rhetorical emphasis placed on "fixing" our broken regime reflects a conception of immigration as a problem to be solved. But migration is a cross-border phenomenon produced by structural and historical factors that will only evolve, rather than disappear, and it therefore requires transnational *management*, rather than a one-time comprehensive legislative solution.

Regulating immigration ultimately requires lawmakers to reach beyond a unilateral "gatekeeping" strategy defined by efforts to stop migration through law enforcement and economic coercion. Because states cannot effectively manage migration in isolation from one another,[1] the United States must approach the issue by prioritizing cooperation with actors outside the United States. In their contributions to the policy debate, scholars increasingly have emphasized the importance of addressing labor and illegal migration through bilateral and transnational frameworks[2]—through accords that would recognize the interdependence of the United States and Mexico and engage our neighbor to the south directly through joint efforts to channel migratory flows.

In this Essay, I seek to contribute to this strand of commentary by focusing on the actual mechanisms of transnationalism and the avenues they open up for advancing a meaningful bilateralism. I demonstrate that the cross-border administrative law space created by these mechanisms is occupied not just by international entities, but also by entanglements between the domestic institutions of different countries. I emphasize the importance of identifying and then building the mechanisms of bilateralism, or the cross-border institutional capacities needed for managing migration, in a manner that promotes burden-sharing, or that ensures that both sides of the bilateral relationship reap benefits and bear costs, in rough proportion.

Many transnational mechanisms of governance already exist, and I use this space to advance the conversation about transnational regulation by mapping some of them and then offering initial suggestions for their development. For the sake of simplicity, I focus on the U.S.-Mexico relationship, not least because immigration to the United States is overwhelmingly Mexican (twenty percent of the authorized population and fifty-six percent of the unauthorized population),[3] and because ninety-eight percent of Mexico's out- migration is to the United States.[4] Our shared border is also itself the source and site of many of the pressures that make immigration a significant public policy issue.

Bringing to light existing institutional frameworks might also help to calm the passions that arise from the popular assumption that the United States and Mexico are locked in an adversarial relationship in relation to migration. This relationship is not without its tensions, of course. Actors on either side of the border have different sets of priorities. Both the United States and Mexico have interests in controlling smuggling, drug trafficking (and the associated extreme violence), and other criminal activity around the border. But on the subject of immigration, Mexico's objectives revolve primarily around protecting the interests of its nationals abroad and facilitating remittance traffic back to Mexico,[5] whereas the United States's interests focus on simultaneously serving the country's labor market needs and preventing immigration from having adverse effects on U.S. workers and federal, state, and local budgets. This divergence of interest makes efforts to cooperate fraught and gives rise to collective action difficulties. The asymmetrical nature of the relationship between the United States and Mexico further complicates the matter; the United States possesses superior bargaining power and economic strength.[6] But it is precisely because of these asymmetries that developing institutional frameworks for cooperation is vital to meeting the regulatory challenge posed by the shared border, and the shared interest in managing migration creates crucial commonality.

I. THE MECHANISMS OF BILATERALISM IN THE U.S.-MEXICO RELATIONSHIP

The mechanisms of bilateralism exist in at least three forms: (1) diplomatic and information-sharing networks that involve consultation and conferencing among cabinet officials and agency heads in both the United States and Mexico;

(2) actual cooperative ventures between administrative officials on both sides of the border; and (3) civil society networks (many of which do not involve state actors) developed to serve the needs of Mexican migrants inside the United States. These frameworks are defined by different degrees of formality and thus have varying relationships to the hard legal regimes of the United States and Mexico. Most of them do not have legal regulatory authority, though they do reflect how the sovereign power and local interests of each nation project across the border. In addition, these mechanisms make clear that migration management depends on activity—sometimes collaborative, sometimes isolated—by officials at all levels of government and in the private sector.

A. Diplomatic and Information-Sharing Networks

The U.S. Department of State and the Mexican Foreign Ministry clearly communicate over issues of mutual concern, but it is also the case that almost every agency head deals regularly and directly with his or her counterpart on the other side of the border.[7] Perhaps the most prominent example of such interaction is the U.S.-Mexico Binational Commission (BNC), originally established in 1981 and envisioned as a forum for cabinet-level officials to meet once or twice a year to discuss regulatory issues related to the binational relationship. Over time, the BNC has become a one-day conference chaired by the U.S. Secretary of State and the Mexican Secretary of Foreign Relations and attended by cabinet-level officials and heads of administrative agencies. The Clinton Administration, in particular, invested heavily in this project,[8] and migration and border security have become prominent among the Commission's agenda items.[9] The governors of border states in both countries have developed a similar network of their own,[10] and mayors in neighboring towns maintain close working relationships. State and local officials in both countries increasingly reach across the border to attract new forms of investment. In the United States, state and local officials also work to respond to the transnational interests of their new popular constituencies of Mexican origin, by facilitating trade, investment, and cross-border traffic.

The tangible accomplishments of these gatherings are few. But formal networks of this kind at least promote information sharing across governments, as well as the articulation of joint priorities. Most important, when taken seriously, these networks can build and sustain the political will necessary to advance bilateral cooperation through the creation of actual legal regimes. They can also help project the particular interests of the United States and Mexico into the domestic political debate of the other country, to ensure that the interests of

U.S. and Mexican citizens receive recognition in the national decisionmaking processes over which they have no direct control.[11]

The Partnership for Prosperity—a public-private partnership initiated by Presidents Bush and Fox in 2001—offers another example of an information-sharing network created by high level officials to advance a tangible reform agenda through reliance on cooperation between bureaucrats and the private sector. The Partnership promotes development in Mexico, particularly in areas with high rates of out- migration to the United States.[12] Former Secretary of State Colin Powell has listed the Partnership's accomplishments as including lowering the fees for transferring money between the United States and Mexico, developing innovative methods for funding infrastructure projects, and establishing an Overseas Private Investment Corporation in Mexico to provide over $600 million in various types of financing to U.S. businesses operating in Mexico.[13]

B. The Cross-Border Work of Administrative Agencies

Administrative agencies on both sides of the border, particularly in the areas of law enforcement and public health, work together to develop actual practices that advance mutual goals, as well as to streamline operations that involve officials from both countries. With respect to border security, cooperation by state officials has been a longstanding practice. Again, this relationship has been complicated by different priorities, with Mexico focused on matters of internal security and protecting the lives and rights of its nationals at the border, and the United States focused on terrorism-related screening and intelligence gathering, as well as drug interdiction.[14] But Presidents Clinton and Zedillo poured considerable effort into formalizing bilateral consultation between consulates and border agencies. In 2002, the two countries entered into the so-called "Smart Border Agreement" (SBA) designed to increase the number of secure documents for frequent border crossers, improve intelligence sharing, and implement security strategies focused not just on the border, but also on the areas where threats originate. Initiatives also have included simplifying the execution of arrest warrants on either side of the border by reducing the legal obstacles that prevent warrants from either country from being honored in the other, as well as removing obstacles to collaboration between law enforcement officials. Perhaps most important, the SBA has brought attention to the need to regularize migratory flows in order to free up larger amounts of scarce law enforcement resources to address public safety and national security issues.[15]

On the subject of public health, perhaps the most formal existing mechanism of cooperation is the United States-Mexico Border Health Commission, which was established under the auspices of Public Law 103–400 and through a Memorandum of Agreement between the governments of the United States and Mexico.[16] Membership consists of high-level government officials from federal and state health agencies in both countries, as well as political appointees. The Commission's primary objective is to deal with mobile public health crises and to address the needs for internal and external forms of communication and technical harmonization.[17] The Commission also continues to work toward facilitating binational health insurance to cover Mexican nationals working in the United States and to address legal barriers to coverage, such as a Texas state law that does not permit HMOs to market insurance plans across the border.[18]

Perhaps the most notable initiative to emerge from the Commission is its support for the Ventanillas de Salud program, through which Mexican consulates (there are fifty inside the United States) collaborate with U.S. nonprofit health organizations to provide services and education to Mexican citizens living and working in the United States.[19] Twelve such programs existed as of 2008, and they provide direct services to 500,000 "consulate clients," reaching an estimated 1.5 million people in the U.S. A combination of Mexican state funds and private grants provides financial support for the programs, which focus primarily on disseminating occupational health and safety-related information and referring clients for services in Mexico.[20]

C. Transnational Civil Society Networks

Several transnational civil society networks have taken shape in the last few decades and have created structures for the delivery of social services and the protection of Mexican nationals' interests abroad.[21] Some of these mechanisms are creatures of the state, such as the Ventanillas de Salud program, and others emerge via networks of private actors. Indeed, emigration countries generally have begun adopting policies to address the rights and interests of migrants abroad, and to provide incentives for them to return home.[22] The attempts by sending societies, such as Mexico, to both provide for and control their nationals abroad simultaneously alleviate some of the burden felt by U.S. institutions and inject the sending state and its civil society into life in the United States.

Two examples of the increasingly vibrant civil society networks that have emerged include nongovernmental hometown associations and the Institute for Mexicans Abroad, which was formed in 2003 to replace the Mexican Communities Abroad Program. The hometown associations and migrant federations have evolved as informal networks that connect migrants in the United States to citizens and organizations in towns in Mexico. They consist of business associations, labor unions, and churches[23] on both sides of the border. In addition to organizing social and civic events, the associations develop positions on binational issues, and their component parts maintain close relations with one another. Some associations actually participate in and help fund development projects in both the United States and Mexico,[24] and the Mexican government finances association projects through its consulates in the United States.[25]

The Institute for Mexicans Abroad similarly exists to provide services to Mexicans living in the United States, while simultaneously promoting understanding of Mexican culture in receiving communities and facilitating immigrant integration. Housed in Mexico's Ministry of Foreign Affairs, the Institute works through the Mexican consulates in the United States and partners with civic actors on both sides of the border.[26] When it was still the Communities Abroad Program, the Institute began the "Tres por Uno" program, through which migrants abroad and Mexican government agencies finance infrastructure projects in Mexico, spending eighty million dollars per year by 2005.[27] Today, the Institute's advisory council consists of Mexican community leaders, Latino organizations in the United States, and officials from the state governments of Mexico.[28] The Institute cosponsors social programs with agencies at all levels of government. In addition to coordinating the Ventanillas de Salud program in the United States,[29] the Institute works with school districts to assess the needs of migrant school children and provides Mexican nationals with financial literacy workshops and English-language and continuing adult education programs.[30] The Institute's objectives also include public diplomacy efforts in the United States designed to enhance respect for the culture and country of Mexico, in order to address the hostility toward Mexicans and Mexican culture generated by illegal immigration.[31] This promotion of understanding helps to create political space for the treatment of immigration as a humanitarian and regulatory issue, rather than as a law enforcement problem.

II. SHAPING THE FUTURE OF BILATERALISM

The existing mechanisms of bilateralism form an intricate constellation of institutions designed to address the multiple needs engendered by immigration between Mexico and the United States. These mechanisms are largely ad hoc, however.[32] Efforts to develop an overarching normative framework could prove stultifying, but some theoretical cohesion will be required to shift the focus of public debate toward bilateralism, given the many different forms of governance needed to negotiate the U.S.-Mexico relationship.

The mechanisms just discussed all embody an ethic of burden sharing and reflect the crucial insight that when countries have large populations in common, both sides of the border should benefit from and bear responsibility for those populations. The civil society networks, in particular, reflect the burden-sharing ethos, demonstrating through actual practice a commitment to treating migration as a binational responsibility requiring transnational mechanisms of governance. The concepts of "burden sharing" (or mutual obligation) and "management" (or regulation) thus offer general but sufficiently substantive umbrella ideas under which to develop the mechanisms of bilateralism. This shared responsibility ultimately can be realized through an agenda that builds the existing institutional capacities described above to (1) address the root causes of migration and (2) manage migration's effects to promote public health, safety, and prosperity, as well as human rights.

With respect to the first set of priorities—addressing the root causes of migration—the concepts of burden sharing and management ought to be highlighted at the diplomatic level as governing principles for the U.S.-Mexico relationship. The foregoing discussion should make clear that the Mexican government takes the interests of its emigrating nationals and the impact of their movement on Mexico and the United States quite seriously,[33] but it remains crucial for high-ranking U.S. officials to apply consistent pressure on Mexico to address the underlying structural causes of migration, especially limited job opportunities and structural inequalities at home. Perhaps more important, the United States should commit diplomatically to assisting Mexico in this long-term, cause-based approach to stabilizing and reducing migration.[34]

At the administrative level, this approach could require diminished reliance by Mexico on remittances as a tool of development, especially since monies sent home from abroad offer only short-term and individualized (rather than systemic) development assistance. It could include devising positive incentives for Mexican migrants to return home, such as business loans or educational grants, to be jointly funded and implemented by Mexico and the United States. Increased funding and technical support from U.S. agencies to arrangements like the Partnership for Prosperity could help expand the reach of preexisting development initiatives. Some commentators also have advocated increased utilization of the North American Development Bank, an institution created in 1994 in a side agreement to NAFTA. To transform the Bank into a collaborative mechanism of development, both its substantive and geographic mandates would need to be expanded beyond their original focus on the environment.[35]

The second set of priorities, which revolves around regularization and management of existing flows, is crucial to creating a climate in which migration is seen as a win-win proposition, rather than as an imposition on the United States and a drain on Mexico. Regularization will require a labor accord of some kind, the details of which are well beyond the scope of this Essay.[36] But at the very least, transnational, interagency cooperation should be part of any new labor regime. For example, federal and state agencies[37] in Mexico can assist in providing crucial data and economic and demographic projections regarding the Mexican labor market and the sources, numbers, and characteristics of likely Mexican migrants.[38] The network of Mexican consulates, which already focuses on the rights and interests of Mexican nationals in the United States, could be cultivated and enlisted in identifying and helping to satisfy the particular needs of migrants, and perhaps also in monitoring employer-employee relations. Indeed, federal policymakers, as well as state and local officials, should regard the civil society networks that have emerged over the last two decades as crucial resources for providing for immigrant welfare and promoting immigrant integration. The hometown associations' and Mexican Institute's simultaneous focus on promoting attachments to Mexico and encouraging community participation and English-language learning in the United States provides an essential model for addressing the inherent tension between wanting to encourage some migrants to return and ensuring that those who inevitably stay for long periods (or forever) integrate successfully.

* * *

To varying degrees, these transnational schemes amount to the extension of sovereignty across borders and the intermingling of different sovereign regimes. They thus implicate one of the central concerns surrounding global governance: accountability to the public. Migration scuttles the social contract on both sides of the border, making one government's decisions consequential for the citizens of the other state. This discussion thus surfaces a question that must be addressed in the shift toward a burden-sharing and management model of migration: How do we simultaneously address cross-border regulatory challenges and ensure that the publics on both sides of the border have adequate voice in what is done? Crucially, this accountability must extend not just from the state to its own citizens, but from the United States government to the people of Mexico and the government of Mexico to the people of the United States.

Interdependence, which is often invoked in the rhetoric that surrounds diplomacy, must ultimately be a core presumption of actual reform debates, and lawmakers ought to make concerted efforts to solidify bilateralism as a working practice. Building transnational networks with ties to public institutions on either side of the border ultimately will promote accountability in immigration policy by ensuring the participation of representatives from both nations in the myriad decisionmaking processes that involve an increasingly transnational public.

ENDNOTES

1. Bimal Ghosh, Managing Migration: Interstate Cooperation at the Global Level, *in* Interstate Cooperation and Migration 109, 111 (2005).

2. See, e.g., Jorge A. Bustamante, Mexico-United States Labor Migration Flows, 31 Int'l Migration Rev. 1112, 1112 (1997) (noting that outmigration in Mexico is perceived as economic and labor phenomenon from which United States reaps benefits, whereas in United States, same migration is perceived as law and order or public safety phenomenon); Jennifer Gordon, Transnational Labor Citizenship, 80 S. Cal. L. Rev. 503, 509 (2007) ("I propose an opening up of the fortress of labor and of the nation-state to accommodate a constant flow of new migrants through a model that would tie immigration status to membership in organizations of transnational workers rather than to a particular employer."); Alejandro Portes, The Fence to Nowhere, Am. Prospect, Oct. 2007, at 26, 28 (arguing that United States and Mexico must develop means to manage massive flow of migration); Marc Rosenblum, The United States and Mexico: Prospects for a Bilateral Migration Policy, Border Battles: The U.S. Immigration Debates, Mar. 8, 2007, at http://borderbattles.ssrc.org/Rosenblum/printable.html (on file with the *Columbia Law Review*) (detailing fraught history of U.S.-Mexico bilateralism and laying out agenda for bilateral accord). For discussion of the history of U.S.-Mexico bilateralism and its limitations as reflected in the World War II-era Bracero program, see Mae M. Ngai, Impossible Subjects: Illegal Immigrants and the Making of Modern America 138–47 (2005); Adam B. Cox & Cristina M. Rodríguez, The President and Immigration Law, 119 Yale L.J. 458, 485–91 (2009).

3. Andrew Selee, Woodrow Wilson Ctr., More Than Neighbors: An Overview of Mexico and U.S.-Mexico Relations 5 (2007), available at http://www.wilsoncenter.org/topics/pubs/Mexico. More%20Than%20Neighbors.pdf (on file with the *Columbia Law Review*).

4. David Fitzgerald, A Nation of Emigrants: How Mexico Manages its Migration 5–6 (2009).

5. In 2005, remittances amounted to approximately twenty billion dollars. See id. At 63. Though the current recession has led to a decline in this traffic of late, see Joel Millman, Remittances to Mexico Fall More Than Forecast, Wall St. J., Jan. 28, 2009, at A3 (noting that amount of money sent home by Mexicans working in United States dropped by 3.6% in 2008—first decline recorded since Mexico began tracking remittance traffic thirteen years ago), the decline in remittances to Latin America may be "bottoming out," Dilip Ratha, Sanket Mohapatra & Ani Silwal, Migration and Development Brief 11, Migration and Remittance Trends 2009, at 2 (2009), available at http://siteresources.worldbank.org/INTPROSPECTS/ Resources/334934-1110315015165/ MigrationAndDevelopmentBrief11.pdf (on file with the *Columbia Law Review*) ("Remittance flows to Mexico declined by 13.4 percent in the first nine months of 2009 . . . However, the decline in flows appears to be bottoming out in most countries across the region.").

6. Selee, supra note 3, at iii; Ghosh, supra note 1, at 121–22.

7. Selee, supra note 3, at 13.

8. Augustin Escobar, Interstate Cooperation: The Americas, in Interstate Cooperation and Migration, supra note 1, at 65, 80.

9. See, e.g., K. Larry Storrs, Cong. Research Serv., Mexico-United States Dialogue on Migration and Border Issues, 2001–2005, at 5–6 (2005), available at http://www.fas.org/sgp/crs/row/RL32735.pdf (on file with the *Columbia Law Review*) (discussing meeting of November 25–26, 2002, during which talks addressed importance of forging bilateral migration accord and joint border security initiatives).

10. The first border governors' conference took place in Ciudad Juarez in June 1980 and resulted, in part, from the efforts of Governor Clements of Texas, who had promised during his campaign to improve relations with Mexico. John Kincaid, The American Governors in International Affairs, Publius: J. of Federalism, Fall 1984, at 95, 111. The conference is designed to enable governors to develop proposals for reform on border- related matters that can be submitted to their respective state and national governments, but through consultation with their counterparts on the other side of the border. The conference consists of thirteen working groups focused on issue areas that include agriculture, border security, crossings, economic development, education, emergency matters, energy, environment, health, science, tourism, water, and wildlife. See Border Governors Conference, Worktables, at http://www.bordergovernors.ca.gov/worktables (last visited Jan. 12, 2010) (on file with the *Columbia Law Review*).

11. Another such network is the Regional Conference on Migration (RCM), a multilateral regional meeting that has occurred annually since 1996. The RCM is attended by eleven member states, including the United States, Mexico, and Canada, and its objectives include promoting the orderly movement of persons and respect for the human rights of migrants. Reg'l Conference on Migration, Conference Description, at http://www.rcmvs.org/pagina_n.htm (last visited Jan. 5, 2010) (on file with the *Columbia Law Review*).

12. P'ship for Prosperity, Report to President Vicente Fox and President George W. Bush: Creating Prosperity Through Partnership 1 (2002), available at http://www.state.gov/documents/organization/16197.pdf (on file with the *Columbia Law Review*).

13. Storrs, supra note 9, at 9–10.

14. Andrés Rozental & Peter H. Smith, Woodrow Wilson Ctr. Mex. Inst., The United States and Mexico: Forging a Strategic Partnership 11 (2005), available at http://www.wilsoncenter.org/topics/pubs/USMEXenglish%20copy1.pdf (on file with the *Columbia Law Review*).

15. Id. at 12.

16. United States-Mexico Border Health Commission Act, Pub. L. No. 103-400, 108 Stat. 4169 (1994) (codified as amended at 22 U.S.C. §§ 290n–290n-6 (2006)); Agreement to Establish a United States-Mexico Border Health Commission, U.S.-Mex., July 14–24, 2000, T.I.A.S. No. 13107, available at http://www.state.gov/documents/organization/126990.pdf (on file with the *Columbia Law Review*).

17. For a history of such efforts, see Julie Collins-Dogrul, Managing U.S.-Mexico "Border Health": An Organizational Field Approach, 63 Soc. Sci. & Med. 3199 (2006).

18. See U.S.-Mex. Border Health Comm'n, Annual Meeting of the United States- Mexico Border Health Commission, McAllen, Texas, March 3–4, 2008: Summary, Actions and Next Steps 8 (2008), available at http://www.borderhealth.org/extranet/files/file_1058.pdf (on file with the *Columbia Law Review*) (reporting on work of H.H.S. Working Group on Binational Health Insurance).

19. See Hilda Bogue, Ventanillas de Salud Program and Community Health Centers, Migrant Health Newsline, Nov.-Dec. 2006, at http://findarticles.com/p/ articles/mi_6843/is_6_23/ai_

n28465712 (on file with the *Columbia Law Review*) (describing goals and benefits of program to decrease barriers to access among consular clients and their families).

20. U.S.-Mex. Border Health Comm'n, NIOSH Information Dissemination on the U.S.-Mexico Border, at http://www.borderhealth.org/files/res_1203.pdf (last updated Mar. 11, 2008) (on file with the *Columbia Law Review*).

21. For a general account of this transnational activity, see Gaspar Rivera-Salgado, Binational Organizations of Mexican Migrants in the United States, Soc. Just., Fall 1999, at 27. For a framing of this civil society activity as political activity and organization by Mexican migrants, see Jonathan Fox, Mexican Migrant Civic Participation in the United States, Border Battles: The U.S. Immigration Debates, Aug. 15, 2006, at http://borderbattles.ssrc.org/Fox/printable. html (on file with the *Columbia Law Review*).

22. See, e.g., Fitzgerald, supra note 4, at 3, 155–64 (describing ways in which Mexican government has attempted to regulate emigration)..

23. The Catholic Church, itself a global, transnational network, has become an important agent for the promotion of migrants' interests in recent years. The Mexican Catholic Church has abandoned its former policy of discouraging emigration in favor of accepting emigration and maintaining connections to Mexicans abroad via partnerships with U.S. dioceses and a "binational migrant ministry," simultaneously encouraging Mexicans to retain ties to Mexican culture and society and learn English and American customs. See id. at 96.

24. See Selee, supra note 3, at 18 (describing cross-border activities of nongovernmental organizations).

25. Rivera-Salgado, supra note 21, at 30.

26. For a detailed discussion of the Institute's structure, see Laureen Laglagaron, Migration Policy Inst., Protection Through Integration: The Mexican Government's Efforts to Aid Migrants in the United States 10–14 (2010), available at http://www.migrationpolicy.org/pubs/IME-Jan2010.pdf (on file with the *Columbia Law Review*).

27. Fitzgerald, supra note 4, at 58–59.

28. Id.

29. Laglagaron, supra note 26, at 29–31.

30. Id. at 1–2, 14–28; see also Rodolfo Figueroa-Aramoni, A Nation Beyond its Borders: The Program for Mexican Communities Abroad, 86 J. Am. Hist. 537, 539–40 (1999) (discussing educational and cultural activities of Institute's predecessor).

31. See Claudia Keller Lapayre, The Institute of Mexicans Abroad as a Mexican Institution of Public Diplomacy in the United States 24 (Mar. 22, 2006) (paper presented at the annual meeting of the International Studies Association), available at http://www.allacademic.com/meta/p99314_index.html (on file with the *Columbia Law Review*) (noting that Institute's programs, though targeted at Mexican nationals, also seek to "improve Mexico's image").

32. See Ghosh, supra note 1, at 115 (observing that existing mechanisms of interstate cooperation act "in an isolated and fragmentary manner and are too narrowly focused to provide an adequate normative framework for a comprehensive approach to migration management").

33. See Fitzgerald, supra note 4, at 155 (noting that Mexico sought from 1900 to 1970 to control "volume, trip duration, skills, and geographic origin of emigrants" through mechanisms such as propaganda, withholding of travel documents, Bracero temporary worker program, and coercion at border, but that failure of such efforts led Mexico to shift strategy to management).

34. For an argument that substantial investment by the United States in Mexico represents the best long-term strategy for reducing illegal immigration, see Jorge Durand & Douglas S. Massey, Borderline Sanity, Am. Prospect, Sept. 24–Oct. 8, 2001, at 28.

35. See Rozental & Smith, supra note 14, at 16 (describing expanding the mandate of the North American Development Bank as one approach to infrastructure development). Of course, this sort of measure could be politically unpalatable, given that NAFTA is perceived on both sides of the border as having failed to deliver the growth in Mexico that would prevent the erosion of jobs and wages in the United States. See, e.g., Douglas S. Massey, Jorge Durand & Nolan J. Malone, Beyond Smoke and Mirrors: Mexican Immigration in an Era of Economic Integration 73–104 (2002) (discussing relationship between NAFTA and illegal immigration).

36. For literature offering various approaches, see sources cited supra note 2. For a critique of temporary worker programs, see generally Cristina M. Rodríguez, Guest Workers and Integration: Toward a Theory of What Immigrants and Americans Owe One Another, 2007 U. Chi. Legal F. 219.

37. State and local governments in Mexico, which have become increasingly independent as the result of the federal government's devolution to them, in the mid-1990s, of authority over education and health care, should not be overlooked as partners in regulation and information gathering. See Selee, supra note 3, at 30 ("Most education and healthcare has been decentralized to state governments, and municipalities are responsible for most basic city and county services.").

38. A reform proposal that has gained prominence would create an administrative agency or independent commission to set visa policy on an annual basis, in the interest of creating an agile labor policy mechanism attuned to facts on the ground. Interagency communication across the U.S.-Mexico border will be crucial to the information-gathering work of such a commission. For a discussion of the commission proposal, see Cox & Rodríguez, supra note 2, at 538–39.

*Cristina M. Rodríguez is the Henry L. Stimson Visiting Professor of Law at Harvard Law School and professor of law at New York University School of Law.

Rodríguez, Cristina M. "Building Capacity for the Transnational Regulation of Migration," Columbia Law Review Sidebar 110, no.1 (February 10, 2010) at http://www.columbialawreview.org/Sidebar/volume/110/1_Rodriguez.pdf.

Migration and Development: The Flavour of the 2000s

by Birgitte Mossin Brønden*

In Hans Christian Andersen's tale "The Emperor's New Clothes", the emperor decides that he has to go through with the procession—showing off his purportedly magnificent clothing—even after an innocent child cries out that the emperor has not got anything on. For quite some time he continues to parade stark naked as noblemen of wisdom maintain that the clothes are magnificent for various reasons . . .

The fairy tale obviously reminds us to make use of our critical senses. It also reminds us that interests sometimes overrule the ability of even the wisest to provide much-needed sharp observations. To this, we add that in order to be constructive and make evidence-based policy recommendations, one must be ready to deconstruct first.

Over a decade has elapsed since the issue of *migration and development* surged to the top of the international development agenda and gained the attention of both policymakers and academics. The "discovery" of the positive role that migration could play in development centred on the potential of migration to deliver remittances to the global South. Thus, in the early 2000s the World Bank, other donors and a range of development actors took a "renewed"[1] policy interest in the migration–development "nexus", a notion introduced in a Special Issue of this *Journal* in 2002 (Sørensen et al., 2002).[2]

Since then, donors have attempted to "make migration work for the poor in the global South"[3] and/or to manage migration better through combined policies that include aid policies, immigration policies in the broad sense, border enforcement initiatives and other aspects of external relations with countries of origin. At the other end, developing countries' governments have directed new attention towards "their diasporas",[4] although often merely wooing them rather than seriously including them. Over the years, the interest has been reflected in the work of institutions ranging from the Global Forum on International Migration and Development to local-level diaspora associations.

Additionally, analysis and discussions of the migration and development nexus have appeared in a plethora of reports, books and articles that, importantly, include the discourse regarding the migrant as a transnational agent in development. This discourse was based on the insight into the transnational lives of migrants that migration increased the possibilities for migrants and their families to live transnationally and adopt transnational identities. This discourse had come into migration studies earlier, through the work of Basch and her colleagues (1994) and Vertovec (1999), and included the notion of social remittances or the transfer of human capital and social ideas and practices, in which the work of Levitt (see, *inter alia*, Levitt, 1999, 2001a,b) became important.

Another part of the picture is that, throughout the decade, the migration and development nexus has been scrutinized and looked upon critically by acknowledged experts in the field who have continued the critical and cautious (when it comes to the intersection with policy recommendations) approach connected to the original coining of the term by Sørensen et al. (2002). These readings of the migration–development hype have, not least, questioned the basis of policy interest in the field and the premises of conventional wisdom on migration and development at each point in time (Glick Schiller and Faist, 2009).

Currently, it is argued by several critical observers—among them, Skeldon (2008) and Glick Schiller and Faist (2009)—that the appealing magic of migration–development policies that purport to be able to bring about "win–win–win situations", where the migrant, the sending country and the receiving country all have a positive outcome has, in reality, served as a façade for a range of other purposes stemming from a North-driven agenda. To mention some of these, migration–development initiatives have been criticized for being used: as the human face of neoliberalism (de Haas, 2010); as a sort of diffraction, or relegation, of more extreme ideas regarding how to stem migration, floating in the interior politics of a donor country (Sørensen, 2010); and as a carrot in the EU's bargains with transit countries (Lavenex and Kunz, 2008).

Others have pointed out that the resources put into migration–development policies in the 2000s are actually rather marginal in comparison to how much talk there has been about them in the donor milieu (see, e.g., Bakewell, 2008).

A decade after this surge of interest started, we find it pertinent to ask where "we"—referring to the international development community, broadly defined—stand today with regard to the migration and development nexus. What has come out of this wave of interest, the policy/practice debate and the critique it has raised? Knowing that the nexus has been variously described as unsettled and, later, as "hype" or a panacea for development, we wonder whether its history can be likened to the story of "The Emperor's New Clothes".

However, not even the most critical researcher would say that there is nothing to the inter-linkages between migration and development, or even that policymakers should not take interest in the migration–development nexus; the emperor is not entirely naked. Nevertheless, the critique suggests that the clothes are not as magnificent as certain agenda-setting men and women (or rather institutions) of wisdom maintain they are, or were proclaimed to be at the outset. All this begs the question of whether this is yet another story of one of the trends in the international development community that dip in and out of fashion.

Our main objective is not to cry out that the emperor is naked. Rather, we hope to use a lucid and critical examination of the actual migration and development nexus to answer the following questions: What new perspectives on migration and development ought the international development community to take into consideration today? What are the possible avenues for future policy-making in the migration–development field? We seek to contribute to a progressive amplification of the insight into the nexus with subsequent improved policies.

With this in mind, we convened a conference at the Danish Institute of International Studies (DIIS) in Copenhagen in January 2011, under the title "The Migration Development Mantra: Retained, Rejected or Reinvented?" We invited scholars who had written extensively on migration and development, together with practitioners who had worked with the migration–development agenda and had insights into the political process connected to the migration–development nexus. We challenged them to address the questions, taking into account how shifting "background policy developments" such as, for instance, transforming geopolitical concerns and changing national policy environments (re-nationalizing endeavours to ensure a so-called "national coherency") have affected the nexus.

The conference embraced very different prisms and examples. The meeting was prefaced by two statements from the UN Special Representative on Migration, Peter Sutherland, who underscored that "the sustained focus on migration and development creates a political space in which governments can focus on the positive aspects of migration" and referred to evidence that "Migration is contributing to the fight against the greatest scourge we face—poverty." It also included a presentation by the Dutch consultancy HIT Foundation that had, at that point in time, under the heading of a *circular migration* pilot project (as part of the Dutch Migration and Development portfolio and in cooperation with the World Bank), initiated a controlled temporary migration programme designed with the clear objective of fulfilling labour needs in the Netherlands and ensuring return and reintegration of the migrants involved (the programme was later abandoned, with the official explanation that it had been too difficult to implement). But, overall, the conference actually bore the impress of several critical perspectives regarding the migration and development mantras. Among these, the contradictions inherent in notions of migrants as both agents of development and as potential threats to host country security were highlighted.

The presentations and discussions from the DIIS conference provide the backbone for this Special Issue. Herein, the authors discuss various aspects of the migration–development discourses currently floating among development actors and shed light on the questions raised above.

Hein de Haas reminds us that migration and development is anything but a new topic. The debate about migration and development has swung back and forth like a pendulum between optimism and pessimism in the postwar period. He points out that these shifts are rooted in deeper ideological paradigmatic shifts, and that that recent views celebrating migration as self-help from below are partly driven by neoliberal ideologies that shift the attention away from structural constraints. Thereby, his paper goes hand in hand with Sørensen's paper, which—later in the issue—explores the nexus between migration, development and security, and alludes to a need to redirect the gaze from individual migrants to structural problems.[5] Migration and development cannot be seen in isolation from wider issues of global power, wealth and inequality.

The simplistic ideas and assumptions among development actors about the relationship between migration and development that appeared in the optimistic phase of the 2000s make up what Mossin Brønden and Vammen, in their paper, argue can be characterized as an "international buzz". Examining how two donor countries have approached the nexus in recent years in the context of the buzz, they add to a description of "where the international development community stands today regarding migration and development policy". They take particular interest in looking empirically at the ways in which it has been feasible to work with migration–development links taking into account various interests and the national political climates regarding development aid and immigration policies.

The theme of whether the buzz or the mantras have a tendency to dip in and out of fashion is taken up by de Haas, as well as Mossin Brønden and Vammen, with the suggestion that we might be past the peak of interest in migration and development—a suggestion that had previously also been made by Skeldon (2008). This points to the necessity of avoiding repeating the same mistakes—especially to avoid oversimplification. All the evidence points to the complexity of the migration–development nexus, and the implications of the studies and insights already out there must be more seriously taken into account. There is no need to throw the baby out with the bathwater—the reaction of those whose high expectations have been disappointed should not be allowed to rule. Only time will tell, however, if the High Level Dialogue on Migration and Development planned for 2013 and/or individual nation-states and international organizations will endow the migration–development debate with renewed impetus and keep it on the international agenda. Currently, situations such as the one following the Arab Spring keeps migration firmly in the loop of public attention, although with a strong securitized and migration management twist.

Two authors deconstruct particular aspects of the migration–development discourses floating among development actors and problematize various parts of the dominant paradigms, opening up a more insightful way of thinking about policy in the field. Sørensen scrutinizes the pairs migration–development and migration–security, and she points out that only by seriously considering (a) the intersection between rising poverty and insecurity levels in the South, (b) the continuous demand for cheap labour in the North, and (c) border enforcement initiatives that knowingly increase the costs and mortal risks of migration can the migration–development nexus become more than a mantra for the actors involved. Ronald Skeldon questions whether *circular migration*—one of the central concepts in vogue in policy circles currently—can be clearly identified as a particular type of population mobility. He examines the antecedents of the idea of circulation and the consequences of circular migration for human welfare, in order to critically scrutinize the role of policy intervention in connection with circular migration and discuss policy options.

In 2008, Castles and Delgado Wise pertinently asked what people in the South thought about international migration trying to redress the balance, by initiating a South–South dialogue on migration and development. The focus of this issue is a discussion of the North's approach to migration and development but, inspired by Castles and Wise, the picture is nuanced through the paper by Hansen that takes up the difficulties faced by poor developing countries to effectively formulate and implement migration–development policies. He argues that current Tanzanian remittance and diaspora policies are not based on knowledge of transnational practices but, rather, on general notions of the phenomena that are circulated among powerful international development institutions. He also points out that the optimism among some Tanzanian government officials in fact collides with other policy considerations of the same government.

Finally, the tendency of policymakers broadly to regard migration as a phenomenon that can and should be managed and controlled is notable across the papers in general. De Haas, Vammen and Mossin Brønden, Skeldon and Sorensen all direct attention to the need to address migrant rights, and the need for legal channels for higher- and lower-skilled migration and for integration policies that favour socio-economic mobility of migrants and avoid their marginalization, if real development outcomes are to be obtained in countries of origin.

The Special Issue is rounded off by a cross-cutting commentary reflecting on the state of the art of migration and development by Glick Schiller, which brings the papers together in a discussion about current and future directions in the field.

A common theme across the papers is that migration is a recurring phenomenon. The understanding of migration as a key aspect of the social transformation affecting all parts of the world today must continue to be the basis of thinking on migration governance internationally and on migration and development. This conclusion in particular calls for migration and mobility patterns in any given developing country to be part of the background knowledge necessary for any development policy. The understanding of the *migration and development nexus* is still essential for the implementation of development policy, and there are both thorough studies and insights and pertinent policies out there. Thus, we need to ensure that the emperor's wardrobe is updated—that it is neither discarded nor overrated, but worn with open eyes.

ENDNOTES

1. As pointed out by Hein de Haas (2010), the debate on migration and development has swung back and forth like a pendulum, from developmentalist optimism in the 1950s and 1960s, to neo-Marxist pessimism during the 1970s and 1980s, towards more optimistic views in the 1990s and 2000s. Therefore, we cannot talk about an entirely new but, rather, a "renewed" interest in migration and development.

2. The focus in the Special Issue of 2002 was on how international migrants in Western countries fuel development in their countries of origin through the transfer of remittances, human capital and return.

3. The Development Research Centre on Migration, Globalisation and Poverty ended a 6-year study with this title in October 2009. They had explicitly drawn attention away from whether more development migration might lead to more (or less) migration and, rather, focused on what migration means for development and poverty reduction. Likewise, they put a focus on South–South migration, internal migration and barriers to movement.

4. For a discussion on the use of the concept of a *diaspora*, see Faist (2009).

5. The need to redirect the gaze from individual migrants to structural problems has also been pointed out by other authors (see, e.g., Delgado Wise and Màrquez Covarrubias, 2009; Hernández-León, 2008; Sørensen and Van Hear, 2003).

REFERENCES

Bakewell, O.
   2008   *"Keeping them in their place: the ambivalent relationship between migration and development in Africa"*, Working Paper 8, International Migration Institute, Oxford.
Basch, L., N. Glick Schiller, and C. Szanton Blanc
   1994   *Nations Unbound: Transnational Projects*, Postcolonial Predicaments and Deterritorialized Nation-States, Gordon and Breach, Basel.
Castles, S., and R. Delgado Wise (Eds)
   2008   *Migration and Development: Perspectives from the South*, International Organization for Migration, Geneva.
de Haas, H.
   2010   "Migration and development: a theoretical perspective", *International Migration Review*, 44(1): 227–264.
Delgado Wise, R., and H Márquez Covarrubias
   2009   "The relationship between migration and development", *Social Analysis*, 53(3): 85–105.
Faist, T.
   2009   "Transnationalization and development: toward an alternative agenda", *Social Analysis*, 53(3): 39–59.
Glick Schiller, N., and T. Faist
   2009   "Introduction: migration, development and social transformation", *Social Analysis*, 53(3): 1–13.
Hernández-León, R.
   2008   *Metropolitan Migrants—The Migration of Urban Mexicans to the United States*, University of California Press, Berkeley, CA.
Lavenex, S., and R. Kunz
   2008   "The migration–development nexus in EU external relations", *European Integration*, 30(3): 439–457.
Levitt, P.
   1999   "Social remittances: a local-level, migration-driven form of cultural diffusion", *International Migration Review*, 32(124): 926–949.
   2001a   *The Transnational Villagers*, University of California Press, Berkeley, CA.
   2001b   "Transnational migration: taking stock and future directions", *Global Networks*, 1(3): 195–216.
Sørensen, N.N.
   2010   "The fate of migration in Danish development policy: opting for the middle ground", *The Broker*, Issue 22, October/November:, 2: 4–26.
Sørensen, N.N., and N. Van Hear (Eds)
   2003   *The Migration–Development Nexus*, International Organization for Migration, Geneva.
Sørensen, N.N., N. Van Hear, and P. Engberg-Pedersen
   2002   "The migration–development nexus: evidence and policy options", *International Migration*, 40(5): 3–73.
Skeldon, R.
   2008   "International migration as a tool in development policy: a passing phase?" *Population and Development Review*, 34(1): 1–18.
Vertovec, S.
   1999   "Conceiving and researching transnationalism", *Ethnic and Racial Studies*, 22(2): 445–462.

*Birgitte Mossin Brønden is section head at the Danish Ministry of Foreign Affairs and an analyst at the Danish Institute for International Studies, Research Unit on Migration.

Brønden, Birgitte Mossin. "Migration and Development: The Flavour of the 2000s." *International Migration* 50, no. 3 (2012): 2–7.

Message on International Migrants Day: 18 December 2011

by The United Nations Secretary-General

Migration affects all countries—and so do myths and misperceptions about its impact.

There are many false assumptions surrounding migration.

One such myth is that migrants are a burden. In reality, migrants make vast contributions to host countries. As workers, they bring skills. As entrepreneurs, they create jobs. As investors, they bring capital. In advanced and emerging economies, they play an indispensable role in agriculture, tourism and domestic work. Migrants often care for the youngest and oldest members of society.

People view irregular migration as a crime. Many think migrants who lack proper documents are a danger to society and should be detained, or that all women who migrate to take up low-skilled jobs have been trafficked.

These and other unfounded beliefs lead to the adoption of migration policies that are irrelevant at best or even dangerous.

States have the sovereign prerogative to manage their borders. But they also have the duty to abide by their international legal obligations. Under international human rights law, all persons, without discrimination and regardless of nationality or legal status, are entitled to enjoy fundamental human rights. No migrant should be sent back to a place where he or she will be tortured. Every migrant woman should have access to health care, including reproductive health care. Every migrant child should be able to go to school.

Human rights are not a matter of charity, nor are they a reward for obeying immigration rules. Human rights are the inalienable entitlement of every person, including the world's 214 million international migrants as well as their family members.

Forty-five countries have ratified the International Convention on the Rights of All Migrant Workers and Members of their Families. I call on all others to join this important treaty as a concrete affirmation of their commitment to protect and promote the human rights of all migrants on their territories.

When their rights are violated, when they are marginalized and excluded, migrants will be unable to contribute either economically or socially to the societies they have left behind or those they enter. However, when supported by the right policies and human rights protections, migration can be a force for good for individuals as well as for countries of origin, transit and destination.

Let us give meaning to International Migrants Day by taking constructive steps to leverage this global phenomenon into a force for progress.

The United Nations Secretary-General. Message on International Migrants Day, by the United Nations Secretary-General, 18 December 2011. © United Nations 2011.

Reprinted by permission.